MW01122020

2007 10 22

Angels & Anger

Angels and Anger
Five Acadian Plays

Selected, edited and translated by
Glen Nichols

Playwrights Canada Press
Toronto•Canada

Playwrights Canada Press
54 Wolseley Street, 2nd Floor, Toronto, Ontario CANADA M5T 1A5
416-703-0013 fax 416-703-0059
orders@playwrightscanada.com • www.playwrightscanada.com

Playwrights Canada Press acknowledges the support of the taxpayers of Canada and the
province of Ontario through The Canada Council for the Arts and the Ontario Arts Council.

Cover design: Corinne Hicks
Cover image: "Angel of Needs" by Gilles LeBlanc 1995. Photographed by Marc Paulin.
Production Editor: Jodi Armstrong

National Library of Canada Cataloguing in Publication

Angels and anger : five Acadian plays / selected, edited and translated by Glen Nichols.

ISBN 0-88754-660-9

1. Canadian drama (French)—20th century—Translations into English. 2. Canadian
drama (French)—New Brunswick—Translations into English. I. Nichols, Glen Freeman,
1961-

PS8315.A54 2003   C842'.5408   C2003-900619-0
PR9196.6.A54 2003

First edition: April 2003.
Printed and bound by AGMV Marquis at Quebec, Canada.

for Louise

ACKNOWLEDGEMENTS

I would like to thank the authors, as well as Jacques Ouellet of Éditions La Grande Marée, for their enthusiastic support of this collection. Special thanks also to Théâtre l'Escaouette, Théâtre populaire d'Acadie, LIVEWIRE Theatre Network, Jenny Munday at Playwrights Atlantic Resource Centre, Moncton Public Library, Université de Moncton (Département d'anglais, Faculté des études supérieures et de la recherche [FESR], Galérie d'art de l'Université de Moncton [GAUM] & Centre d'études acadiennes [CEA]), CBC Radio One and Two, Nathalie Arseneault, Chris Budd, Philip André Collette, Corinne Hicks, and David Lonergan. Also a very special thanks to Angela Rebeiro of Playwrights Canada Press for her work on this project, as on so many through which she has helped bring Canadian drama to a wider audience.

—*GN*

TABLE OF CONTENTS

PREFACE

This anthology presents in English for the first time five plays from the contemporary Acadian repertoire. Other than the earlier plays of Antonine Maillet, several of which have been available in English translation for many years, no other Acadian playwright has work published outside its original language.** The purpose of this project was to introduce in a small way the vivid world of contemporary Acadian dramaturgy to a broader non-francophone audience.

The goal was to reflect what has been happening most recently in Acadian theatre, but with a few exceptions the number of new Acadian plays being produced professionally is less than it was a few years ago, so the time parameters slid a little further back to 1987 for the earliest play in the collection, *My Husband's an Angel* (*Dark Owl* was originally produced in 1975 but the text translated here is from the revised 1997 version). There are many reasons for the diminished number of new Acadian productions, as outlined so well in David Lonergan's introduction to this volume and in his brief history of Théâtre l'Escaouette published in 2000. But I would suggest one factor is the lack of a playwrighting component in the otherwise superb dramatic arts program at the Université de Moncton. For over a quarter of a century this program has provided the foundations for the professional theatre in Acadie. It continues to train excellent actors, designers and technical personnel, but a stronger emphasis on playwrighting would be a significant help in building the next generation of dramatic writing.

Establishing criteria for selection of texts is always frought with difficulty, but when the texts are intended for a collection in translation the challenges are compounded. I wanted plays that not only reflected trends in contemporary Acadian dramaturgy, but which also could be playable in English outside of the region. The final collection includes plays by leading Acadian playwrights which received professional productions in the recent past. The three principal geographical areas of Acadie in New Brunswick are represented (the Moncton area: Herménégilde Chiasson; the Acadian peninsula: Laval Goupil; and Edmundston: Gracia Couturier). Nova Scotia is represented indirectly through Ivan Vanhecke's adaptation of the Nova Scotian children's story *Le tapis de Grand-Pré*. Theatre for young audiences, an important component of professional Acadian theatre especially through the efforts of Théâtre l'Escaouette, is also represented by Chiasson's play for teens, *Cape Enrage*. Political, social, economic and aesthetic questions are explored in *Alienor* and *Dark Owl, or The Renegade Angel*, while *My Husband's an Angel* provides the comic relief and a quarky example of the extended dramatic monologue, another quintessential Acadian form since Maillet's *La Sagouine*.

The plays have been translated with attention to developing their potential as texts for performance in English, while adamantly maintaining their "acadianness." To that end, after numerous drafts and consultation with the authors or others involved in the original French production, each of the plays was subjected to a rigorous workshopping process concluding with a public performance in the form of a staged reading.

I felt it was important the translations make a bridge between Acadian dramaturgy and potential English-language performance. I wanted neither "museum piece" academic treatments of Acadian otherness, nor plays with all traces of their origins rewritten out of them. So, the plays have not been "adapted" except superficially, such as in the dense word-play of *My Husband's an Angel* and *Dark Owl, or The Renegade*

Angel; they remain as Acadian in theme, form, and content as possible while being prepared through performance workshopping as playable English texts.

The title of the collection, *Angels and Anger*, is the result of an interesting accident of content and theme. Each of the plays deals with an underlying sense of anger, some more obviously than others. It may be anger at being poor, at being young, at being unjustly accused of a crime; even in the comedies there is an underlying frustration that drives the characters: frustration at being unable to find the magical yarn that will complete the ancestors' enchanted legacy, or at simply being a man, pregnant and misunderstood! It would be far too simplistic to say these are only metaphors for the frustrations and anger of a francophone minority group on the fringes of an anglo continent; the plays are much more complex than that.

The presence of angels, characters who bring clearer understanding to the problems in the plays, points the way to resolutions which make the texts both highly specific and broadly human. In varying ways, each of the plays deals with an expatiation of the past as a means of moving beyond the confines of traditional nostalgia and historical fetishism into a new world, uncertain and unexplored, but full of possibilities.

—*GN*

** Herménégilde Chiasson's *La vie est un rêve* has been translated recently by Jo-Anne Elders in Fredericton for publication in the near future.

Originally from Ontario, **Glen Nichols** has spent the last six years happily learning about life as a Maritimer. Part of that process has been the joy of discovering the richness of Acadian theatre, and this anthology is a way of sharing that discovery. Glen teaches Canadian literature and drama in the English department at the Université de Moncton. He has published articles on theatre history and theatre translation in *Theatre Research in Canada, Port Acadie, l'Annuaire théâtrale,* among others as well as in several collections of essays. Along with Louise Ladouceur at the University of Alberta, he is co-editing a special issue of *Theatre Research in Canada* on theatre translation in Canada.

A History of Acadian Theatre in Five Plays? Why Not?
by David Lonergan – June 2002

If I were to pick five Acadian plays to translate, which ones would I choose? Choosing is always a risk because, inevitably, more examples must be left out than included. Glen Nichols has made the current selection of five plays for his own reasons. So what can be said about his choices when we look at them in the larger context of Acadian theatre?

In 1975, when Productions de l'Étoile, located in Caraquet on the Acadian Peninsula in north-east New Brunswick, created Laval Goupil's original version of *Dark Owl*, Acadian theatre was still a wholly amateur enterprise. In Moncton, the Feux Chalins and Théâtre amateur de Moncton (TAM) competed for the same audience by offering traditional plays while also trying to encourage new works.

And so that was how the Feux Chalins happened to create *La Sagouine* in 1971 with the then amateur actor Viola Léger in the title role. Starting in 1972 they presented puppet plays for children by Jean Péronnet who brought to the stage the now famous *Pépère Goguen*. They attempted political theatre with *Qu'est-ce qu'on fait Monsieur le Maire?*, a Monctonian adaptation of *Médium saignant* by Françoise Loranger in 1973 (the Moncton mayor in question being the infamous Leonard Jones who was spurned for his anti-French politics), and explored the technique of collective creation, very much in fashion at the time, with *Le sucre est trop salé* in 1975.

Théâtre amateur de Moncton was not to be outdone. In 1975, having learned the art of collective creation two years earlier with *Acadie actualité*, TAM created *Les tombes de Madame Mélanie* by Huguette Légaré, who had won the Cercle du livre de France prize for her novel, *La conversation entre hommes* in 1973. They also produced *Kouchibou Quoi?*, a play for young audiences about the expulsion of people from lands expropriated to create the Kouchibouguac National Park along the eastern coast of New Brunswick. The play was written by Roger LeBlanc, at that time a student in the drama department at the Université de Moncton and later a co-founder of Théâtre l'Escaouette.

Back on the Acadian Peninsula, the Théâtre des Élouèzes was creating plays written by its founder Jules Boudreau starting in 1973 with *L'Agence Belœil Inc.*, and followed shortly afterwards by *La Bringue*. Boudreau would go on to write or co-write seven plays for Théâtre populaire d'Acadie (TPA) between 1975 (*Louis Mailloux*, with music by Calixte Duguay) and 1991 (*Des amis pas pareils* with Jeannine Boudreau-Dugas).

For its part, the Université de Moncton drama department, which had just been established and which would graduate its first students in 1978, was also creating new works. In 1974, the students mounted *As-tu vu ma balloune?* by Raymond Guy LeBlanc whose first collection of poetry, *Cri de terre*, had been the first book published by Éditions d'Acadie in Moncton in 1972. In 1975, the department mounted *Becquer bobo*, the first play by Herménégilde Chiasson who had just published his first collection of poetry, *Mourir en Scoudouc*, in 1974, also with Éditions d'Acadie.

Dark Owl, or The Renegade Angel

The founders of Productions de l'Étoile (which became Théâtre populaire d'Acadie in 1976) were determined to "work for the promotion and development of all aspects of the arts and theatre" and to eventually become professional as Réjean

Poirier emphasized in a 1975 press release. The late Laval Goupil (1945-2000), a native of the Acadian Peninsula and, like Réjean Poirier, an active participant in Feux Chalins, was one of the founding members. Productions de l'Étoile chose Goupil's *Tête d'eau* for its first show which was coproduced by Feux Chalins: the transition from one company to the other thus being seamless. It would then tackle the process of collective creation with *Cérémonie* in 1974, and mount *Dark Owl [Le Djibou]* in 1975 under the direction of Poirier and with a cast of actors more amateur than professional. The play was a terrific success while surprising audiences more by the crudeness of the lines than by his use of popular language. The still young Éditions d'Acadie published the play soon afterwards and it quickly became for both the audience and the theatre world one of the first "classics" of Acadian drama alongside the early plays of Antonine Maillet who was already famous thanks to the legendary good fortune of *La Sagouine* and her novels.

From the critics, however, the reaction was less enthusiastic. In Quebec, after pointing out the weaknesses in the text and in the characters, Pierre Lavoie tempered his assessment by concluding, "Laval Goupil has talent, maybe even a lot of talent" (*Livres et auteurs québécois* 1975). In Acadie, Yves Bolduc did not temper his review which he concluded with the callous statement, "As far as I'm concerned, I would forget most of the first 69 pages and then reconstruct the play using the poetic tone and intensity of the last 20 pages. There we find the seeds of a great play... which remains to be written" (*Si Que*, automne 1978). But the critics are just critics, and TPA would remount a new version of the play, *Le Djibou, ou l'Ange déserteur*, with success in 1997. This version was immediately published by Éditions La Grande Marée in Tracadie-Sheila, New Brunswick, and Glen Nichols has chosen to base his translation on this later version which is somewhat better than the original.

My Husband's an Angel

The second play chosen for translation here, *My Husband's an Angel [Mon mari est un ange]* by Gracia Couturier, dates from 1987: twelve years later, and the theatrical landscape had changed a great deal: Feux Chalins, TAM, and Élouèzes had disappeared. TPA had become the main Acadian theatrical institution, dividing its energies between canonical plays and new works (fourteen new Acadian plays out of forty productions). The Théâtre l'Escaouette Cooperative, founded in 1978 by Marcia Babineau, Philippe Beaulieu and Roger LeBlanc, all recent graduates of the Université de Moncton drama department, Bernard LeBlanc from TAM, and Gracia Couturier who had an education degree, dedicated itself to creating new works: in ten years and with a lot fewer resources than TPA, the company produced eighteen new plays encompassing a full range of genres and catering to all ages. By the late 1980s, these two professional companies were well established. And yet, only Jules Boudreau at TPA (six plays between 1975 and 1987), Herménégilde Chiasson at Théâtre l'Escaouette (eight plays between 1980 and 1987) and Antonine Maillet at Théâtre du Rideau-Vert in Montréal (nine plays between 1972 and 1987) had made a name for themselves as playwrights.

In 1988, Gracia Couturier was considered an emerging author. She had already written and produced *La couche aux fesses* (1981), *Et le filet n'est pas percé* (1982), *Les enfants, taisez-vous* (1983) and *Les ordinatrices* (1984), all at Théâtre de saisons, a company created by students from the Shippagan campus of the Université de Moncton where Gracia was director of Campus Recreation from 1981 to 1984. Her professional debut came in February 1986 with the creation of *Le gros ti-gars* by

Théâtre l'Escaouette and followed in December of that year with *Les ans volés* by the Université de Moncton drama department. Although *Enfantômes suroulettes*, produced by Théâtre l'Escaouette and published by Michel Henry éditeur in 1989, would be the last of her theatrical output for several years, Zénon Chiasson couldn't know that when he wrote in an article for Dalhousie French Studies that Gracia "was without a doubt the most prolific playwright in Acadie today" (Fall 1988, p. 75).

But still more and more theatre artists were coming out of the Université de Moncton drama department, itself an active producer, while the literary scene was bubbling over with new works. The two companies couldn't possibly absorb all the enthusiasm and ambition for creating new plays.

So that is why Gracia Couturier and her partner Philippe Beaulieu decided to self-produce *My Husband's an Angel* as part of the 1987 summer season at the Jardins de la République, a provincial park near Edmundston in north-west New Brunswick, Gracia's home town. She wrote the script and Philippe took the solo role. After twenty-five performances that summer, the play toured around New Brunswick and Nova Scotia in the winter of 1988, was published by Michel Henry éditeur later that year and adapted for television by Radio-Canada in 1989. *My Husband's an Angel* was the first self-produced professional Acadian show and out of the six plays published by Michel Henry éditeur (out of a total of twelve books published in its four-year existence which ended in 1989) four were by Gracia Couturier. After ten years of "silence," Gracia published her first novel *L'antichambre* in 1997, followed by *Je regardais Rebecca* in 1999, both with Éditions d'Acadie and both demonstrating a complex writing style which appears to contrast the directness of her plays. Nevertheless she has not completely abandoned writing drama. In 1996 Radio-Canada produced her radio play, *Le prisonnier*, and her one-act play *Tu te fais du mal pour rien* was one of the four pieces presented together as *Et moi*, the Université de Moncton drama department production in 1999.

Twelve Strands of Wool

In 1989 TPA and Théâtre l'Escaouette decided to co-produce a show, something they had not attempted before. Both companies had created several plays for children and had experienced a great deal of change. Katherine Kilfoil, named artistic director of Théâtre l'Escaouette in the fall of 1987, continued the work of Eugène Gallant, her predecessor, to professionalize the company's productions. At TPA, Andréï Zaharia, also named artistic director in 1987, was trying to introduce works from a broader range of sources. The two directors decided to join forces, inspired by the short-story *Le tapis de Grand-Pré*. Born from the imagination of Réjean Aucoin and Jean-Claude Tremblay, and illustrated by Herménégilde Chiasson, the story had been published by the Centre provincial de ressources pédagogiques at Church-Point, Nova Scotia, in 1986 and had won the France-Acadie prize for literature in 1987. This "Christmas tale for all ages" presented a stimulating theatrical challenge for the stage adapter, Ivan Vanhecke, whose play *Promenade en haute mer* Théâtre l'Escaouette had produced just the summer before. The play was a phenomenal success and became one of the cultural and media events of the year in Acadie. Nevertheless, at the core of Théâtre l'Escaouette, fear of amalgamation with TPA fueled discussions even before the play left on tour. It would be another ten years before the two companies would coproduce together again, this time Herménégilde Chiasson's comic hit *Laurie ou la vie de galerie* in 1998.

Cape Enrage

After its inaugural production, Laval Goupil's *Ti-Jean*, Théâtre l'Escaouette decided to focus on young people as its primary audience. In turn, Marie Cadieux, Raymond Guy LeBlanc, Gérald LeBlanc and Roger LeBlanc all tried their hand at this specialized genre but none of them stuck with it. In contrast, Herménégilde Chiasson was inspired by the form, and between his *Histoire en histoire* in 1980 and *Le cœur de la tempête* (co-written with Louis-Dominique Lavigne) in 2001, he wrote seven theatre-for-young-audience plays for Théâtre l'Escaouette. First produced in 1992, *Cape Enrage* was the sixth play in the cycle and the second one to feature teenage characters (the other one was *Pierre, Hélène et Michael* produced in 1990). *Cape Enrage* explores the problem of teen suicide, a taboo subject if there ever was one. And while the theme aroused certain reservations on the part of teachers at its first production, it was outright censored at the time of its remount in the spring of 1999 after four students at the local Marthieu-Martin High School had taken their own lives over a period of a few months. The artistic director, Marcia Babineau, had no choice but to ask Chiasson to change the ending so that the suicide became an accident. The rewriting allowed the play to be presented in the schools, but it meant sacrificing the play's effectiveness and relevance. Unfortunately, neither this play nor the adaptation of *Le tapis de Grand-Pré* has been published in French. In general, theatre for young audiences has never received much interest from Acadian publishers; for example, out of the eleven plays for youth of all ages that Chiasson created for Théâtre l'Escaouette, only one, *Atarelle et les Pacmaniens*, has ever been published (1986 with Michel Henry éditeur). As a result and somewhat curiously, these plays are appearing here for the first time in print, in English.

Alienor

In 1993, Théâtre l'Escaouette decided to start producing plays for adults more regularly and to present them in the theatre at the Aberdeen Cultural Centre in Moncton where the company had its offices. Since 1981 five of its seven plays for adults had been produced for summer theatre and were, consequently, comedies. Faced with the multiple challenges of space and profitability, Théâtre l'Escaouette gave up its summer season. At the same time, Chiasson was beginning to explore greater thematic depth in his dramatic writing. In 1989 he had written and performed the self-produced show, *Ed(d)ie*, in his workshop at the Aberdeen Cultural Centre. This play represents Chiasson's first attempt to explore aesthetic concerns through dramatic writing. Building the play around Shepard's *Fool for Love*, he skillfully interweaves extracts from the American piece with his own dialogue. For the first time Chiasson was no longer writing only according to the demands of his audience, but from himself. With his next play for adults, *L'exil d'Alexa* (Théâtre l'Escaouette, 1993), Chiasson explored the relationship between language and identity. With *La vie est un rêve* (Théâtre l'Escaouette, 1994), he focused his text on more universal themes of identity. Finally, *Alienor*, created by Théâtre l'Escaouette in 1997, brought to a close this thematic trilogy on his quest for Acadian identity, the theme which forms the keystone of all his works regardless of the media he is using, by giving it a metaphoric dimension. Central to the works of Chiasson, these three plays were equally important to Théâtre l'Escaouette because they brought to the company a decidedly modern discourse; however, the company was not able to take full advantage of the plays at the level of *mise-en-scène*. It wouldn't be until 1999 and the production of *Pour une fois* that a director, in this case Philippe Soldevila, would succeed in fully expressing Chiasson's theatrical universe.

Conclusions

Since 1997 the theatrical landscape in Acadie has been transformed. That year a new professional company was created, bringing together the multi-talented director, lighting designer and professor from the Université de Moncton drama department Louise Lemieux, the musician Jean Surette who is a member of the rock group Les Païens, the actors Amélie Gosselin, Lynne Surette, and Philip André Collette, as well as the writer France Daigle. This collective created Daigle's first play, *Moncton Sable* which became the name of the company. The creation was experimental, based on an exploration of sand [*sable*] as an element of nature. In 1999, *Craie* [Chalk] mines the poetic dimensions of those little limestone sticks used to write on blackboards. In 2000, *Foin* [Hay] followed a parallel process, and the sweet smell of meadow grass filled the Grange-Théâtre at the Université de Moncton where the group has always performed. *Bric-à-brac*, in 2001, transformed the barn [*la grange*] into a veritable pawn shop. Because of Moncton Sable's emphasis on innovative scenic design, the black-box theatre was arranged to accommodate only about 50 spectators and the collective offers fewer than ten performances per production. This reflects Moncton Sable's interest in addressing a very specific and somewhat limited audience. However, the originality of their approach has had a major impact on the theatrical scene in Moncton. The company has seen its professional status recognized by The Canada Council for the Arts and the New Brunswick Arts Council. It recently became the fourteenth member of the Association des théâtres francophones du Canada.

In a completely different genre, Daniel Castonguay created Théâtre du Bocage in 1996. Situated at Ste-Anne-du-Bocage, a community in Caraquet, this private theatre was built in a small barn with space for about sixty spectators, presenting shows over the summer season. Because it is not subsidized and because it targets a broad audience, this theatre offers comedies which, according to Castonguay, bear more than a little resemblance to vaudeville. Nevertheless, the first production, *Alice* (1996 and remounted in 1997) co-written by Castonguay and Jeannine Boudreau who also acted in it, was of a more serious tone. Since 1997 the theatre has offered two plays each summer, most of them written by Robert Gauvin. The titles clearly suggest the genre: *Au tour de Zénobie* (1998), *Lange et Lique* (1998), *Bye Farnand!* (1999), *Les Co-co* (2000), and *Les années peppermint* (2001), texts intended to make people laugh and give audiences a little pleasant diversion, but which remain more sketchy than polished. All the plays are self-produced; the box-office receipts are divided among the members of each cast and a portion is retained by the theatre.

Other experiments, all collectives, have appeared since 1996, but none up until now has managed to mount a second production. In 1996, Théâtre Ent'quat'dieux created a cabaret-style show which was relatively well received, but then disappeared. Two of the members later helped found Moncton Sable. In 1999, Productions de la Mouvance presented a play by Marc Poirier, *Le mythe du masque à Ray*, which received the Éloizes for theatre that year (the Éloizes are the annual awards given by the Association acadienne des artistes professionnel.le.s du Nouveau-Brunswick) and then disappeared. In 2001, Le Masque de Neptune created *Le poil public*, a somewhat unpolished collective creation designed to be presented out-of-doors and based on *commedia dell'arte*. This company is still trying to figure out a permanent structure for itself.

Contrary to appearances, Acadian dramaturgy is faced with a serious problem: a lack of playwrights. Laval Goupil might have written, let's say, thirty plays but for reasons that should be explored some day he never succeeded in transforming his intuitions into works which fully realized his vision. Ultimately *Ti-Jean* was his last original play produced professionally. *Garrochés en paradis* marked the end of Antonine Maillet's Acadian dramatic output in 1986. On the other hand she continues to supply texts for the characters of the Pays de la Sagouine, a tourist attraction built around the pantheon of her characters which opened in 1992 at Bouctouche, New Brunswick. Since 1991 Jules Boudreau has continued to write, but none of his new plays has been picked up by TPA even though they are looking for plays by Acadian authors.

Symptomatic of this difficulty is the quasi-monopoly Herménégilde Chiasson has at Théâtre l'Escaouette (eleven plays out of the fifteen created since 1990) and the near-disappearance of new works from the stage of TPA since 1995 (only two new Acadian plays one of which was a resounding failure, and two co-productions, *Laurie ou la vie de galerie* and *Pour une fois*, which really came out of the imagination of Théâtre l'Escaouette). This is in sharp contrast to the seventeen new works the Caraquet company had created in the previous twenty years. Théâtre l'Escaouette has been trying for some time now to encourage new projects by organising various workshops, play readings, mentorships and so on. And while the number of participants has been relatively large, none of the "writers" to date has managed to bring a play to production. TPA is involved in community and student festivals which have been taking place for several years, but here again, there have been no convincing results.

Clearly other plays merit translation, but the five pieces chosen for this collection, while they don't represent every facet of Acadian theatre, do give an excellent overview. It remains to be seen if English-language companies will pick them up and give them that unique dimension born of the passage from one language and culture to another...

—translation, GN

David Lonergan is originally from Quebec where he helped found two professional theatre companies. He has lived in Moncton since 1994. He teaches at the Université de Moncton and contributes regularly to the francophone media in the region.

Dark Owl

or

The Renegade Angel

Laval Goupil
translated by Glen Nichols

Laval Goupil was born on July 15, 1945 in Shippagan, New Brunswick. He studied literature and theatre in Quebec, Sherbrooke and Paris, also completing a Masters degree at the Université de Moncton. He began his remarkable career as co-founder of La Batture, a production company and roadhouse in Shippagan in 1966. Later he would participate in the founding of Productions de l'Étoile in 1974 and Théâtre l'Escaouette in 1978. He wrote nearly 30 plays including the inaugural shows for both Productions de l'Étoile (*Tête d'eau*) and for Théâtre l'Escaouette (*Ti-Jean*), as well as several adaptations (*Rouv'e canne* at TPA in 1988 and *Aléola* also at TPA in 1995). Although most of his plays and other writing remain unpublished and many were never produced, he was an important force in contemporary Acadian theatre during its formative years. He is most remembered for his play *Djibou*. Laval Goupil passed away March 29, 2000.

Photo courtesy of Centre d'études acadiennes, Université de Moncton: Fonds Théâtre acadie, P186.B108N.

INTRODUCTION TO *DARK OWL, OR THE RENEGADE ANGEL*

Dark Owl, or the Renegade Angel by Laval Goupil is the most complex play in the collection. When a good-looking stranger appears in the village, a dysfunctional family is forced to confront their involvement in a tragic rape that occurred in the neighbourhood a few years earlier, triggering acts of revenge and a near repetition of the previous tragedy. These events seem to exorcise ghosts of the past which have driven a wedge between the family members as well as between themselves and their community, causing them to stagnate and decay emotionally.

The family's dysfunctionality is reinforced by the dramatic structure of the play which mixes realism and surrealism, contrasting direct-address monologues with dialogue scenes using traditional fourth-wall conventions. Four siblings aged 18 to 24 occupy the main action set in the living room of a somewhat run-down house. They argue more than talk, constantly bickering, picking open old wounds, and dredging up unpleasant memories. Their energies are eventually directed towards tricking the handsome stranger they ogle outside their house into visiting the neighbourhood girl who had suffered the rape a few years earlier. This precipitates a violent encounter and the final resolution of the play.

Meanwhile the father, Utrope, spends the play voluntarily isolated from his family out in his wood shop, framing the play with his monologues about the decline of his family which he attributes to the horrors of the neighbourhood rape years earlier. The mother, Victorine, only appears in the middle scenes of the play, first to chastise her children for having woken her up with their noise, then to deliver an extended Sagouine-like monologue on her life as a fish-plant worker.

In the end, as the play becomes more and more surreal, the violent outcome of the siblings' vengeful trick brings mother and father together for a tentative reconciliation. They eventually join their children in a choral expression of hope that they will all be able to climb out of the hole they find their life has become.

In addition to the extensive monologues by Utrope and Victorine, the play's brutal naturalism is also relieved by various structural and metatheatrical devices which add to the complexity and power of the piece. For example, each of the siblings "performs" other characters the audience otherwise doesn't see. First, within the boundaries of realistic conventions, Delicia "performs" her hilarious phone call to the dark stranger pretending to be the girl next door, and Amandine "performs" her rendition of the neighbour girl for the amusement of her siblings. Later "performances" become surreal when the rape is "replayed" by Amandine and Nicolas as remembered by the family, and Flora re-enacts the memory of her coming together with the original Dark Owl.

Despite the violence, socio-economic deprivation, isolation, stagnation and despair of the characters, the play is inflected with subtle but jarring glimpses of hope. The vicious bickering of the siblings is underscored by the playfulness they knew as children. Amandine's naivete and Nicolas's determined attempts to see light in the darkness of their carnage both contrast the cynicism of the older sisters. The humour of the mother's terrible descriptions of her work picking worms out of cod filets contributes to the compassion she feels for her co-workers' acts of kindness.

The family, perhaps as a microcosm of the society they are part of, is under tremendous pressure because of change and loss of control over their lives. These changes are metaphorized by the black magic of the first "Dark Owl of sorrows," the visitor who acquired mythic qualities as a harbinger of evil and who is said to have cast a spell of revenge on the family before he moved on. But in fact they are faced with real socio-economic forces as jobs are lost and families and lives adjust to the natural cycles of life. The father reacts to the loss of control by cutting himself off from his family and the world, by escaping to his workshop, a clear metaphor for the natural world as he calls it himself, "like a sheep's meadow deep in a dark woods." The mother reacts with angry confrontation. Whether its against her family or her bosses, she has learned to stand up and make herself heard in no uncertain terms! The siblings present a range of options. The older sisters, Flora and Delcia, act out revenge through subterfuge and viciousness. Nicolas is striving to create harmony through his writing, and Amandine, the more innocent one, seeks balance and peace.

The play's rich theatricalism is matched by Goupil's incredible use of language which he chose to construct using a transcription of the Acadian dialect from north-eastern New Brunswick, reminiscent of Michel Tremblay's use of Montreal *joual*. Through a diversity of lexical and formal variations he creates a vivid sense of character and immediacy. He also weaves a strong pattern of images, especially bird images, throughout the play. What struck me about this use of language when seen in the context of these particular characters, with their harsh social-economic situation, their bitter struggles with each other and with the outside world, and their strong inner sense of human potential, was the parallel with the fictional world of David Adams Richards. For that reason, in seeking voices for the translation, I allowed myself to be strongly influenced by Richards' evocation of Miramichi speech patterns.

Another significant factor in the translation was dealing with the extensive scene that is built on the interplay between English and French language and cultural tensions. In the original French play, Delicia phones the handsome stranger, whom the siblings believe is English, and attempts to talk to him in her broken attempts at that language. Eventually she learns that he speaks French, but of a more refined dialect than her own which precipitates still more amusing misunderstandings. I decided to simply reverse the polarity of languages here with Delcia now having to make the call in broken French to someone who actually speaks English, but with an accent that causes problems later in the conversation. To carry over the implied cultural tensions of the original scene I chose to place the stranger's dialect from outside the region, from "the States," a traditional source of wealthy "come-from-aways" in maritime lore.

With its highly fluid sense of theatrical form, the characters' constantly shifting temporal positions, the complex interplay of myth and reality, and the poetic density of its language wrought from the raw material of the playwright's own community, Laval Goupil's *Dark Owl, or The Renegade Angel* is a testimony to the development of Acadian drama. Produced as it was in the very earliest days of professional theatre in Acadie and then reworked and remounted in the more recent past, the play provides a particularly apt frame for this collection.

—GN

Dark Owl, or *The Renegade Angel* by Laval Goupil

Le Djibou was first performed on May 18, 1975 by Productions de l'Étoile in Maisonnette, New Brunswick, with the following cast under the direction of Réjean Poirier:

François Godin	Eutrope, the father
Olida Godin	Victorine, the mother
Jeannine Boudreau	Flora
Francine McClure	Delcia
Ginette Poirier	Amandine
Bernard Dugas	Nicolas
Robert Thériault	The Djibou

This version was published in 1975 by Éditions d'Acadie.

A new version of the play, *Le Djibou, ou l'Ange déserteur*, was coproduced by the National Arts Centre and Théâtre Populaire d'Acadie following a series of workshops carried out under a play development program with Brigitte Haentjens. The performances took place during the winter of 1997 under the direction of René Cormier with the assistance of Maurice Arsenault.

Albert Belzile	Utrope
Sandra LeCouteur	Victorine
Denise Bouchard	Flora
Amélie Gosselin	Delcia
Lynne Surette	Amandine
Philip André Collette	Nicolas
Philip André Collette	The Dark Owl, voice played by Nicolas
Lynne Surette	The Simpleton, voice played by Amandine

This version was published in 1997 by Les Éditions de La Grande Marée.

The translation here was workshopped during the Moveable Feast playwrights colony sponsored by Playwrights Atlantic Resource Centre and hosted by Live Bait Theatre in Sackville, New Brunswick, from July 21 to July 31, 2002 with the following cast:

Bill Forbes	Utrope
Nicola Lipman	Victorine
Gay Hauser	Flora
Jenny Munday	Delcia
Krista Laveck	Amandine (+Simpleton)
Bryden MacDonald	Nicolas (+Dark Owl)

Special thanks to Sarah Stanley for her work as dramaturg on this text during the workshop.

CHARACTERS

Utrope, father, in his 50s
Victorine, mother, a bit younger
Flora, oldest daughter, 24
Delcia, Flora's sister, 1 year younger
Amandine, the youngest daughter
Nicolas, the "baby", 19
The Dark Owl, voice played by Nicolas
The Simpleton (Bernadette), voice played by Amandine

SETTING

The action takes place in four different locations.

Utrope spends most of his time in an old shack which he uses as a carpentry workshop. In addition, we see the living room of the house with a staircase leading to two bedrooms. One door is open a bit, revealing a small bed with squeaky springs; the other door is closed, boarded up, out-of-bounds…

The time of the action has not changed: it takes place at the beginning of the 1970s.

Dark Owl
or
The Renegade Angel

by Laval Goupil

—•— PROLOGUE —•—

DELCIA

So… Nicolas… "The Dark Owl"…. (*FLORA gives DELCIA a deadly look to show her opposition, but says nothing. She addresses NICOLAS.*) You gonna read it or what? (*Same reaction by FLORA, this time directed towards NICOLAS. She says nothing.*)

NICOLAS

(*pause*) I'm not gonna tell our story; it's not worth it anymore.

AMANDINE

(*playing the disappointed kid*) Oh no! C'mon! Every time he says he's gonna read one of his stories, he always changes his mind! (*FLORA mocks her. They hear the bed springs squeak upstairs.*)

DELCIA

(*holding herself back from speaking too loudly*) No way, Nicolas, you ain't gonna quit now, half-way into this just 'cause mom's grumpy as a jeeseless bear. It's way too much fun! (*FLORA is upset again, but still doesn't say anything.*) Now come on, start readin'! (*She forgets where she is and speaks loudly, like a preacher.*) "The kingdom of heaven is like treasure hidden in a field…"

NICOLAS

(*trying to quiet his sister*) Sssshht! I'm not telling that story, so just forget it. And stop bugging me about it, okay!

DELCIA

(*impatient*) Listen you! Yer not still crapping yer shorts at yer age, are ya? Gutless little arse-hole!

NICOLAS

Look, Delcia, I just really don't want another big fight with Flora. Sure she drives me crazy sometimes, but she never refused to help me when I was in trouble at college. Which is more than I can say for you.

DELCIA

(*She loses her temper.*) Okay, shithead little brother. Fine! Don't read your damned fairy tale then. But we'll hear it again one of these days! Oh yeah, we'll hear it yet.

VICTORINE
(*She suddenly turns on the ceiling light in the bedroom and rolls out of bed.*) Jesus, Mary an' Joseph! You bloody brats! Jus' wait'll I get down there!

THE SIBLINGS
(*terrified*) Oh God! The squall's on its way! (*Everyone freezes.*)

—•— ACT ONE —•—

Scene One

UTROPE *is in his workshop. He's putting the finishing touches on a rocking chair he has just made.*

UTROPE
So, mayswell tell ya right up front: me, I ain't playing the game anymore. Kids? Same as the rest. I don't give a good goddamn. (*He puts down his work to roll a cigarette.*) Must be, oh, 'bout year an' a half now, two years maybe since I talked to 'em hardly at all. I mean, besides the basic necessaries, you know, eatin', drinkin', tellin' 'em to turn down that friggin' record player b'fore the whole house comes down like the walls o' Jericho, or 'mindin' Flora, my oldest girl, not ta let herself get carried away again with stories 'bout men she don't even know. Nope. Other than that, I ain't got much to say to them kids anymore. Jus' keep me mouth shut. (*He strikes a match against his backside.*) Jus' keep me mouth shut an'... (*He lights his cigarette.*) an' listen to 'em mouth off at each other, pickin' on each other like hens what got teeth so's they can peck all the harder... fer hours an' hours on end! 'Til I jus' get fed up. Jesus fed up. So I put on me cap an' come lock meself out here in the shack. Away from all that racket, all that n'ver endin' gripin' an' moanin'.

Goes for the wife, Victorine, too. She ain't talkin' much to 'em either these days. Course, I think... well, there's somethin' else bothrin' her. Victorine.... Goddamn it! Since when did she ever talk to those kids sensible-like anyway. She don't talk to 'em, she yells at 'em, she screeches at 'em. Slaps 'em in the head from here to kingdom come like they was pulp wood in a jeeseless pulp mill! Friggin' fool idea knockin' 'em senseless every time they turn around, those poor kids. An' when it's not the kids she's after tormentin', it's me. Goddamn it ta hell! "Oh you were right willin' ta make 'em fer sure" she says. "But when the time comes to give 'em a damn good thrashin', when I can't stand 'em bein' 'round the house anymore 'cause they're getting too smart-ass fer their own good... ah! Then yer tune changes.

Victorine
(*voice from offstage*) Yer tune changes all right, Utrope Nazaire Joseph, ya fat-assed spider! Like father like son! Ya piss off out to yer shack, tellin' me, "It's none o' my business!" Then no one sees your mug again 'til I'm after given 'em a good thrashin', every one of 'em from the oldest to the youngest. An' 'til after

they're all upstairs in bed, their bottoms warmed so's they can't sit fer a week, you betcha!" (*silence*)

UTROPE

Now, jus how're s'pose to discuss anything serious-like with a woman ornery as that? (*pause*) Yeah, okay. I know I was real willin' to make 'em, for sure. Oh yeah, real willin'! The daughter of old Louis Frogger was quite a looker y'know! But to go from that, to now, to beatin' the kids black'n blue in order to teach 'em how to behave like decent folk… no way, ma'am, no jeesly way! I had enough of me own dad givin' us so many boots to the backside and swats to the head when we was little that he ended up turnin' my baby brother, poor little Thomas, into a simpleton. But never you mind, eh. Cause there is a god in heaven after all, …me ol' man ended his days draggin' hisself along on a wooden cane from the house to the garage, from the pantry to the livin' room. And b'fore ya knew it he was cartin' hisself 'round in a wheelchair from his bed to the rockin' chair then from his bed to the cemet'ry. God help his soul now, the old bugger!

Nope, I tell ya, I jus' ain't playin' the game no more. A family's like a person's body: it's a fine thing 'til it gets sickly. Me, I think I done about everything I could to make it work; but it ain't workin'. An' I don't give a damn anymore. I'm outta the game. All I ask of this son-of-a-whorin' world is to keep sendin' me EI cheques when it gets too cold to work shinglin' houses. From then on, I'm just like a deer way back in the woods. I lock meself out here in the shop every day with my workbench, an' my chisels, an' my saws an' all my stuff, an' turn me hand to makin' rockin' chairs out of slabs o' wood. (*He goes back to work.*) It can take hours an' hours on end workin' with a hammer an' chisel to decorate the backa one chair with fancy patterns o' trees an' birds. But this here is my own little bit o' paradise. It's clean at least… no stink o' rot out here, far from it. Here it smells like fresh-cut wood… just like a sheep's meadow hidden away deep in a great dark wood.

Scene Two

FLORA, DELCIA and NICOLAS are at the window. Behind them, AMANDINE is holding a big sandwich which she is eating with gusto. Off to the side is a solid-looking rocking chair like the ones their father makes.

FLORA

Hey, Delcia, did ya get a look at the buns on this guy out here? Ya see 'im, Amandine?

AMANDINE

(*playing the slow-witted girl*) Ya mean the one leanin' on that mother of a big Plymouth out there?

FLORA

Yeah!

AMANDINE
The one with the fuzzy-balls… on the aerial?

FLORA
Yeah!

AMANDINE
(*not very enthusiastic*) Yeah…

DELCIA
(*sharp tongued*) Yeah. He ain't my type. I only go for men with some size. Less'n six feet an' they just don't turn my crank; I'm fussy about men.

AMANDINE
Good grief! What's your problem? This guy's not short. I mean, he ain't big, big. Okay, he's no, like RCMP, or anything, but he's no runt either.

DELCIA
Well, as far as I can see, he's short, okay. Too short. Kinda stumpy if ya ask me.

FLORA
Yeah, well, aren't you a hard one to please, Delcia. As if you've got anything to brag about. (*They give each other scornful looks.*) Just take a look at those shoulders, eh. He's no pansy, lemme tell you.

DELCIA
(*turning her nose up*) Whatever…. (*AMANDINE bites into her sandwich and chews loudly.*) Hey 'mandine, can ya cut the racket, eh? Ya sound like a cow chewin' 'er cud. You're drivin' me nuts.

AMANDINE
(*shrugs her shoulders*) Hmmmf.

FLORA
He's damn well built, that's fer sure. From this far, eh, he uh… he reminds me of my favourite singer. Y'know, the good-lookin' one…

DELCIA
Yeah, we know, Flora. Everybody knows. Harry Belafonte. Every man on earth: black, yellow or white who's more'n skin an' bones, brushes his teeth with Pepsodent and has short curly dark hair reminds you of Harry Belafonte. Yes, my dear, everybody knows that now…. (*pause*) Christ! She ain't half gettin' on my nerves with her *chomp, chomp, chomp* right in my ear! Can ya quit stuffin' your face for two seconds, 'mandine? You're gonna bust yourself! Doesn't matter we're watchin' good-lookin' fellas go by the house, 'mandine here's gotta be fillin' 'er face. Can't help exercisin' 'er chops, non-stop. I betcha if we saw Elvis Presley himself cruisin' by real slow in a shiny black Buick with the top down right smack in front of the house, 'mandine would run out and give 'im a kiss with 'er fat baloney sandwich still in 'er gob. She can't help it; shovellin' it in

and chawin' it up like a friggin' garburator! Christ, though! Can't ya give it a rest for just a minute? You're drivin' me crazy.

AMANDINE

Well, you're drivin' me crazy with your "you're drivin' me crazy." So there.

DELCIA makes a grab for the sandwich; they push each other a bit.

NICOLAS

(*turning back to his sisters*) Hey, you two pains in the ass. Stop screwin' around. Cripes a'mighty! Can't a fellow look at the scenery in peace, eh? (*He turns back to the window.*) It's true, y'know; I can see what you mean; the guy out there's not bad lookin'. (*DELCIA and AMANDINE start to imitate their brother's little gestures. He doesn't notice and continues to relate his impressions.*) Though he doesn't look like my... I mean... I'm not sure I could spend much time chatting with this guy. On the other hand, to be fair I mean... cripes... (*pause, like a confession*) ...he is cute all right! (*His sisters applaud.*) Hey! Watch out! He's lookin' this way! (*All four scatter away from the window. In her rush, Amandine lets her sandwich drop on the ground.*)

AMANDINE

(*to DELCIA*) Hey, watch what you're doin' you! (*to FLORA*) Every time I get myself a sandwich, Delcia always bumps me and makes me drop it somewhere.

FLORA

(*on her way to get a washcloth*) Food all over the floor again! And you, Delcia! It's obvious you're not the one keeps this place clean when mom's at the fish plant. (*to AMANDINE*) Well!? You get that picked up right now, geez. (*AMANDINE cleans the mess. She puts the bits of sandwich on the seat of the big rocking chair. FLORA returns with the washcloth.*) And I just finished washing this floor.

NICOLAS

Hey girls, ya better come and take a look at studly again before he takes off! (*The three sisters rush over to the window, pushing NICOLAS.*) Watch what you're doin'. Cripes! You don't have to all crowd the window at once. Hey, you're squishing me, ya bunch o' hooligans! (*They continue to crowd him, almost climbing on top of him so he is forced lower and lower until he's on all fours. He escapes by crawling out from under them. He stands up rather ruffled and offended. He tries to put his clothes back in order. His sisters laugh at him.*) Just look at my good silk shirt... my brand-new silk shirt!

DELCIA

(*mimicking his delicate gestures*) That's what ya get for being such a never-endin' pain, cripes!

FLORA

Oh no. He's not leaving, is he?

AMANDINE

No. I don't think so. Maybe he's just starting up his car to show Joe-Fish how big his motor is.

DELCIA

Take it easy, Flora. Your prince charming ain't takin' off. Y'see, he's gettin' out of his car again.

AMANDINE

Lucky, eh…

NICOLAS

Any chance I might get a peek too?

FLORA

He sure don't walk much like the fellas from around here; that's for sure. Compared to him, the guys we know all walk like ducks. Don'tcha think so, Amandine? Look…. (*She imitates a kind of waddling walk. AMANDINE quickly picks up the step and follows behind her.*) Y'ever notice that, Delcia? (*DELCIA starts to quack like a duck. They all find this very funny.*)

NICOLAS

(*decides to join his sisters, but in a different style… his butt tucked in like a ballet master*) Un peu de souplesse, mes demoiselles!

FLORA

(*returning quickly to her observation post*) Hey, where's he gone to? (*pause*) Ahh! There he is. (*pause*) Wow! Don'tcha think he's just too cool? I wonder where he came from, eh?

DELCIA

Straight from the finance company; that's obvious, ain't it?

FLORA

Oh stick a sock in it why don'tcha!

DELCIA

Fuck you. D'ya think anyone's gonna buy a boat like that 'cept on credit? (*pause*) I mean… don'tcha think he looks a little too snob, y'know, with his big black shades? And y'see the way he keeps lookin' around and around, strutting about like he's some kinda millionaire. Sure likes to put on a show anyhow.

NICOLAS

If you got it, flaunt it.

DELCIA

No. But look at 'im, I mean look at 'im. Look how he keeps glancing around to see who's watching him… he looks like a puppy what's lost his ball!

FLORA

Oh no! Don't say that, Delcia! Lost his ball! I feel faint! (*She pretends to faint. The others catch her.*)

AMANDINE

Oh doctor, hurry! Doctor! He's lost his ball! (*They break into laughter. NICOLAS is uneasy.*)

DELCIA

Bulletin! Bulletin! The millionaire's lost his ball and Flora's losing consciousness! (*She laughs even harder.*)

FLORA

My God! My God! What are we going to do?

DELCIA

Hey, Nicolas, it wasn't you who snatched the handsome stranger's ball, was it?

The joke cuts a little too close to home for NICOLAS. Insulted, he sits on the rocking chair. In that instant he realizes that he has just sat on AMANDINE's sandwich. He makes a terrible face. His sisters stop laughing, especially AMANDINE who realizes what's happened. He gets up and pulls off a slice of baloney that was stuck to the seat of his pants. His three sisters double up in laughter again. NICOLAS is caught between wanting to laugh and wanting to cry.

NICOLAS

Cripes! Cripes!! My good pair of velvet pants! Look! Brand-new! I just put these on for the first time this morning! Cripes a'mighty! Flora, do something!

FLORA

Ah no! I've done enough moppin' up for today. (*She changes her mind.*) Well, yeah okay. Hand me yer handkerchief there, I'll clean it all up fer ya.

DELCIA

Amandine you stinker! Wouldn't ya know it… she takes her best shots when she doesn't even mean to!

NICOLAS

Yeah, well, it's not funny. And you practically ruined my pants. Don't worry; from now on… I've never done anything to you, but you better watch yourself, keep your eyes peeled. One of these days you might just plop yourself down on a carpet tack, and that'd deflate your balloon a bit wouldn't it, you hypocritical little tramp.

AMANDINE

I didn't mean to do it, Nicolas…

NICOLAS

(*aping her*) I didn't mean to do it, Nicolas…

DELCIA

Didn't I tell you she was a bit simple? Simpleton!

AMANDINE

Hey you guys! I don't like being called that. Havin' one next door is bad enough.

FLORA

She's right, Delcia. Don't call her that. She hasn't done anything bad enough fer you to treat her like that. (*to NICOLAS*) There you go; it's all off now. Your butt is clean, clean, clean, little brother.

NICOLAS

Thanks, Flora.

FLORA

Gee, y'know what? I was just thinkin' it's been a long time since I had to wipe your bum, eh! (*NICOLAS reacts.*) Oh, c'mon, don't play high'n'mighty with me. Delcia and Amandine know very well that when you were little, a single day didn't go by without you crapping your shorts at least twice.

NICOLAS

Knock it off, Flora! What's got into you?

FLORA

Hello! This is my childhood I'm talking about here, Nicolas. My "golden youth" like they call it in your fancy books… yeah, golden all right: spent wipin' up your precious crap, the golden boy, our dear little brother Nicolas. Oh, you should be interested in this, an educated lad like you. I can still hear mom yelling for me from the kitchen, "Flora!" Hey Nicolas get your pencil out, you should be writing this down! "Flora! Yer little brother just crapped his diaper again an' it's stinkin' up the kitchen. I got my hands covered in flour. Ya gotta change yer little brother. So, kin ya go get a clean diaper outta the bottom drawer of the dresser. And don't screw up this time and grab a hand-towel like ya did yesterday. (*Until now NICOLAS hasn't batted an eyelid.*) Hurry up Flora, he's startin' to play with his turd. An' don't forget to put the dirty diaper in the basket out on the porch after. (*provoked by her brother's stoic reaction*) D'ya hear me? Hurry up! Nicolas is after puttin' the shit in his mouth! Dirty little pig!"

The three sisters think this is funny as hell. NICOLAS blushes with shame and anger.

NICOLAS

You're the one full of crap, Flora! You've gone way too far. I'll never forgive you for this! Never! (*His sisters continue to laugh at him.*) It's not my fault I was born with three fruitcake sisters who can't think of anything better to do than laugh at their brother, put me down, drive me crazy! Keep this up, an' I'm taking off for good this time I swear. And it won't just be for college… d'ya hear me?

DELCIA

Oh where then? Montreal maybe… all those topless dancers at the big clubs?

FLORA

Oh c'mon Nicolas, c'mon… ya little pooper you! (*NICOLAS tenses up even more.*) Oh all right, all right. I'm sorry. No really. I was just kidding; I didn't mean to flip ya out like that; I just wanted to remind you of some memories I have of my own tender childhood. Y'know, in case ya might wanna write about it someday… 'cause y'know, girls, our pretty little baby brother Nicolas here, on top of everything else, is turning into a poet!

DELCIA & AMANDINE

(*mocking naive*) No! You don't say!

FLORA

Oh yes, girls. A poooet!! Just like Leonard Coooohen. He's 'bout all I remember from grade eight, y'know… good ol' Lennie-I-got-a-deep-voice Cohen!

NICOLAS

How did you find out, eh? Were you snooping in my things?

FLORA

Oh no. I don't go scrounging through my sisters' jewellery boxes, like some people. No, it was just by accident. I was sweeping your room this morning…

NICOLAS

What the hell were you doing in my room again? (*He gives her a terrible look. Almost shouting.*) Flora, my room is MY room! Not yours, MINE! You have no business sticking your nose where it doesn't belong! (*to the rest*) When the hell are you going to understand that? When, eh? My room is the only place I can get away from the rest of you, find a little peace and quiet. My room is sacred!

FLORA

Well, if it's as sacred as all that, you'd think you'd run a broom over it once in awhile! (*NICOLAS refuses to answer.*) Look at him: he dresses like a prince and sleeps in a pigsty. (*NICOLAS gives in. FLORA picks up her story again less harshly.*) As I was saying… I was sweepin' under his bed when I brushed up this little piece o' paper. Before throwing it in the garbage, I thought I better make sure it wasn't important. So I read it. Ahhh… a hot little love poem! Don't worry, Nicolas, I put it back in your dresser drawer under your silk hankies; I wouldn't dare keep it! It was a real pretty poem though. Signed Nicolas Latendresse…!

NICOLAS

Flora, don't start again. Just be quiet, okay!

FLORA

Don't worry, mama's-boy, I didn't understand a thing; I haven't been to university, have I?

DELCIA

So, how'd it go, this "hot little love poem?"

AMANDINE

(*playing the fool*) Oh yeah. I'd love to hear it! I just love hot little love poems!

FLORA

Well, okay. Just one line as an example… if I can remember…. Hmmmm…. How did it go?

NICOLAS

Flora. Do you want me to tell you in clear, simple English…. Shut Up!

FLORA

Yes, it was quite simple…

NICOLAS

Flora, you stupid cow, I'm not going to say it again, shut the fuck up!

DELCIA

My goodness! This can't be our refined, sweet, little Nicolas, can it… all ruffled up like a wet hen?

FLORA

Oh I got it now. Listen to this…

NICOLAS

(*threatening*) Flora!

FLORA

(*She thumbs her nose at him and continues…*)
The day dawns again with golden gems
Each time I think of you and dream of love

DELCIA & AMANDINE

(*playing vestal virgins*)
The day dawns again with golden gems
Each time I think of you and dream of love

FLORA

Stuff those falsies' girls! Nicolas is after showing off the family jewels! Chink! Chhing-a-ling! Chink! Chhing-a-ling!

NICOLAS

What is your problem? What's wrong with it, eh? Besides I was only fifteen when I wrote that. Haven't the rest of you ever been in love?

DELCIA

(*She bursts out laughing.*) Nicolas... in love!

AMANDINE

In love?

FLORA

Sure, why not in love? But not with girls, eh!

DELCIA

(*She can't get over it.*) Nicolas in love!

NICOLAS

So, what of it? It's better than those stupid country and western records you play all day long. They're so *passé* y'know, Wilf Carter, Johnny Cash; I mean, c'mon. Gee, it's too bad I can't "warble a few tunes" for ya like mom says sometimes. Maybe that'd settle ya down a bit, eh.

AMANDINE

Hey that's a good idea! C'mon Nicolas, warble us a coupla love stories like the ones in the country an' western songs.

NICOLAS

I'm telling you, I can't "warble" anything! And after what you just did to me, don't even consider pesterin' me about it.

AMANDINE

Oh c'mon Nicolas, you can do it.

NICOLAS

Will ya just leave me alone? (*frowning*) Cripes!

AMANDINE

Just a little one... Nicolas...

NICOLAS

No! Bugger off!

AMANDINE

Just one verse, Okay?

NICOLAS

No! I've already told ya! Go ta hell! (*He pouts and starts rocking very fast in his rocking chair.*)

AMANDINE
Okay, fine then! Mama's-boy! (*She joins her sisters who have gone back to the window.*)

THE THREE SISTERS
(*to NICOLAS, unhappy*) Fine then!

> *AMANDINE puts her hand on FLORA's shoulder. FLORA doesn't react. DELCIA, on the other hand, looks at her and the two stare each other down while FLORA continues to watch out the window at the visitor who moves from one side of the stage to the other. NICOLAS continues to rock back and forth in his chair like a maniac.*

Scene Three

In his workshop.

UTROPE
Yeah, I know very well when it comes to being a pain in the ass, there ain't many kin top 'em. Those damn kids're a pain all right! Course they ain't kids no more. Ya jus' hafta look at 'em. Flora's damn near an ol' maid, if she don't watch out, an' Delcia's not far behind her; 'mandine's no little girl anymore; an' Nicolas just had his nineteenth birthday las' April or May…. Yep they're near all grown up. But it's funny, ain't it; we keep callin' 'em kids, eh, as if they were still seven, eight years old. Jus' like I used to yell at 'em first thing in the morning, "Hey you kids up there! Shake a leg an' get your butts down here for breakfast. There's baloney fryin', an' molasses an' good homemade bread. I ain't waitin' much longer for ya, kids."

Yeah, but if ya think they're crazy for all that, Victorine, ya sure got the wrong end o' the stick. No. No way. They ain't crazy an' don't even try ta make me swallow that one. Backwards? Maybe! But crazy? Not one Jesus bit. The proof? …Well they're just too sharp. No way. They're not mad, or mean; 'cause when you scrape away all the crap, they… well, they're not all that bad, really. No, far as I'm concerned they're just kinda… well, they're like… what's the word I'm looking for…? Uhh… I know… deadwood! That's exactly what they are: deadwood! They don't budge anymore. Nope. They ain't goin' backwards, but they ain't goin' forward, either: they're just deadwood. Full-stop. An' ya can't tell 'em anything; they won't listen to ya. Don't even notice themselves. They're like blind… or… like people what got mixed up in some kinda black magic or witchcraft. Like people… whaddya call it… hypnotized… or somethin' worse, possessed. Don't have a clue what they're doin'. Not the slightest clue.

But lemme tell you something: there was this ungodly, what they call a dark owl of sorrows came sniffin' 'round my girls… 'bout four, five year ago. He was an odd sorta jigger lemme tell ya. A workin' stiff 'peared to be lookin' for a job. A big scrawny sonuvabitch. Like an animal, with clumps of fur growing out all over his body. An' I noticed this weird tattoo on his left shoulder…. But more'n

Albert Belzile as Utrope
Photo by Rufin Cormier.

anything else I remember, it was those eyes of his, blazing out of his head… they were a funny colour, sorta blue-grey… like the scales of a fish! Those eyes gave me the creeps sometimes. You'd be talkin' to him an' after a while he had this way of lookin' at ya with a cold stare like an owl tryin' ta paralyze ya. Flora, 'specially, was bewitched by this sweet-talkin' tramp with ears big as a barn door!

Well it didn't last long, course. Just like all the other dark owls we'd seen before, one day he just up an' shits in our face.

Scene Four

The kids have not noticeably moved, but since the end of Scene Two the door to the mother's bedroom has been opened.

FLORA
So, can ya tell where he's gone to now?

AMANDINE
No idea. Can't see him anywhere.

FLORA
He sure disappeared in a hurry, eh. We hardly turn our backs and he's headed over to the plant.

AMANDINE
…unless he turned around first and disappeared like a bolta lightning round the curve in the road at the top of Whooper's hill.

DELCIA
Well, whaddya expect? Soon as he noticed none of us was gawkin' at him from the window anymore, he left to show off his new set o' wheels someplace else.

FLORA
God, you're in a grumpy mood, you! (*to the rest*) She can't open her trap without mouthin' off at somebody. (*DELCIA stares at her, but says nothing.*) Well I for one think it's just a cryin' shame he didn't hang around a little longer in front of Davi's store. I woulda put on my coat and headed over to look for something I'd be sure ol' Davi don't have in stock… just ta get a closer look at him.

AMANDINE
An' I woulda been right beside ya, Flora.

FLORA
We coulda both checked out if he mightn't have hidden somewhere a little pimple what needs squeezin', eh, Amandine?

DELCIA

Jeesus! Ya've fallen arse over kettles for him pretty quick, haven't ya?

FLORA

Well, it ain't the first time I seen him, is it, our mystery peacock there. An' every time he just gets more'n more mysterious.

DELCIA

What!? You know him already?! (*FLORA laughs.*) Why didn'ya tell us that before? Sneaky bitch.

FLORA

(*insulted*) Sneaky! (*mysterious*) Well, I don't have to tell you all my secrets, do I.

DELCIA

Secrets! Listen to her talk now! (*to NICOLAS*) Since when has our big sister ever started chasin' after some guy and we didn't end up hearing all about it?

NICOLAS also starts to laugh at FLORA.

AMANDINE

Well, I'd sure like to hear your secret, Flora. I really like secrets.

DELCIA

(*fed up with AMANDINE*) Sookie baby! (*She prefers the company of her brother.*)

FLORA

(*to AMANDINE*) The first time I saw him was at the *Enfant-Jésus* hospital, y'know, when I took mom in to see about that embargo that's been botherin' her for awhile.

NICOLAS

(*serious, spiteful*) Lombago… you twit!

FLORA

(*turning her back to him*) Whatever! I saw him go down the hall. What a sight! He was dressed all in white: white shirt, white pants, perfect white shoes, and a cute little sky-blue jacket overtop.

NICOLAS

Cripes! Sounds like what you saw was the Virgin Mary dressed up as a man.

FLORA

More like a doctor! A real doctor!

DELCIA

Course he might be nothin' more'n a nurse who wipes up everyone else's mess.

NICOLAS

Or maybe just your ordinary ambulance driver who picks up what's left of people all smashed on the pavement after an accident, any time of the day or night.

DELCIA

Ain't nothin' ta be too proud o' there, Flora.

AMANDINE

Oh you two think you're so smart, don'tcha? Who knows? Maybe he is a doctor after all. Didja get his name at least, Flora?

FLORA

Well, no. Not really. A candy-striper told me his name, but I can't remember it. It was something odd... like Paul Wallet or Wellet or Walton.... A funny kinda name.

NICOLAS

That's it! Saint Walden and the Virgin Mary all wrapped up in one man! Wow! That must've been something to see!

DELCIA falls to her knees in front of NICOLAS who poses like the saint in a romantic painting.

DELCIA

Oh give me my sight, oh Saint, my sight!

NICOLAS

(*harshly*) No. I'm saving it for the others! (*They faint. The other two find them very silly.*)

AMANDINE

Well, I'm sure he was really good-lookin'. Don't pay any attention to those two, Flora.

FLORA

He was one gorgeous hunk, lemme tell you, 'mandine! You can be sure I wouldna hurt our fine peacock there if I coulda got him alone in a dark little corner of the *Enfant-Jésus*!

DELCIA

"Fine peacock!" You make me laugh. A fine blackbird, don'tcha mean. A black bird what becomes a kinda crow after a bit... (*moving close to FLORA to emphasize her point*) ...then a real dark owl of sorrows; that's what he is if ya ask me !

FLORA

Good God Delcia! What are you driving at now?

DELCIA

(*pinching FLORA in the abdomen to tickle her*) Oh c'mon, Flora; you know very well what I mean...

FLORA

(*can't help giggling*) Stop it! Your claws are sharp!

AMANDINE

What's a dark owl of sorrows Delcia?

FLORA

Never mind. She thinks she's so smart with all her stories.

DELCIA

What! You don't know what a dark owl of sorrows is yet Amandine? You don't know that? God you're ignorant. Ya sure they don't teach you that at school? (*AMANDINE responds with silence.*) No, I don't s'pose it's changed much since I last set foot in that shit-hole. Well, it's about time you got smartened up 'bout real life little sister. All the same, there was a time mom used that expression quite a bit around the house here. Isn't that right, Flora?

FLORA

Don't start...

DELCIA

Why don't you tell us what a dark owl of sorrows is, Flora. G'won, tell us.

FLORA

Delcia, I'm warning you, shut your fuckin' trap or it's gonna get real ugly 'round here.

DELCIA

What!? What's got into you? Who's got her claws out now?

FLORA

I don't want you to talk about that stuff, understand. What's past is past. Jus' drop it!

DELCIA

For your information, you got no business bossin' me around. (*pause, then gently*) Besides, what've you got against birds anyhow? An owl is just an owl, isn't it, Flora. And 'mandine here has a right to know the difference between an owl an' a seagull, don't she? You got somethin' ta say against that, eh, big sister?

AMANDINE

What stuff, Flora?

FLORA

You just mind your own business, you! 'K? (*AMANDINE is hurt.*) Oh, don't go playin' the martyr with me! That'll teach ya not to listen to Delcia!

DELCIA

Hey, Nicolas, you've been to your fancy college; why don't you tell us what makes a seagull a seagull, an' an owl an owl. C'mon, Nicolas, explain it to us. (*Seeing where this is leading, NICOLAS doesn't want to get involved.*) Oh, our little golden-boy brother's still pouting, eh. The fatted calf ain't done sucklin' yet, I guess. (*She sits on the arm of the rocking chair next to NICOLAS and really tries to coax him.*) Now, remind me again, who was it that upset our little brother so badly a few minutes ago?

FLORA

Look Delcia, don't you try rilin' Nicolas up against me. There's been enough trouble around here already.

AMANDINE

(*to DELCIA*) She's right, y'know. We've had enough of you. Troublemaker!

DELCIA

Oh yeah, right. As if I'm the only one ever wanted to crap on this goddamn shit-house of a family.

VICTORINE

(*yelling from her bedroom upstairs*) Jesus, Mary an' Joseph! Ya screamin' bunch o' brats! Is it too bloody much to ask for a bit of peace an' quiet. Sounds like a goddamn whorehouse down there!

The kids freeze for a moment.

FLORA

Sounds like mom's tossin' an' turnin' a bit up there.

Deathly silence.

DELCIA

Must be havin' a nightmare. I can't believe it.

AMANDINE

(*after a pause*) I think we better sit tight. One heck of a storm is gonna let loose down those stairs.

DELCIA

(*starting to rock again*) C'mon, we're not gonna all drop dead of a heart attack just because of her.... So now, my one-and-only baby brother ain't pissed off at his second big sister, is he? Amandine, come over here on the rocking chair with Nicolas and me. We can tell each other stories jus' like we used to on the porch swing when we were little. (*FLORA tries to hold AMANDINE back, but she gets away, hesitates a moment, then goes to join NICOLAS and DELCIA. She sits on the other free arm of the chair. Feeling very vulnerable, FLORA becomes more and more anxious.*) Okay, c'mon Nicolas, we're all settled here now; why don'tcha tell my little sister an' me the delightful story of the dark owl. You know, the story of the old maid… (*She corrects herself.*) …the silly old virgin who took a dark owl for her lover an' got all messed up when the owl found himself all alone with her. In the dark! (*She lets out a few fake cries of fright. The others gesture her to spare her dramatic effects.*) G'won, tell us the story you wrote about her. You know, the one you hoped would win you a prize… or a medal… or whatever. C'mon… tell us!

FLORA

(*holding herself from speaking too loudly*) Nicolas. I don't want you to tell that story!

NICOLAS

I'll read it if I bloody well want to, cripes! (*He gets up to look for his scribbler, then sits down again.*)

DELCIA

It's okay, my one-and-only baby brother. Don't let her bother you. I'm all for you bein' a writer.

AMANDINE

I've never heard this story, Nicolas.

FLORA

It's not a story to be tellin'. It's just a story what makes fun o' the gospels. That's all it is.

NICOLAS

Huh? Since when did you start payin' attention to the gospels, sistah? Cripes a'mighty, when all this happened, lemme tell ya, the stories about Mary Magdalene weren't exactly your guiding light…. (*He gets ready to read.*) Isn't that right, Flora? An' the dark owl sure wasn't our Saviour, eh! An' the whole village couldn't help but know what was goin' on.

> *FLORA is very embarrassed. She doesn't know what to say. She is close to tears.*

DELCIA

Hoh! Hoh! Our one-and-only baby brother can sure talk when he decides to, eh. What? The cat got your tongue, Flora? Where's all your spit an' fight now? All your fancy slang like a cocked-up slut, eh? Chicken-shit. (*FLORA goes after her sister.*)

VICTORINE

(*flicking on the ceiling light in her room*) Delcia! You shit-for-brains little fart! Don't make me come down there! 'Cause if I do, you won't know what the hell hit'cha! I'll tan yer hide b'fore ya can turn around! (*She sits on the edge of the bed, disheartened.*) Utrope! Can'tcha keep the brats quiet down there fer just a little while? They're drivin' me crazy with their gawdawful racket!

FLORA

(*a little frightened*) Dad isn't back yet, mom.

VICTORINE

Ahh, that bugger. He always makes himself scarce jus' when I need him. Flora, you tell yer sisters an' yer brother ta keep their traps shut 'cause mother-o'-god if I hafta come down there, it won't be a pretty sight (*The kids are speechless.*) D'ya hear me, Flora?

FLORA

Yes, mom.

VICTORINE

(*She turns out the ceiling light and goes back to bed, grumbling. We can hear the bed squeak.*) Those kids are a pain in the ass. At their age, they oughta have more sense. Bunch o' bird-brains.

DELCIA

Well, looks like Amandine's storm's gone back under the covers. (*They relax a bit. They start rocking again. Pause.*) So… Nicolas… "The Dark Owl"…. (*FLORA gives DELCIA a deadly look to show her opposition, but says nothing. Then she talks to NICOLAS.*) You gonna read it or what? (*Same reaction by FLORA, this time directed towards NICOLAS. She says nothing.*)

NICOLAS

(*pause*) I'm not gonna tell our story; it's not worth it anymore.

AMANDINE

(*playing the disappointed kid*) Oh no! C'mon! Every time he says he's gonna read one of his stories, he always changes his mind! (*FLORA mocks her. They hear the bed springs squeak upstairs.*)

DELCIA

(*holding herself back from speaking too loudly*) No way, Nicolas, you ain't gonna quit now, halfway into this just 'cause mom's grumpy as a jeeseless bear. It's way too much fun! (*FLORA is upset again, but still doesn't say anything.*) Now come on, start readin'! (*She forgets where she is and speaks loudly, like a preacher.*) "The kingdom of heaven is like treasure hidden in a field…"

NICOLAS

(*trying to quiet his sister*) Sssshht! I'm not telling that story, so just forget it. And stop bugging me about it, Okay!

DELCIA

(*impatient*) Listen you! Yer not still crapping yer shorts at yer age, are ya? Gutless little arse-hole!

NICOLAS

Look, Delcia, I just really don't want another big fight with Flora. Sure she drives me crazy sometimes, but she never refused to help me when I was in trouble at college. Which is more than I can say for you.

DELCIA

(*She loses her temper.*) Ok, shithead little brother. Fine! Don't read your damned fairy tale then. But we'll hear it again one of these days! Oh yeah, we'll hear it yet.

VICTORINE

(*She suddenly turns on the ceiling light in the bedroom and rolls out of bed.*) Jesus, Mary an' Joseph! You bloody brats! Jus' wait'll I get down there!

THE SIBLINGS

(*terrified*) Oh God! The squall's on its way!

> *VICTORINE comes down the stairs throwing furious glances at her kids. NICOLAS and DELCIA are dumbfounded. AMANDINE takes refuge in FLORA's arms. They expect the worst.*

VICTORINE

(*She stops at the bottom of the stairs.*) Nicolas! Up to your room! (*He is terrified, unable to move from his chair.*) Nicolas! Don't make me go get'cha! (*He moves like a zombie, trying to get up the stairs as far away from his mother as possible to avoid the smack she gives him at the bottom step. Stunned, he climbs the rest of the stairs to his room.*) And you, Delcia, git over here! (*DELCIA goes over, head bowed like a little girl caught red-handed. She stoically takes the cuff her mother gives her across the head.*) There! You damned little vulture! That'll teach ya to act a bit more yer age, shit-for-brains! An' you two, yer no better than her, a packa bird-brains, the whole lot'a ya! (*She gives them a furious stare. They all hang their heads.*) I work all night long in that filthy cod an' flat-fish crawlin' with white worms. Wear myself out at that plant every night the good Lord sends. When I get back home, dog-tired, I drop into bed 'cause I can't stand up anymore... then just when I'm finally beginnin' to close my eyes what do I hear? The goddamned screechin' racket of the brainless floozies I have for daughters. The never-endin' bitching an' snipin' like a flock o' buzzards rippin' into each other with no feelin's whatsoever. Goddamn vultures! That's what you are! Even when you were no bigger than this... (*The three girls recite along with their mother's familiar tirade.*) ...all you did was pull each other's hair, throw stones at each other an' tear each other to pieces like a bunch of wild animals. (*end of the recitation*) That's right, you jeeseless bird-brained little brats! Wild animals! Scrappin over here, pickin' on each other over there... (*The girls recite right to the end of the sentence.*) an' pilin' inta one another like... like vultures! That's right; you're not real people! Yer nothing but a race a... (*all together*) vultures!

How old are you anyway? (*She collapses into the rocking chair.*) Ahh, Jesus Murphy! What did I ever do to deserve the good Lord saddlin' me with such backward, dim-witted daughters like you? You're old enough to have husbands, kids, a house of yer own to look after… but what are ya doing instead? Wastin' yer time scrappin' with each other. Christ! When're ya gonna grow up? When's it gonna end… all the trouble ya cause me? When I'm six feet under, I s'pose… when I'm six feet under. (*She sobs.*)

FLORA
Now, mom…

VICTORINE
When I'm six feet under. Is that what'cher waitin' fer, eh? (*Her sobs grow louder.*)

AMANDINE
(*going over to her, sympathetic*) No, mom. Of course not. No…. (*She consoles her mother. Gives her a tissue to wipe her tears.*)

VICTORINE
(*after a moment*) Where's your father?

AMANDINE
In his shop…

VICTORINE
Oh God, that man. He's somethin' else. If he'd jus' give me a bit of a hand sometimes… but no. Can't count on him. "It's none of my business." Jus' wipes his hands o' the whole thing, the jeeseless wimp.

Scene Five

UTROPE
"Poor men are born to trouble as the sparks fly upwards." (*pause*) It was a scandal. (*pause*) A scandal the likes of which'd hardly ever been seen in the history of the parish. (*finding it painful to talk about*) The girl… Planteen's only daughter, the neighbourhood simpleton next door…. Anyway, the dark owl jumped her. An' the story of the rape sure got all the fat tongues round here flapping: "It was his fault." "It was her fault." "No, I tell ya, he forced her." "C'mon! She was askin' for it." It was like that for months an' months. After a while the whole lousy affair was so mixed up ya couldn't make head nor tail of it anymore. 'Cept for us… neighbours started treatin' us like the village scum. Y'see the dark owl had stayed here, and no one would talk to us anymore. Yep, we were the ones had to pay for a crime we didn't do. (*pause*) So, ask me if I think there's any justice in the world, eh. (*pause*) The dark owl just took off back into the bush where he come from. By an' by, people got tired of it all. The Simpleton stopped talkin' about it; Planteen didn't do anything; we hardly heard anyone talk about it anymore…

But that's not the whole story. The day that goddamned dark owl disappeared for good, that very day… I… well I tell ya…. A kinda curse… I got proof too.

Everything jus' sorta stopped... turned unnatural.... My wife wouldn't let anyone get close to her anymore; men didn't want anything more to do with my girls; an' Nicolas...

Well, that's what the dark owl did to us. Ever since he made tracks outta here, nothing acts natural anymore. He put a spell on us, a trance, like in the story o' "Sleepin' Beauty": time stopped an' we're all messed up. A curse on our family... ta get back at everybody else.... (*UTROPE holds his hand over his heart.*) I swear. An' I have the proof!

Scene Six

AMANDINE brings VICTORINE a glass of water so she can swallow her pill.

VICTORINE
If I could just calm down a bit once I got to work, but no... There ain't no calm for folks like us. (*She pulls herself together.*) What time is it?

AMANDINE
(*looking at the clock in the kitchen*) A quarter to six, mom.

VICTORINE
Good lord! I gotta be at work by ten. An' by the time I get ready...

FLORA
But mom, you got lotsa time...

VICTORINE
No I don't. We got word there's gonna be a union meetin' tonight at seven. I better shake a leg if I wanna be ready on time. Flora, have you seen my smock and rubbers anywhere?

FLORA
Ahhh, they should be hangin' in the hall closet as usual.

VICTORINE
Oh Jesus! Where's my head these days? (*She goes up to her room; she stops in front of NICOLAS, who is sitting on the steps, and lectures the kids.*) And you better keep your goddamned traps shut, 'cause so help me God, if I gotta come back down here, I promise ya won't sit for a week.

AMANDINE
(*in a whisper*) Phew! Well that storm was a real old blower, eh? (*They stifle their laughter.*)

NICOLAS
Cripes! Has she ever gotten bitchy!

FLORA

No half friggin' way! Must be 'cause of her pills! (*more muffled laughter*)

AMANDINE

Don't laugh. I feel sorry for mom.

FLORA

Oh yeah. As if she ever felt sorry for us. (*silence*)

DELCIA

(*speaking in a whisper*) Hey, you guys! Come over here: There's somethin' I wanna tell ya. (*They gather around her.*) Just a minute. (*She goes to the foot of the stairs to make sure her mother is not on her way down.*) The hurricane's gettin' dressed; we got a minute to talk.

NICOLAS

Ok, but don't talk so loud this time. I don't want another one of her smacks.

DELCIA

Don't be such a cry-baby; you'll live. Besides, mom isn't really all that scary anyway. Look, listen to me good. Mom don't want us to fight anymore, right? Fine. But she didn't say we couldn't have a little fun! So… I had this great idea while she was doin' her woebegone mother routine.

FLORA

I don't know if I trust your ideas.

NICOLAS

Let her say her piece, Flora. Mom'll be down again in a minute.

AMANDINE

So what's your great idea, Delcia?

NICOLAS

Be quiet, Amandine.

FLORA

Oh shut it, Nicolas.

DELCIA

Shhhht. Shut up. Let me talk, eh. (*all listening*) Y'know the guy we were watching just now out the window…?

FLORA

Yeah… my mystery peacock from the hospital…

NICOLAS

Ssshhht!

DELCIA

Ssshhht! (*She takes another look up the staircase.*) Okay. We're gonna have a little fun! When mom goes to get her supper, I'll go find out where our feathery friend is nesting; then when mom goes off to the plant, we kin call him on the phone an' wind him up a bit. Okay?

AMANDINE

(*not understanding*) …wind him up?

NICOLAS

(*to DELCIA*) You're kidding right!

FLORA

Yeah, well, it's an interesting idea…

AMANDINE

But what do you mean, Delcia?

DELCIA

It's pretty simple. We find his phone number… that shouldn't be too hard with a name like his; there can't be too many Paul Walton's around here… then when we get him on the phone, we'll just chat him up a bit! How's that sound?

NICOLAS

Hey, I'm with ya one hundred percent. Flora and Amandine'll go for it too.

DELCIA

Trust me; we'll have a hoot! You'll see. But one thing, we can't let on to mom and dad what we're doing, at all.

AMANDINE

That's not gonna be easy.

FLORA

Oh c'mon Amandine, they won't even be home.

DELCIA

That's right. There, now all we have to do is wait… an' look innocent.

VICTORINE

(*voice offstage*) Flora? Did you put the salt-herring on to soak for supper like your father asked you to?

FLORA

Yes, mom. It's been soakin' since this morning. I was gonna put it on the stove in a few minutes.

DELCIA

Oh God, is time ever gonna drag until she gets off to work, eh!

NICOLAS

What'll we do while we're waitin'?

DELCIA

Well, mom said we couldn't talk loud, but she didn't say anything against warblin' a few little love songs, did she…? C'mon! We can practice our harmony.

NICOLAS

(*already fed up*) Ah no!…

AMANDINE

…Yeah, the Fish-Plant Warblers.

DELCIA

No, no. The Fat-Assed Spiders! (*She goes and stands in front of the others and imitates the gestures of a parish choir director. Or else she might pick up a guitar from somewhere and accompany the group… or perhaps do both at the same time etc.*) Okay ladies, your attention please! This evening we are going to begin our practice with a very lovely song from around here: "Danny's Song." One. Two. Three! (*They begin to sing the first few lines of the song. The girls can barely keep a straight face.*)

DELCIA

(*stopping them*) No. No, I have a better one than that. You know it. It's easy: "Please Release Me."

FLORA & AMANDINE

Oh yeah! That's great! Let's do it!

NICOLAS

Oh no. Not "Please Release Me."

AMANDINE

C'mon, sing with us, Nicolas. (*He makes a face. They begin singing.*)

> *VICTORINE, who has just put on her work smock, comes down the stairs carrying her little boots and goes straight to the kitchen. The kids put on their best behaviour…*

> *NICOLAS ends up singing the harmony part.*

—•— ACT TWO —•—

Scene One

VICTORINE is seated in the rocking chair, finishing her cup of tea. She's the picture of a typical fish-plant worker: green, pale-yellow or white smock belted in the middle, little rubber boots and her hair carefully tied up under a fine hair net.

VICTORINE

Another night of work ahead of us… a whole bloody night pickin' worms outta cod filets. I no more'n get outta bed an' I gotta get dressed an' go to the goddamn fish plant to spend my night pickin' worms outta fresh cod tails. Goddamn cod tails! Sometimes, seems like summer's never gonna end, y'know…

An' it's like that every friggin' day the good Lord sends. I get up 'bout quarter-ta-six, six o'clock, my butt draggin' on the ground, my eyes like two piss-holes in the snow they're so wrecked from starin' at fish all night. But I get up on my pins best as I can, get dressed… and what do I see in my head? Goddamned fresh cod tails! So I head down to the kitchen, cut me off a slice o' bread, make meself a cuppa black tea, a little fresh cow's milk… and wham! first thing I know, all I can think of is fresh cod tails! Cod tails with slimy little worms crawlin' through 'em!

Ah God, just the thought of it makes me wanna puke. But I don't puke 'cause I ain't got nothin' on my stomach to bring up. So I leave my slice o' homemade bread an' come an' drink my cuppa King Cole in the living room here. Ahhh, a spell in the rockin' chair an' I start to feel a bit better. The cod tails leave me alone for a bit! (*She drinks her tea.*) Only thing is, I know very well it ain't gonna last. Tony Stretch is gonna come by pick me up with the other worm-pickers, Cami Degracci, Olive Hynes, Gaye Anne and that fat Fredda Marius. Three in the front an' three in the back. But no matter, I know too well what's in store for me: a whole night with these friggin' big tweezers diggin' jeesely little worms outta disgustin' fresh cod tails! (*She finishes her tea.*)

Fredda Marius, y'know, she says it don't bother her no more; she's used to it she says. She says it ain't so bad as all that after all, 'cept for havin' to perch like a bunch a chickens for hours an' hours on those damn stools with no armrests. I dunno; it's more'n I can take sometimes. There's nothing to think about 'cept…. (*She shudders.*) I really hafta force myself every time I see one o' those goddamn slimy little maggots squirmin' away in a fresh cod filet. Ugh! Before I know it, my stomach's turnin' inside out like an ol' wool sock! I'll never get used to it! (*confidentially*) My God.

There are times, y'know, I'm just gettin' into Tony's car… an' it hits me! I imagine I see those maggoty worms squirmin' in the sunset! And that's when I start thinking about death, an' about what goes on in graves… in the cemet'ry.... My doctor give me some pills for the nerves... ahh... diamarzapan ten or somethin'; they're supposed to stop me gettin' the shakes. Cause... well... you just try pickin' out those Jesus little worms when your hand is shakin' like a leaf! It ain't easy. You have ta keep pickin' away... pickin' away... 'til your filet ends up all mushy and the worms are just laughin' at'cha. Ahh! Jesus, Mary and Jehoshaphat! I feel sorry for the 'merican what ate my first filets! Woulda got a little extra protein, if ya know what I mean.... He musta been dancin' the shake for a spell afterwards, I bet'cha! (*She laughs heartily.*)

Oh well, it's not as bad now as it was in the beginning, I guess. Shouldn't exaggerate: Camilla never misses a chance to laugh in my face every time I go "yuck!" an' I nearly puke 'cause I just found another worm. Camilla? She's the clown o' the worm-pickin' room. Always got a joke to tell ya, even if us worm-pickers aren't s'pose to talk to each another on the job. An' at midnight break, oh my God! She's a wild one! If you could see her carryin' on.... She's right loonie I tell ya! An' she pulls some great jokes on the filettin' girls! They're jus' a bunch o' sluts anyway. Yep, if I managed to tough it out 'til now, it's thanks to Camilla. She seems to take everything like a joke, she does. Even those little white maggots in the fresh cod tails. She calls 'em.... Oh. No. I can't repeat what she calls 'em.... (*She goes for it.*) Ah heck. She calls 'em... (*secretively, to the side*) ...bishops' little peckers! (*Then, as if she'd just said nothing funny at all, she calmly checks her watch.*)

Oh my goodness, those guys are gonna hafta show their face pretty quick. I better get my coat on. (*She goes up to the alcove under the stairs to get her coat. She takes a look out the window and sits in her chair again.*) I don't know if there's any point in still waitin' for 'em at this hour. (*weary*) Hey Flora! Give Fredda Marius a call. Ask her if Tony's still comin' to pick us up like usual, or if we hafta get there on our own tonight.

FLORA

(*from her room*) Okay, mom! I hope the line's not busy like every other time.

> *FLORA comes running down the stairs. Passing by the door of the boarded-up bedroom, something seems to hold her back for a second. Then she comes the rest of the way down in order to use the telephone hanging on the alcove wall.*

VICTORINE

Thank God I got Flora here to keep the house clean when I hafta go turn a buck at the plant. Delcia an' Amandine aren't worth a hilla beans. Jesus! If it were just up to them, this hell-hole of a house here'd be a pigsty in no time. All they ever think about doing all summer long is eatin' an' sleepin' an' helpin' Flora as little as possible, an' course watchin' guys go by in fronta the house. They're a paira goddamned good-for-nothings! The whole world could be goin' to hell in a handbag, an' they wouldn't lift a bloody finger, I tell ya. It's pretty clear they take after their father. But don't worry, one o' these days I'm gonna grab 'em by the scruff o' the neck, you jus' wait an' see.... They'll get a belt around the ears an' a hidin' they won't soon forget!

FLORA

(*hanging up*) Mom? Fat Fredda says to tell ya they'll be here in a minute. Seems Tony had some trouble gettin' his car started 'cause his slimy little kids spent the afternoon messin' around in it. They should be here any minute now. 'K?

VICTORINE

Okay Flora. Hey, your father ain't still out in his shack, is he?

FLORA

Yeah. Think so. (*going back to her room*) He took off right after supper. (*The attraction she felt when passing the boarded door is repeated, but she frees herself quickly and disappears upstairs.*)

VICTORINE

(*griping under her breath*) Oh that Utrope. He was against me goin' ta work at the plant, y'know. As far as he could see a woman's s'pose to stay home. Can't understand why a woman my age'd feel the need to go out an' earn a few bucks for her old age. As far as he's concerned, *he*'s the breadwinner: huh! (*Eyes to the sky, she sighs.*) Well one day I'd had just about enough of gettin' my ears chewed off with that crap. So, I let 'im have a piece o' me mind. I said to 'im, I said, "Listen to me Utrope Nazaire Joseph ya fat-assed spider, I been sluggin' away me whole life trying to raise these kids. They nearly killed me more'n once. And you?! You ain't been half a father to this family; you've never lifted a bloody finger to help me give 'em a proper bringin' up. An' now they're damn near growed up, don't come cryin' to me.

I don't want anything to do with your money anymore just so's I can go out, or so's I can buy some clothes, or have a little fun in the time I have left. I'd like to be able to go to the Legion when I want to, an' on Sunday night don't be lookin' for me… I'll be in the church basement cryin' "Bingo! Jesus, Mary an' Joseph!" (*She takes a second to catch her breath.*) Don't worry, Utrope didn't have any more to say on that score. No. You bet'cha! I mean, I woulda scratched his beady little eyes out I was that pissed off I was. As if a woman's gonna stay chained up to a kitchen stove her whole life long in this day an' age! So that's why I went over to the fish plant like all the other women I know from round here. An' I became (*proud and mocking at the same time*) …a cod-fish worm-picker!

Oh, I woulda really liked to get the job'a putting together the cardboard boxes, or maybe as one of the packers… y'know the ones what put the little packets'a cod-filets into the cardboard boxes… it's not such dirty work an' not nearly as disgustin' for sure… but seems I hafta wait a bit for that; it's a kinda promotion for later on. "Well, if there ain't no other jobs," I said to 'em, I said "then I guess it's hip-hip-hooray for the cod-fish worm-picker!" (*She laughs.*) Course no need to tell ya Utrope's still gripin' 'bout it all. Oh, not to me face, no. He wouldn't dare do that. No. But under his breath, like, an' when he's off with his buddy Albert Squid-face. Well he can just chew his gums all he wants; I say every woman's gotta look out for herself. Me, I spent twenty-five years up to last summer puttin' up an' shuttin' up. (*Her throat tightens with emotion.*) Well,

Sandra LeCouteur as Victorine
Photo by Rufin Cormier.

I ain't gonna say any more about it. (*She can hardly hold the tears back.*) I s'pose one day he'll understand.... (*She wipes away her tears.*)

Now then... (*changing topics to something less painful*) ...well I don't really know if I got the time to tell ya this or not, but... (*She chooses her words carefully.*) ...well they say there's trouble brewin' at the union office. Seems they're startin' to push the idea that the women are gettin' paid a heck of a lot less than the men, an' that the men, from what I can gather, are gettin' paid less than men in the rest o' Canada. But don't worry, I let 'em know what I had to say about it all, sure as I'm sitting here. "Give it to 'em, eh Pierre. Go for it, Matti! G'won, face up to those company big-shots and don let 'em get away with it. We're with ya all the way, us bottom women." Yep, that's what I told 'em at the las' union meetin'. Right in front o' everyone too! Fat Fredda grabbed me by the shirt-tail an' tried to make me sit down. She told me after that I was wound up like a maniac. But I just kept on talkin'. Didn't matter I had a big lump in me throat like a new potato; just made me yell all the louder. "We're sick o' workin' in all that shit an' in those damn cod worms! Sick o' gettin' screwed by every goddamn company for nothin' but starvation pay! The better our pay, the more we could start livin' like everybody else, Jesus Murphy! An' the more food stamps we could get to help pay for flour an' lard what's costin' us an arm an' a leg these days!" At that point, I don't know what I was saying no more, but everybody started clappin' an' shoutin' an' whistlin' like a bunch o' school kids! When I saw I couldn't talk no more over the racket, I sat back down beside Fredda who was red as a beet!... An' the meetin' went on. (*She catches her breath.*) Oh I dunno what came over me to do a thing like that.

FLORA

Mom? A car just came in the door-yard and they're all out there waitin' for ya. Hurry up. You're gonna be late.

VICTORINE

(*jumping to her feet*) Okay! I'm comin'. (*She bends over to pick up the empty teacup she set beside the rocking chair, then straightens up.*) Now I get it. Now I know what made me get up off my chair at the las' union meetin'.... Those lousy worms I can't stand the sight of! (*triumphant*) That's it, yep! Well, you goddamn cod-fish maggots, ya better watch out! Here I come! (*She leaves.*)

Scene Two

UTROPE has finished putting his workshop in order. He turns his attention to an old crucifix, which he can't decide what to do with. Finally he hangs it up over the workshop door. Through his window, he notices and watches VICTORINE's departure.

UTROPE

Well, there's Victorine off for another nighta glory. (*pause*) Though with all the pills she puts down her gullet, I don't know how much longer she's gonna be able to tough it out. (*We hear the noise of car doors closing and then the putt-putt of an old motor starting up. The noise fades and disappears.*) Before Victorine got really bad, I used to like teasin' her a bit. I asked her once why she didn't go an' throw her hat into the politics there? Oh ya could see she didn't know what to make o' that; she looked at me straight in the eye an' asked me, "Whaddya mean by that, Utrope?" Well it's pretty obvious, isn't it, I said. In politics y'know ya could pick on all the slimy vermin ya wanted!

Scene Three

We can hear yelling and laughter from the girls upstairs. Irritated, NICOLAS comes down the last steps, a notebook in his hand.

NICOLAS
Cripes! Where in the heck am I supposed to go so I can finish my writing? (*He sits in the corner of the room.*) Now where was I? (*He tries to concentrate by re-reading aloud the last few lines he's written in his notebook.*) "He was the one who set everything in motion. If I were to write about what's happened since that moment when... since that moment when..." (*Still bothered by the noise of the party upstairs, NICOLAS's efforts are in vain.*) Oh shut up! Cripes! "...when I first set eyes on him. The need I felt... drawn to my father, his wall of silence... (*more laughter from upstairs*) his don't-bother-me-now looks when I needed him most. The desire, strong, hidden, hopeless... hopeless..." (*He tries to write the rest of that sentence. It's a lost cause.*) How the hell am I supposed to write anything half-serious about my search for inner peace... when I have to put up with these damned lunatics in the house? (*He tries really hard, but...*) Oh! Fuuu...! (*He gives up.*) All right, there's no point blowin' a fuse. (*with feigned friendliness*) Hey Flora! And all the rest of you darling big sisters! Mom's gone. The field is clear! C'mon on down! (*Like a mad whirlwind, they come down the stairs.*)

THE THREE SISTERS
Yippy! Yahoo! She's gone! Hurray! Outta sight! Finally!

FLORA
God, I couldn't wait.

AMANDINE
Me neither.

DELCIA
I didn't think they were ever gonna leave...

AMANDINE
Yeah, they went off in that piece o' junk what's more beat up than the old kettle we used to keep on the stove before...

FLORA

You can say that again! An' that Tony Stretch! He ain't half enough ugly, is he?

They all agree.

DELCIA

Okay. Okay. We got better things to do'n sit here gossipin' like a bunch o' old ladies. Let the fun begin! Nicolas, bring that rockin' chair over here by the telephone. Oh, 'mandine, better go help your sooky brother there before he hurts hisself: wouldn't want him to break a nail now or anything would we.

NICOLAS does not appreciate this sort of remark; he pushes AMANDINE out of his way and brings the chair over by himself.

FLORA

(*a little nervous*) Are you sure it's okay what we're doing?

DELCIA

Oh c'mon Flora. Don't tell me you never done this before. It's lotsa fun! The last time we did it ta Freddy Chase. Y'know him, Isadora Chase's big lug of a kid…. (*She sits in rocking chair near the phone. FLORA shakes her head.*)

AMANDINE

Oh yeah, he's the one everyone calls Isadora's "Dopey" on account he seems to be missin' a few screws somewhere.

DELCIA

(*to AMANDINE*) Yeah, yeah. That's him. Fer sure ya know him. I was with Geraldella over at Leo's restaurant. We were laughin' like ya wouldn't believe. 'Specially when he got to the restaurant to pick up his blind date, eh! Tryin' not to let on like…. God ya shoulda seen 'im. An' he stunk like he was wearin' a whole bottle o' Old Spice or somethin'. Eventually he figured out I wasn't his blind date, that it was Geraldella who phoned him. If you coulda seen what an idiot he looked like! God! I nearly pissed myself I was laughin' so hard.

FLORA

(*no more amused than necessary*) Oh yeah, I can imagine…

NICOLAS

(*amused*) He oughta been happy!

AMANDINE

(*copying FLORA*) I don't blame him… puttin' that great big lug together with tiny little Geraldella!

DELCIA

He was so pathetic, God! His arms were practically draggin' on the ground.

NICOLAS is quite cheered up now.

FLORA

So… uhhh… about our good-lookin' hunk, eh… Mr. Mystery Peacock, are you gonna tell us if you found his phone number or what?

DELCIA

(*pretending not to know what FLORA is talking about*) …mystery peacock…. (*The others don't believe her. But she drags out the suspense a bit more, then…*) Yes! (*Everyone cheers.*) But don't talk to me about it. It was no fun tryin' to flush out a bird like him. His number wasn't even in the phone book.

FLORA

Good God. So how did you find it?

DELCIA

Well, I called the operator, but the bitch wouldn't give it to me. I tell ya…. So then I tried Geraldella's sister, the one works at the hospital, an' she was able to help me out.

AMANDINE

D'ya know his first name?

FLORA

Or just his last name?

AMANDINE

Is he stayin' around here?

FLORA

Is he really a doctor or what?

NICOLAS

(*mocking*) Doctor, nurse, or… undertaker?

> FLORA, *especially, groans.*

DELCIA

Nurse's aide, dear Flora. That's what Geraldella's sister says anyway an' she's an RN, so she should know. That's right, Nicolas, "RNA" (*She gives him a handshake.*) But other than that, he's just the man yer lookin' for: handsome, new in town, and… hungry! Handsome – at least he sure thinks he is in any case… new around here, not married… hey, I checked everything! Flora, he'd give his left nut to catch a good-lookin' girl like you. (*pause*) …At least for one night, anyway! (*FLORA protests again.*) No, Flora. Trust me. I know about this sort of stuff; he's just the kinda guy ya need.

> FLORA *doesn't want to believe it.*

NICOLAS

(*impatient*) So what's his name then?

AMANDINE

Yeah, stop stringin' us along... c'mon!

FLORA

Yeah, what's his name?

DELCIA

(*She's looking for a slip of paper she has hidden in her bra.*) Wait a minute while I take a look on my shelf.... (*She finds it.*) Aha!... his name is... are ya ready? (*in English*) Paul... (*in French*) Ouellette (*Everyone looks at her, uncertain.*)

FLORA

(*in English, incredulous*) Owletta!

DELCIA

(*scornful*) Yeah... that's almost the same as Walton, eh! Walletta, a big shot no doubt. Must be French. Or maybe 'merican with a big "wallet!"

NICOLAS

(*in English*) Paul... (*in French*) Ouellette.... You're sure it's Paul?

DELCIA

Well...

AMANDINE

Paul.... (*She makes a face.*) Paul... I don't really like that name. Now if he called himself... (*in French*) Paul... y'know like Paolo or Ricardo or Michel... I like those names.... (*Nobody is listening to her.*)

FLORA

(*She tries to pronounce it very carefully: first in English.*) Paul (*then in French*) Ouellette? Are you sure about that? He seemed to me more...

NICOLAS

Well, it's pretty odd if you ask me. Cripes a'mighty! What are they doing hiring French RNA's for anyway? Some bright idea to kill off patients with embarrassment?

DELCIA

...or garlic breath!

NICOLAS

Well it sure ain't because they're bilingual, anyway.

AMANDINE

Bilingue don'tcha mean? Just like all the future bilingue secretaries like me... *comme moi!*

FLORA

(*pensive*) Paul Ouellette… RNA…. (*to DELCIA*) Is he staying around here for awhile?

AMANDINE

Yeah… did Geraldella's sister tell you where he lives?

NICOLAS

Ouellette…. Well he sure ain't a local, that's obvious. Do you know where he comes from, Delcia?

DELCIA

(*mysterious*) Nobody seems to know… 'cause people like that aren't real people like the rest of us. They live nowhere, come from nowhere…. (*lively all of a sudden*) They just appear an' disappear with no warning! A flashy peacock: that's what he is, really! (*She passes her little scrap of paper over to FLORA.*) Here! Call him! (*Her sister remains frozen.*) Well, g'won, call him!

FLORA

(*after a long pause*) No.

DELCIA

What?! No? (*FLORA merely laughs rather stupidly.*) You goddamned bird-brain! (*She grabs the scrap of paper from FLORA and picks up the phone.*)

NICOLAS

You're going to call up a complete stranger? Just like that?

DELCIA

Right now! It's no big deal. I'm gonna do it right now 'cause I don't like mysteries. I'm gonna clear things up right now. This very minute!

FLORA, AMANDINE & NICOLAS

In French!?

DELCIA

Well I ain't about to start parleyvooin' this guy in Chinese am I? Yeah, that'd really take the cake wouldn't it. No, we're gonna have ourselves a real party. Course I'm going to talk to him in French. An' I don't have to turn myself inside out to do it either. *Par se quer je savoir aussi Fransez quer une froggé…* can… croak. *Daccorde*? Now give me some space; I'm callin' him! (*She dials the number while FLORA and AMANDINE get more and more excited and giggly.*)

FLORA

She's crazy! Completely crazy!

AMANDINE

You got that right! She's crazier'n a bag o' hammers.

NICOLAS

(*serious all of a sudden, as if it were a matter of great importance*) I can help you with your French. I took it in school, Delcia.

DELCIA

(*phone to her ear*) It's ringing.... (*suddenly, into the phone*) *Mesewer* Paul Ouellette? (*pause*) *Murrcy bowkoo.* (*to NICOLAS*) That wasn't him, but he's not far away. They're gonna go get him. (*She imitates the voice of a man.*) "*...une menute... see voo play.*" That's what he said, the chief of the owlette tribe. Oh! This is great!

NICOLAS

(*in a loud whisper*) Must be his landlord, or maybe a roommate.

DELCIA

Whatever. (*suddenly, into the phone*) *Wee*, hello! *Bonejoor!* (*to NICOLAS*) He said, "Hello" (*back to the phone*) *Mesewer* Paul Ouellette? (*pause*) *Je suis une amie voos aplay... par se quer...* ahh... cause... ahh...

NICOLAS

(*whispering*) *Je voudrais mieux te connaître.*

DELCIA

Huh?

NICOLAS

(*whispering*) *...parce que je voudrais mieux te connaître.*

DELCIA

(*into the phone*) *mure te connetre* (*pause*) *Je suis une amie voos aplay...* ahh *par se quer je voo connet mure...* ahh *quer voo!* (*Her sisters burst out laughing.*)

NICOLAS

No!

DELCIA

No!

NICOLAS

(*still whispering*) *...parce que je voudrais mieux te connaître.*

DELCIA

No! *Wee! Par se quer je voos...* ahh.

NICOLAS

(*still whispering, but finding it harder and harder to keep serious*) *...mieux te connaître!*

(l to r) Lynne Surette as Amandine, Denise Bouchard as Flora, Amélie Gosselin as Delcia & Philip André Collette as Nicolas.

Photo by Rufin Cormier.

DELCIA

…*mure taqinnet!* (*Her sisters are splitting their sides.*)

NICOLAS

No! Cripes!

DELCIA

No! (*She listens to the phone for a minute. Her expression changes.*) Huh? Oh, you speak English! (*General reaction from the others. DELCIA speaks to them.*) He says his name sounds French, but he's English because of his mother. (*to the phone*) Ahh well, so in that case you're English! From around here? (*pause, then to the others*) He says he ain't from around here, that "thaht would be a verah lohng storah" (*to phone*) You got a funny accent, y'know! (*pause*) Ah well, Mr. Ouellette…. (*pause*) Paul… I really don't think I want to tell ya my name after the joke about speakin' French on the phone. Ya must think I'm a real idjit fer sure. (*pause*) Oh. Well that's good. (*to the others*) He says it happens to him a lot. (*pause*) Yeah, well, I like it even better that you're English too. We speak the same language anyway. (*pause*) Huh? (*pause, then to the others*) He's says sometimes you don't hafta say anythin' to understand each other! (*pause*) You're a pretty fast talker, aren'tcha!

NICOLAS

Ahh. That's an American for ya… I saw him coming a mile away.

DELCIA

He's falling for it! (*The conspirators celebrate.*)

FLORA

I didn't know they could be so fast on their feet.

NICOLAS

Fast? You're kidding! They're as quick as greased lightning and as hot as apple pie!

AMANDINE

What is he saying now, Delcia? What's he saying?

DELCIA

(*She speaks into the phone. We sense she is trying to speak very correctly, but not too successfully.*) No, really Paul, I can't tell ya my name. I was just callin' ya… calling you… for the pleasure o' talkin' to ya. (*She winks at the others. Pause.*) When? (*to the others*) He's asking me when I saw him. (*pause*) Me? Well a few times, but I don't think ya… uhh… you… would remember me. (*pause*) Wasn't it you was hangin' around in front of Davi's convenience store? (*pause*) The self-serve; that's right. (*very coy*) You're not bad lookin', y'know. (*Pause. She gives FLORA a jab in the ribs and laughs out loud as if the person on the phone just said something rather daring.*)

FLORA
What's he saying, Delcia?

DELCIA
(*She continues to laugh.*) Me? My "ovahall appairance"? (*pause*) My looks, ya mean. (*She laughs again.*) Ahh. Same as you, I s'pose. I'm not too hard on the eyes. Well, I'm no Brigitte Bardot, course, but I ain't no hard lookin' ticket at all. My friends tell me sometimes I ain't hard lookin'. (*pause*) Ain't hard lookin'? (*to the others*) He says it's the first time he ever heard that expression! He's starting to be a bit of a pain.... (*pause*) A more precise description? Ahhh.... (*She's stuck on this one, all the more so because she's no painting herself. Suddenly she thinks about FLORA and she makes her stand in front of her. FLORA lets her do this. She even has a bit of fun miming some of her sister's lines.*) I'm average tall, not fat... slim. I have naturally blond hair.... (*FLORA has brown or black hair.*) Ahhh...

NICOLAS
(*whispering*) I often get compliments on my eyes, my mouth...

DELCIA
I often get compliments on my mouth, my blue eyes, my cute button nose, my face.... (*pause*) Yes, that's right. I'm rather pretty actually. (*pause*) My "mensahrations"?! Good grief! What are you talking about?! (*descriptive gesture from NICOLAS*) Oh! My measurements! That's what you mean...! (*FLORA takes a "femme fatale" pose. AMANDINE pretends to measure her.*)

AMANDINE
Thirty-two, twenty, thirty-two.

DELCIA
Thirty-six, twenty-four, thirty-six. The last time I checked. (*pause*) No. I'm serious. I'm not kidding.

NICOLAS
(*still whispering*) I once took part in a Miss New Brunswick contest.

DELCIA
(*into the telephone*) Well, you know, I once took part in some contests... (*pause*) beauty contests, a'course. As if I'd be takin' the prize at a craft show or somethin'! (*NICOLAS has to hold his stomach to keep from laughing out loud.*) Yes. Oh for sure. I'd love it if we could see each other up closer... "look intah each ahthah's eyes" as you put it. (*to the others*) Hey! No kidding. This guy's goin' a hundred miles an hour here! (*speaking into the telephone as FLORA starts to show signs of getting nervous*) It's not everyday I get to meet a good-lookin' guy like you. (*pause*) Where? Where could we meet? (*FLORA gives a sign to DELCIA that she doesn't want to go that far.*) Well, I don't know.... Maybe at the restaurant... or maybe...

FLORA

(*whispering in her ear*) Delcia! I don't want anything more to do with meeting this guy.

DELCIA

(*pause*) Ah, can you hang on a minute there? I think there's somebody out the back door… uhh, at the kitchen door. (*to FLORA*) He really wants to meet you somewhere…

NICOLAS

…ready to rock an' roll…

FLORA

What! Are you crazy? As if I'm gonna hook up with that guy now.

DELCIA

What's your problem? All he wants to do right now is check out your 36-24-36. He seems really nice, an' he talks like a dream.

FLORA

That's just the problem, ain't it. He talks way too good for me. I'd melt right through the floor in front of him the minute he opened his mouth.

NICOLAS

My! My! Now look at who's crappin' her shorts, eh! You're backin' out, Flora. If ya back out again this time, you're gonna end up an old maid…

DELCIA

An' I'm gonna look real stupid, ain't I, if I don't make a date with him now, you retard.

FLORA

(*thinking*) Wait. Wait a minute.

DELCIA

(*into the telephone, very carefully*) One moment, please.

AMANDINE

C'mon, Flora, this is your chance!

NICOLAS

Cripes, if I were in your place, I'd lay on my Sunday best and make 'im work for it!

DELCIA

Move it, Flora, move your friggin arse before he hangs up on me.

FLORA

No. I've got a better idea. (*She becomes very serious.*) You called me a retard a minute ago…. Listen ta this, Delcia, you tell him to go visit that slut next door, Planteen's goddamn Simpleton! Then we'll see some real fun tonight!

NICOLAS

Yeah! Yeah, Delcia! G'won!

DELCIA

Okay. That's a good idea.

AMANDINE

(*frightened*) Hey, you guys, be careful. Maybe…

FLORA

(*serious tone*) Planteen's goddamned fool of a daughter!

NICOLAS

This is gonna be great fun!

DELCIA

(*into the telephone*) Paul? Oh, I'm glad you're still there. (*pause*) No, No. It was nothin' at all. (*pause*) So ahh…. (*pause*) Well, yeah sure. I can't think of anything better than "gettin' tah know each ahthah mo deepla" as you say. (*pause*) Look. Why don't you come over here. Y'see, my folks ain't… uhh aren't home right now. (*pause*) "On vahcation," yeah, that's right, for sure. Afterwards we can go wherever you like. (*pause*) Where do I live? (*to the others*) Gamin' Street… number thirteen! (*They burst out laughing.*) Ssshht! (*pause*) Oh it's not hard to find. Y'know Davi's store? (*pause*) Well it's just the other side o' the road, first house on the right. (*pause*) Not the one right across, no. The one beside it, to the right.

FLORA

(*in a whisper, but with force*) The house is pink and green.

DELCIA

(*transmitting the message*) It's pink and green. (*pause*) Yeah that's the way the house is painted. You can't miss it. (*pause*) You're comin' right now? (*pause*) That's fine. I'm all kit up. (*pause*) "kit up?" …it means… ahhh…

NICOLAS

(*very feminine*) I'm all reddah for ya!

DELCIA

It means I'm all ready! (*She laughs.*) Whadja call it? (*pause*) "…Kwen'en Ruull"? (*pause*) Ah! "… kwentlah rourall!" (*pause, then to the others*) He says my expressions have a "kittenla rohll!" Do any of you know what he's talkin' about? (*NICOLAS is nearly in hysterics.*) Okay, that's it. (*pause*) Yep. See y'inna bit…

right, see you soon! (*She hangs up the telephone and while the others applaud she takes a deep breath.*) Give me some space! Some air. I need some air!

FLORA

That was unbelievable!

NICOLAS

Delcia, you are quite an actress!

AMANDINE

I wouldn't have believed you could do it.

DELCIA

Oh, c'mon now. I may not be as beautiful as my big sister, Flora. Maybe I don't have her 36-24-36, but crafty girls with smarts like me, well, they don't make 'em like that anymore!

NICOLAS, AMANDINE & FLORA

You can say that again... they sure don't make 'em like that anymore!

Scene Four

UTROPE slams his wooden mallet against the workbench. He is furious.

UTROPE

That goddamn dark owl! Wasn't jus' my wife an' my kids he hurt either y'know, inside like. But me too. If there's one thing in this son-of-a-whorin' world I wanna keep clean, it's my shop here where no one—d'ya hear me? no one— comes dump their shit like they do everywhere else. My shop, well maybe to you it's just a shack, hardly big enough to turn around in, but what a shack! Clean an' tidy an' smellin' o' pine an' cedar an' hemlock enough to send ya to seventh heaven. A few square feet like you ain't gonna find no place else! "A sheep's meadow deep in a great dark wood." But then I already told ya that, didn't I?

So just think, it was here. Here! Goddamn it. He dragged that Simpleton over here so he could do his filthy business. Here! In my wood shop! Hellish fiend! Damn him. It doesn't happen to me often, but that time, I really lost my head. One swipe I took my hammer an' some wood an' I boarded up the whole damn lot: the shop, Flora's bedroom where the dark owl an' her used to... mess around! (*He is silent for a minute, but he can't contain himself.*) No! Not in my shop! Not in my house! (*pause*) He couldna hurt me more if he'd gone an' stabbed me in the heart! (*UTROPE shows the signs of great inner pain.*)

Scene Five

AMANDINE is alone at the window. She has a strange look on her face. At the back, in shadow, FLORA, DELCIA and NICOLAS are sitting motionless. They are watching her very carefully.

AMANDINE

(*She stares into the distance and calls out with the "celestial" voice of Bernadette the SIMPLETON.*) Cheeep-Cheeep, Cheeep-Cheeep…. (*She listens for a moment in the hope of hearing a response. Getting none, she starts again.*) Cheeep-Cheeep, Cheeep-Cheeep-Cheeep, Cheeep (*She listens again, not understanding why there's no response.*) Papa? Where've they gone, eh? (*She looks through the window into the void.*) They ain't here no more. They're all gone 'way. (*She imitates the plaintive cry of a small defenseless bird.*) Cheeep-Cheeep. Here little birdies; here, little birdies…. Cheeep-Cheeep, Cheeep-Cheeep. Come to your mommy. (*She listens one more time, then*) Cheeep…. (*No response. Worried and sad, she looks around the room and up to the ceiling.*) Where've they all gone to? Where've all my little friends gone to, Papa? My little birdies… They sang so sweet, so pretty, so sweet. My little birdies…. Cheeep-Cheeep. (*Her voice breaks. She lets herself fall into the rocking chair in front of the window and sobs.*) So sweet. What've I done to 'em, Papa? They've been gone for days an' days… I keep callin' to 'em an' callin' to 'em 'till I just can't anymore… an' still they're hidin' from me… Papa, what've I done to 'em?

NICOLAS

(*jumping up with a cry of impatience*) It's fall, Bernadette! It's fall! (*Everyone starts to laugh. They applaud as if at the theatre.*)

NICOLAS, FLORA & DELCIA

Bravo! Way to go! Bravo Amandine! Bravo!

DELCIA

Hey, you're a helluva actress too, y'know!

FLORA

Oh my God! That was so good I had a lump in my throat an' it nearly brought tears to my eyes. One more line an' I woulda been bawlin' like a kid.

AMANDINE

But that's not the whole story. Planteen was wastin' his breath repeatin' his, "It's fall, Bernadette! It's fall!" That bloody Simpleton didn't understand a thing about it. She just shut herself up with her daydreams and every chance she got, "Where are they, Papa? Where're all my little birdies?" As for Planteen, well, after listening to that for a while, he just wanted to shut her up! But she was still far off in her own little world, and you know what idea she got into her head then?

FLORA & DELCIA

(*pretending not to know*) No…

NICOLAS
C'mon Amandine, you've only told us this story a hundred times already. (*to the others*) But it's always fun! (*to AMANDINE*) You're off to a good start… go on.

AMANDINE
Well, she got it into her head that her sweet little tweety-birdies were sulking and ignoring her 'cause she hadn't taken good enough care of them. So, get this, you're not gonna believe it, she hauls out all the Christmas lights and starts to decorate that Jesus big shack she kept her birds in… stringsa blue, white, red, green, yellow…

THE OTHERS
…and orange!

AMANDINE
…every colour of the rainbow! So there she was, up on the ladder, all tangled and wrapped in strings o' Christmas lights, hammerin' and poundin' away on the roof of the bird shack. Planteen tried everything he could think of to get her to change her mind. But in the end he was afraid she was gonna fall off that ladder and break her fool neck. So he went an' hooked up the damned strings himself… blue, white, red, green, yellow…

THE OTHERS
…and orange!

AMANDINE
…every colour of the rainbow! An' me, I used to be over there from time to time, and God I found it so damned funny I nearly pissed my pants sometimes! (*Everyone is laughing.*) But then at the same time, I felt kinda… well, I mean, it was pretty pathetic too…. (*Together they cut short their laughter and exhale a collective sigh of mock empathy.*)

When the whole shack was decorated and lit up, with the strings going on and off, on and off, just like the front window of the Two-Lanterns massage parlour, Bernadette the Simpleton settled back into her rocking chair… she seemed almost hypnotized… started rocking back'n forth muttering to herself, "I'm sure they'll come back now. I'm sure my birdies'll come back now, Papa. I'm sure they'll come back…"

THE OTHERS
…next spring!

AMANDINE
No! "At Christmas!"

DELCIA
You tell a heck of a story, 'mandine.

FLORA

(*sarcastic*) A terrible tragedy!

NICOLAS

I really should write that story down, y'know.

DELCIA

Then at Christmas, she had to be happy with a few little sparrows squackin' around the house.

AMANDINE

All I know is she was a pitiful sight the whole winter long.

FLORA

Oh she's pitiful, all right. You can say that again! Crazy bitch!

DELCIA

Well your sad times are about to end Bernadette. Your days of doing without are almost over! You're gonna have a visitor, you cagey little bird-brain!

FLORA

(*Her frustration has been growing in her for the last few minutes.*) So all she wanted was her sweet little birdies, eh! That's all she was lookin' for, huh, the damned slut. Well, she's gonna get her bird all right! One hell of a bird. And I hope... I hope he knocks her up real good this time!

DELCIA and NICOLAS move to calm FLORA.

NICOLAS

Whoa, now...

DELCIA

...take it easy...

AMANDINE

Hey! C'mere, guys! Our peacock's already here! (*Everybody crowds in front of the window.*) Look! His car's parked right over there.

THE OTHERS

Where? Where?

AMANDINE

There! Right in fronta the house!

NICOLAS

Yeah, she's right!

DELCIA

That's his car all right. The Plymouth.

AMANDINE

Must already be inside the house.

DELCIA

Yep... well, there doesn't seem to be too much happening right now.... (*Silence as they keep watching.*)

NICOLAS

It's awful quiet. (*silence*)

FLORA

The calm before the storm...

NICOLAS

Could be...

DELCIA

Yep, that's probably what it is...

AMANDINE

It is strange though, eh.... (*She looks at FLORA.*) Don't you have anything else to say, Flora?

FLORA

Me? I get the feeling it's not going to turn out quite the same way this time.... Wait just a bit more.... Just long enough for the slut's senses to warm up a bit. You're gonna see what happens when her old memories of the dark owl come back an' smack her in the face... you'll see! She'll take a fit like dry kindlin' going up in flames... I promise you!

Scene Six

UTROPE has still not recovered from his depressed mood in the previous scene.

UTROPE

Burning! Deep! Like a knife in the heart! (*He does his best to pull himself together.*)

A coupla days later, I heard the whole story straight from my oldest daughter; in the morning I came back out here to work... try to figure things out. So I took off the boards I'd nailed up... opened the door.... (*At the memory, he recoils in fright.*) I couldn't believe what I saw! There, nailed to the door, right on top of the crucifix that'd been hangin' there for years... I couldn't believe it... a large bird... crucified! (*hand on his heart*) I could hardly breathe... like a sleepwalker, I go look at the poor creature... dead. His wings stretched out, nailed to the wood, his head slumped down in front. (*pause*) Imagine.... Why that? (*He takes the pose of Christ on the cross.*) Who?... How?... What kind of evil mind…? To think someone would dare do such a horrible, cruel thing, here, in my little kingdom? Why take it out on me? I never did anything to anyone, ever…. (*Pause as he gives up trying to figure out this part of the mystery.*) Was it him? The neighbours? Never found out. (*pause*) I really wanted to talk to Victorine about this, but she woulda just laughed at me, treated me like a fool. It was the same with the rape. Her daughter hadn't been touched; she never wanted to talk about it with me.

VICTORINE
(*voiceover – trying her best to control herself*) Stop it, Utrope! Stop draggin' up the past all the time an' broodin' over it. What good does that do? Just tell me that?

UTROPE
"What good does that do?" (*grimace*) Even Albert told me he don't believe in the devil: the stories about fortune tellers an' charlatans an' black magic. "It just ain't really the way folks do things any more, y'know" is what he says. He figures it was just a coupla harebrained kids who'd been out huntin' an' figured they'd play a trick on me; musta managed ta get inta the shack here without bein' noticed.

But I just can't get it outta my head that before he took off, the stranger musta put a curse on us… made sure we knew he didn't appreciate the way we treated people. The proof… a sure sign of evil: the eyes of the bird had been gouged out of its head, an old barn-owl…. Imagine taking his hellishness that far…. (*silence*) The blood still dripping down the poor creature's chest… the colour of flames!

> UTROPE is overwhelmed. After a brief moment of silence, we can hear the sound of a car stopping near the shack, a few voices saying goodbye etc, a car door closes and the car moves away. UTROPE goes to his little window. What he sees draws him out of his morbid thoughts.

Scene Seven

> The kids also hear the car stop and leave again. They look towards the kitchen, expecting someone to knock on the door or come in. They listen closely and speak in whispers.

NICOLAS
I don't hear anything else. (*silence*)

DELCIA
Who could it be at this hour?

> NICOLAS shrugs his shoulders. Silence.

Scene Eight

The door of the workshop opens. VICTORINE comes in. The sense of uneasiness between her and her husband is palpable.

Scene Nine

Still whispering.

AMANDINE

I think there's someone goin' around the house…. (*In fact we can hear—or perhaps only Amandine hears—the flutter of wings like those of a bird in flight.*) It's like a rustling noise…. (*The noise grows louder, then fades and disappears.*) Don't you hear it?

NICOLAS

No. I don't hear anything.

FLORA

Me neither. (*silence*)

AMANDINE

The dark owl… maybe he's come back to give us a scare…

FLORA

(*forgetting herself and laughing*) Dark owl! What dark owl?

AMANDINE

Not this one…. The other one, with a face like a werewolf…

DELCIA

A werewolf, now…!

FLORA

(*in a normal voice*) What d'ya think you're tryin' to do bringin' up the dead like that? You're just tryin' to scare us. No. It must be someone come to see dad in his workshop. Albert or… wait! I'll go look out the kitchen window. The rest of you keep an eye out for our peacock; make sure he don't pull a fast one on us before he takes off. (*She heads for the kitchen.*)

Scene Ten

VICTORINE and UTROPE move a little closer to one another. She has a small bandage on her forehead. She speaks first.

VICTORINE

…passed out just after I got to work… felt myself goin'. First time somethin' like that ever happened to me. Fredda Marius and Gaye Anne picked me up off the floor in front of my seat. I hit my head on the edge of the table when I fell. When they brought me round… I was bleedin'. Tony and Fredda give me a ride home. Ahh, they're good to me, those guys. I won't forget 'em; they're good souls. (*She looks at her husband. She is very tired.*) Utrope, I…. (*UTROPE doesn't appear to be listening to her the way she's wants him to.*) Utrope, look at me for a second. If I took the trouble to come out here to see you, if I swallowed this mucha me pride, you know as well as I do that it's not jus' fer the fun a botherin' you. (*She softens her tone.*) I have a question to ask ya, seriously.

> *UTROPE hesitates, but finally looks at her… aslant.*

Scene Eleven

> *Scene Eleven overlaps short monologues and speeches from the two performance areas.*

NICOLAS

(*surrounded by his sisters*) It's funny. I know you're going to think I've gone soft, but all of a sudden I realize that… well, we haven't argued all night. All four of us are here watching the neighbour's house, playing the same game without ripping each other apart. Don't you think it's better like this, eh? (*Sensing the others' uneasiness, he dares not go on. FLORA especially rebels against his idea.*)

VICTORINE

The question I wanna ask ya is, well, a little embarrassing. (*pause*) Do you think I been showin' my age a lot more these days? (*UTROPE is the one embarrassed.*) Answer me straight, okay? Am I right to think I'm starting to get old lately?

NICOLAS

Wouldn't it be great if we could stop playing these games but keep the fun we can have together?

VICTORINE

(*worry showing on her face*) I wanna know. Is it true I'm gettin' too old to work now? (*UTROPE doesn't dare say what he's thinking.*) Utrope, is it true?

> *The sound of a siren begins very faintly in the distance and begins to approach. NICOLAS becomes more and more desperate.*

NICOLAS

I want to know. Why couldn't we stop these terrible games without wrecking the happiness of just being together? Like when we were little kids. Like when we were real brother and sisters. That's what I want to know.

VICTORINE

No. What I want… what I really really want to find out is if there is any love left in your heart for me. That's what I want to know.

FLORA

(*She is furious.*) Stop it Nicolas! Kids! You know damn well what I think of that. I never had a chance to be a "kid," did I?

DELCIA

(*stoically*) That's enough, Nicolas. Don't go tryin' your fancy speeches on us.

The siren is getting louder and louder.

FLORA

You know damn well the only childhood I had was yours, shafted with havin' to take care of you all the time. I was cheated. I've always been cheated, always. One day I loved a man an' that damned bitch next door ripped him out of my reach! (*flashing of red light*)

NICOLAS

(*on the edge of panic*) Don't you get it? We're playing with fire here! If we keep going on like this, everything we've got left will go up in flames. We've got to stop.

FLORA

No! Not until we settle my score with that Planteen slut, we don't. Not until we've fixed her.

NICOLAS

No more pretending innocence! No more dreams! Amandine! Save yourself! Get out of here! We've lit a fire all around our lives. Everywhere!

The siren is at its loudest point. Red emergency lights now sweep the stage.

DELCIA

Oh my God! What's going on?

AMANDINE

(*a little lost*) Nicolas! What is it? Flora?

VICTORINE

What's going on out there?

Everyone rushes to the windows, except NICOLAS who remains fixed in place.

NICOLAS

No! This can't be happening!

DELCIA
(*Suddenly panicked, she speaks to FLORA who doesn't understand.*) An
ambulance has pulled up at the Simpleton's house. An ambulance, Nicolas!

UTROPE
Is that the police over at Planteens? No. It's an ambulance.

VICTORINE
An ambulance?

THE THREE SISTERS
(*dazed at first, then…*) Oh, no!

VICTORINE
But what's it doing there? (*UTROPE has no idea.*) Maybe old Planteen's taken
sick again?

THE KIDS
No! No! My God! Oh no! It can't be true! No!

UTROPE
I don't know. I just hope…. C'mon, Victorine, let's not stay here. Let's go see if
we can help 'em. C'mon. (*They go out.*)

Scene Twelve

THE KIDS
(*They don't want to believe what's happening to them.*) It doesn't make any
sense! My God! No! It can't be true! An ambulance!

> *They don't know which way to turn; there's another moment of confusion,
> then…*

AMANDINE
What've we done, Flora?

FLORA
(*lashing out at DELCIA*) Well you've made one helluva mess of things, haven't
you Delcia!

DELCIA
What!? We ain't done nothin'. Who knows what happened? We don't know for
sure it was because of us.

FLORA
(*grasping onto this idea right away*) She's right! There's nothing says it was
because of us!

NICOLAS

(*slightly reassured, at the window*) They're bringin' somebody outta the house...
in a white jacket...

His sisters rush to the window.

FLORA

Oh no!

NICOLAS

It looks like her.

DELCIA

They're taking her away. Oh my God! It's the Simpleton. It's her!

AMANDINE

Are you sure?

DELCIA

Yeah, I'm sure it's her!

More lights are added to those still sweeping the stage.

DELCIA

(*to NICOLAS*) Look! A police car! (*They all look outside. AMANDINE's nerves
crack and she begins to sob in silence.*) Look! D'ya see that? It's mom and dad!
They're over there.

FLORA

(*to herself*) Nothing. It's pointless. Nothing happened.

AMANDINE

(*through her tears*) It's not our fault is it?

NICOLAS

Hey! They're bringing someone else outta the house... on a stretcher!

DELCIA

It's not...?

FLORA

(*suddenly very alarmed*) Oh my God! Not him! Paul! (*She makes a dash for the
kitchen door, but DELCIA grabs her and holds her back.*)

AMANDINE

Where are you going Flora? (*crying*) Flora!

DELCIA

No, Flora. Stay out of it. Stay here! You can't let mom and dad, and especially the police, see your face over there! (*Bit by bit, FLORA gives in.*)

NICOLAS

That's our visitor…. He's got blood all over his clothes. The Simpleton must have gone nuts.

AMANDINE

That's our guy, all right. Blood on his face, blood… on his undershirt!

FLORA

(*to herself*) Nothing. Nothing's happening. It's just a bad dream. It's not real. It's not our fault.

> The siren begins to wail again. The kids cover their ears with their hands to cut the noise. The ambulance starts up and pulls away. Gradually the siren and emergency lights fade away; the kids begin to speak and move again.

NICOLAS

Nothing. Nothing's happening. We're not responsible.

DELCIA

No. We're not responsible. We're not to blame…

FLORA

(*to NICOLAS*) That's right…. We're not to blame…. It's…

NICOLAS

…there's someone else behind all this..

AMANDINE

Someone else to blame…

DELCIA

(*to FLORA*) Someone to blame…

FLORA

The dark owl! That's who. He's to blame.

NICOLAS, DELCIA & AMANDINE

That's it! It was him! He's the one who's really guilty!

FLORA

(*to herself, seeming distraught*) I was crazy about him…. (*The following is spoken under and in counterpoint to what NICOLAS is saying.*) Completely crazy about him! (*like a stabbing pain to the gut*) My desire for that man… my fear of getting knocked up… the strength to resist him… how could I resist him?!

NICOLAS

We were only his instruments. The tools of the stranger who possessed us all and then betrayed us. He's to blame. The one really responsible. Guilty.

FLORA

Oh yeah! I was crazy about him. He held me close and begged me… tears in his eyes he wanted me that bad. It took everything I had, every fear I had to say "No. No." …fear of mom and dad, the neighbours, the priest, of getting knocked up, especially of that. He wanted me so bad. One day he said to me, right out of the blue, he said if I didn't make up my mind, he'd go see the Simpleton. I thought he was joking. Except, I knew she would do it. Planteen's hypocritical little Simpleton. (*pause*) Ahh, if only I knew what was coming! Everything he was gonna do to us! (*with immense regret*) If only I could've foreseen…

Scene Thirteen

The kids, gripped by their collective memory of the rape of the SIMPLETON, hear the muffled cries and noises of a struggle between the dark owl and Bernadette who tries desperately to get away from him.

SIMPLETON

No! No! I don't want to!

DARK OWL

Keep quiet, I'm warning you.

SIMPLETON

No! Leave me alone! I don't want anything to do with you! No!

THE KIDS

In papa's workshop. In the dark!

DARK OWL

You've been wanting this for a long time. Well, you're gonna get it!

SIMPLETON

Leave me alone!

DELCIA

It's coming from the workshop! Don't be scared!

DARK OWL

Stop it! Dammit! Stop! I'll kill ya! (*the sound of a struggle and cloth ripping*)

THE KIDS

He's ripping her clothes off…!

SIMPLETON
(*crying, begging*) Stop! Please! No! No!

THE KIDS
Then all of a sudden...! (*They all stop.*)

AMANDINE
He saw us!

FLORA
...just for a second. (*She shakes her head "no" and moves away.*)

NICOLAS, DELCIA & AMANDINE
The eyes of the dark owl: just a glance, his eyes red with blood!

Silence except for the sobs of the SIMPLETON in the dark.

Scene Fourteen

AMANDINE and NICOLAS speak in counterpoint.

AMANDINE
I was really young then. I didn't ask many questions, but he frightened me.... When I realized what he'd done to my friend—oh we used to play together all the time when we were little—just how serious it all was for her... phew! (*Wiping her brow with the back of her hand.*) I said to myself, I said, "That was a close one, 'mandine!"

NICOLAS
He was the one who set everything in motion. If I were to write about what's happened since that moment when I first set eyes on him: the need I felt; drawn to my father... his wall of silence... his don't-bother-me-now when I needed him most. The desire, strong, hidden, hopeless... that I had for this stranger. Then suddenly...! (*He looks for and finds his notebook, opens it, presses it to his chest, then throws it down in front of him: inspired.*) The tale of the Simpleton! The rule of silence: no one talks about it! My first days at university! (*like an avalanche*) Ahh! My first love! The men's residence! Jean-Guy! Caught. Judged! Forced to see the psychologist! Then... then—my mother, my sisters, my father never really wanted to know—my getting kicked out of university! (*With a gesture, indicating his notebook.*) I could write a novel about my growing up! (*pause charged with emotion*)

But what I miss the most, what never stops tormenting me is still the image of my father's hands, the hands of a carpenter! (*pause*) The other one, the dark owl, was just an "affective transfer" ...that's what they told me at the university.

DELCIA

Me? I was jealous. I couldn't take it anymore.

AMANDINE

I was just young. What do you expect?

NICOLAS

I was his best friend; that's what he told me. Yeah. Me. I often imagined he was a kind of renegade or escaped convict.... At fourteen, the idea really blew my mind...

DELCIA

I couldn't take it anymore. I wanted to scream! Just scream!

NICOLAS

When he left, I really felt betrayed. Oh, not only me. My sisters, my parents, everybody! And after we'd taken him into our home! To do something like that and then just disappear? I know, in one way it's not really right, but... but sooner or later...

NICOLAS & DELCIA

...someone's gotta pay for what he did!

DELCIA

I was jealous of Flora. Every time I saw 'em together, I felt sick... like somethin' eatin' away inside me, gettin' bigger an' bigger, more an' more painful... I asked myself, "What's Flora got that I don't to attract guys like that?" Cause he...
I don't know what it was, but he had this kinda real charm. An' he knew it too... oh yeah, he knew it all right. God, how he could get me to like him again after one of my tantrums...

NICOLAS

(*recalling the words of the dark owl*) "You wouldn't bring me a nice glass of cold water, would you, my pretty little Delcia?"

DELCIA

(*also remembering*) ...make me get things, run little errands, do favours for him! Christ! Make me dream about him! Then he hurt me too. "Ugly brat!" That's what he called me when I wouldn't do what he wanted anymore.
I couldn't stand it that he liked my sister better'n me.

AMANDINE

I was young, but I knew damn well there was somethin' not right about him, inside.

NICOLAS

It wasn't hard to figure out their little games. Flora was crazy about that dark owl. He was a real ladies' man! When they... it tortured me!

DELCIA

(*as if calling the lovers*) Flora! Get down here! Mom an' papa are comin'! (*pause*) But she wasn't scared, no, she was too smart: the oldest in the family. She wasn't scared o' getting caught, no, not her. But him, he came down those stairs with his arrogant looks an' prowled around an' around me just to drive me crazy. Then he realized what I said wasn't true, that mom an' dad weren't comin' in; he looked at me with those strange eyes like hellfire an' said...

NICOLAS

(*He has been prowling around her for a moment.*) Go fuck yourself, you ugly brat!

DELCIA

I was young, but those things... ya understand them pretty quick, an' they stick... for a long time. That's when I started to think, "One day, you'll see; one day somebody's gonna pay for this!"

DELCIA, NICOLAS & AMANDINE

We were nothing but puppets.

NICOLAS

The instruments of a craving for vengeance against the stranger who possessed us all and then betrayed us.

THE KIDS

He's the one to blame. Responsible. Guilty.

FLORA

(*She heads towards the staircase as if under some kind of spell.*) The dark owl is in my room. He's waiting for me. The others don't want me to go, but my angel has come back.... Stronger than me. I'm drawn to him. He's calling me.... (*She has already started up the stairs.*)

DELCIA, NICOLAS & AMANDINE

(*following her as if to stop her from going further*) Flora! (*Her name may be repeated by each character individually.*) Don't go up there! Don't go. Stay with us. (*louder*) Flora, stay with us!

Scene Fifteen

Carried away as if by a magnetic force, FLORA tears herself away from the others despite their best efforts. She dashes for her bedroom, grabs the bar of wood blocking the door and rips it off. At that moment the door becomes translucent, the bedroom bathed in a surreal light. A very attractive man, a kind of guardian angel, is revealed standing in the room, leaning over FLORA's bed. He calls to her softly, but with a voice full of temptation.

DARK OWL

Come, Flora…. Come to me, my dear…. Come closer…

FLORA

Yes, my angel…

DARK OWL

Come to my arms my lovely little owlette… let's fly away together.

FLORA

(*She laughs in a very sensual way.*) He called me his little owlette! (*She throws herself into the dark owl's arms. They disappear into the darkness.*)

Scene Sixteen

AMANDINE

(*alone*) Poor Bernadette… I hope they don't lock her up this time. (*pause*) What's going to happen to me in my life? What am I going to do in the world? I don't know, but sometimes, it's like I'm afraid.

Scene Seventeen

VICTORINE and UTROPE return to the workshop.

VICTORINE

I can't believe it…

UTROPE

The Simpleton just staring like that, the guy's face all smashed up, blood everywhere… I shouldn't've took you over there. You shouldn't've had ta see that, Victorine.

VICTORINE

It doesn't matter.

UTROPE

No. Not in the state you're in. You're tired. I'm sorry.

VICTORINE

It just doesn't make sense in this day an' age to leave a young girl, who's been messed up like that, alone all by herself!

UTROPE

Yeah, I know, I know… but it's just that old Planteen can't keep himself cooped up all year round. Nobody can do that…. (*He looks at her.*) Even you, Victorine, you can't either; I understand that, y'know.

VICTORINE

What if that happened to our kids… getting attacked like that by a complete stranger. We're not safe anywhere anymore, not even in our own house these days. The country is at the mercy of every bugger who wants to take just whatever he can get. (*pause*) Utrope. Utrope, listen to me and listen good. I'm tired. I've had my fill of slavin' my life away at that plant. We still have grown kids at home. So that's okay… I'm gonna try to finish out the season but then, well then we'll have to see…. (*UTROPE was not expecting this.*) But there's something else; we gotta talk to each other. It's our last chance! Do you understand, Utrope? Before it's too late, we gotta talk to each other!

UTROPE looks at VICTORINE, hesitates a moment, then finally shows his agreement by placing his big hand over hers.

Scene Eighteen

DELCIA

A great dark hole, a deep pit full of vengeance where mistrust an' fear trapped us even before we really began to live.

FLORA

A gaping dark hole opened under my feet just as I was gettin' ready to escape all this.

AMANDINE

Two holes, two empty pits! The cold, staring eyes of the dark owl!

NICOLAS

The queer eyes of the dark owl, open graves on the devastated landscape of our green years, subject of my first novel! My sisters and I had to fall very deep, buried alive at the foot of our rage, before tasting the desire to escape.

FLORA

To escape! Find a way out! That's all I'm waitin' for!

UTROPE

Yes Victorine, we must find a way out of this hole!

DELCIA

Now, we must climb out of our pit!

VICTORINE

Yes, we must find a way out of this hole!

AMANDINE

We have to find a way to climb out of this hole, Nicolas!

UTROPE & VICTORINE

Now, we have to get out of this hole!

THE KIDS

Now, we have to get out of this hole!

ALL

We have to get out of this hole! We have to…

The end.

My Husband's
an Angel

Gracia Couturier
translated by Glen Nichols

Gracia Couturier was born in Edmundston in 1951. She did an education degree at the Université de Moncton, but in 1977, she switched her classroom for the stage, helping to found Théâtre l'Escaouette for which she wrote two plays, *Le gros ti-gars* (1986) and *Enfantômes suroulettes* (1989) which she also directed. In addition, for ten years Gracia wrote the pedagogical material accompanying the plays Théâtre l'Escaouette toured to regional schools. In 1981, in Shippagan, she founded Théâtre de saisons which she directed for three years and for which she wrote four plays. Back in Moncton, she wrote and directed *My Husband's an Angel* (*Mon mari est un ange*) in 1987; the one-man show played by Philippe Beaulieu toured across the Maritimes and was produced for television by Radio-Canada. Gracia also worked for Radio-Canada as researcher and cultural reporter, for Le pays de la Sagouine as program director and actress, and for Les Éditions d'Acadie as editor and director of production. She obtained a masters degree in French literature from the Université de Moncton. Now a freelance writer, she is currently writing her third novel, following on the success of *L'antichambre* (1997) and *Je regardais Rebecca* (1999). For several years she has been interested in the haïku form of poetry and contributed to three anthologies published by Les Éditions David in Ottawa. She also writes screenplays for documentaries and fiction.

INTRODUCTION TO *MY HUSBAND'S AN ANGEL*

The ironic underpinning of Gracia Couturier's one-man play, *My Husband's an Angel*, is evident from the first appearance of Tarzan Mazerolle, middle-aged and bearded, "dressed in his wedding suit, shakily playing the wedding march on a harmonica" and showing the unmistakable silhouette of advanced pregnancy! Tarzan, who is described as "your average guy," explains why he let himself get pregnant, *in vitro*, in order to let his opera-star wife, Jane, pursue her singing career. He is "pleased as punch" to be carrying his wife's baby, but has discovered that being pregnant brings all sorts of physical and mental upsets he didn't expect. His unique perspective gives him, and the audience, new insight into certain aspects of motherhood. On top of that, Tarzan is still a "real man" and struggles to maintain his masculinity as he is gradually overwhelmed by the intensely feminine condition he finds himself in. The result is a lighthearted, ironic look at what motherhood is all about, what being a parent is all about. *My Husband's an Angel* looks at the trials and upsets of pregnancy from a decidedly masculine point of view and the result is a very funny, yet poignant reflection on relationships and family.

The one-man show is loosely structured around a series of episodic narratives. Tarzan relates such events as his wedding and subsequent commitment to get pregnant, his encounter with police officers who suspect him of shoplifting ("Hey buddy whaddaya got swallowed down there?"), the consternation of fellow prenatal class students, and his futile fight to get paternity leave and EI benefits. These are connected by Tarzan's philosophical observations about women's rights, his insecurities about his wife's fame and love of travel, the pros and cons of reproductive technology, his inner fears, as well as his joyful anticipation of the imminent experience of childbirth, among others. The result is a piece easily adaptable to varying performance conditions and playing times.

Tarzan's frequent refrain that "Nothing's changed. No. Nothing's changed at all," when indeed things have changed a great deal, points up the intended irony of the play. This irony is reinforced by Tarzan's exaggerations, for example his parodizing of the wedding ceremony conducted by a priest with "angelic, nay seraphic air," his mother-in-law's oversized reactions to his condition, his description of the men in his prenatal class, and the excuses he's given by the EI bureaucrat for being refused benefits. The playfulness extends as well to his self-perception as he laughs at his "own idiocy." He pokes fun at his profession ("psychologists like me always come up with these great theories that've never been tested in practice"), at the rashness with which he offered to console his wife by carrying the baby, at men's overweening pride, and at the peculiar motivations of scientists. These examples, which are only the tip of the iceberg, give a sense of the rollicking richness of this text.

This richness extends naturally to the language of the play as well, with its constant stream of puns and wordplay which made *My Husband* a surprisingly challenging play to translate. More often than not strict denotation had to be sacrificed in order to create a target language in the same spirit of lightness and irony as the original. So things like the description of Jane's tantrums as "*déclencher tout un délire de diva déchirée*" [lit. "let loose a whole delirium of a torn diva"] became "detonate a full teary-eyed diva tantrum;" "*mères porteuses… porteuses de malheur*" became "surrogate mothers… counterfeit mothers;" "*moton au coton*" became "stem to stern;" and his worries about his breasts not bouncing back to their youthful tightness because after the age of 35 skin gets more like government funding: "*plusse pendante pis moins élastique*," became "more and more wrinkles, less and less flexible."

Jane's last name presented a unique problem as well. In French, the "d'" in "d'Aracadie" suggests the aristocratic pretensions of her family (plus the homophonic allusion to "acadie"). I was fortunate to be able to work very closely with Gracia and her partner, Philippe Beaulieu, who created the original role in French and who workshopped the translation with me. Together we decided to go with "McAracadie" which, while not necessarily "aristocratic," allows a new kind of irony in the joke about "McJobs" when Tarzan is contemplating a name for the baby. This is a typical example of the kind of unavoidable shifts in translating a play of this density. One can only hope these shifts still allow full justice to the spirit and sense of the original while creating a text that is playable and meaningful given the particular restraints of the target language.

Overall the trick was to find the correct balance between the sheer comedy of the words and the sensitivity of the character, without making Tarzan into a buffoon on one hand or into a victim on the other hand as he suffers increasingly painful labour cramps in the last moments of the play: he is neither silly nor tragic nor offensive. In the classic mode of comedy, Tarzan is simply a character out of his element, struggling to keep his balance as he learns his way through a series of challenges his gender has not prepared him for. As a human being, however, and perhaps in spite of his masculine inhibitions and the pain and fear he is feeling, he experiences the astonishing joy of bringing new life into the world. The audience is invited to laugh at Tarzan's foibles and the unusual challenges he has to face, but through his growing joy we are given a new look at a part of life that connects us all.

—GN

My Husband's an Angel by Gracia Couturier

My Husband's an Angel (*Mon mari est un ange*) was created for a summer theatre on the stage of the Jardins de la République, a provincial park near Edmundston in north-west New Brunswick. Twenty-five performances were given in the summer of 1987 followed by a tour of New Brunswick and Nova Scotia in February 1988. The play was adapted for television and produced by SRC Moncton in 1988.

Tarzan Mazerolle	Philippe Beaulieu
Directed by	Gracia Couturier

The play was published in 1988 by Michel Henry éditeur.

This translation was workshopped and given a staged reading in Moncton, June 2002, with Philippe Beaulieu in the role of Tarzan. Directed by Glen Nichols.

CHARACTERS

Tarzan Mazerolle teaches psychology at the university. He's your average guy, an intellectual open to all the innovations and possibilities of science, politics, society, religion and so on. He's a softy, a humanist. He shows his complete devotion to those close to him with the greatest liberality and humility; what more can I say, he's an angel!

On the other hand, Tarzan carries with him certain relics of a macho education which surface from time to time when he least expects it, especially when he's caught off guard, when he's having trouble with his situation as a pregnant man.

My Husband's an Angel

by Gracia Couturier

Scene One

TARZAN Mazerolle enters dressed in his wedding suit and shakily playing "The Wedding March" on a harmonica. He is obviously very pregnant.

TARZAN

It changed nothin', y'know…. Nothin' changed at all. Sure, we got hitched like everybody else, same church as everybody else, same script as everybody else. And it was all over every bit as quick.

"Do you, Jane McAracadie, take Tarzan Mazerolle, present and accounted for on your left, as your lawful wedded husband? Do you promise to be faithful to him in ecstasy and in misery, to no longer listen to any other voice but his, to be obedient and serve him in sickness and in heartbreak, in catastrophe and war, 'til death do you part?"

And she answered in her most exquisite hifalutin opera voice, "I do."

Then the high priest turned to me with angelic, nay seraphic air, so pure and chaste, and asked me in candid calmness, "Tarzan, do you take Jane McAracadie, present and accounted for on your right, as your lawful wedded wife? Do you promise to treat her as if God fashioned her from your own rib cage? Do you promise to hold her… to her obligations, her duties and your rights?"

And I answered "OOOOooooooOOOO (*He jumps as he remembers the jab in the ribs Jane gave him.*) Okay." That's the only opera note I know.

At that the priest declared us husband and wife: bound together in holy fetters, shackled for life, a lump in the throat and everything. A wedding is, well, after all just a wedding. It's the same for everybody… lots of ceremony, lots of emotion. But it changes nothing, really, nothing changes at all.

Then, as she left the church, Jane started to sing:
Daarling…
If life has made me diva
Ohh death… ohh death
If life has made me diva
Death will see me still a diva;
And on heaven's opera staff
I will be forever diva!
And the notes for singing
Sharps and flats,

Tremolos and scales in C and G
Will be my way, my truth, my life,
Will be my way, my truth, my life,
Will be my way, my truth, my life…

And she wouldn't stop. She wouldn't stop singing… even in our wedding pictures, taken on the church steps, she's got 'er mouth wide open belting out the word "way." The photographer, the priest, even the janitor had taken off and she was still warblin' away… "my way, my truth, my life…"

I had to do something to bring her back down to earth, so I stood up straight'n'tall right in front of her and I said, "My dearest Jane, now we can have a baby."

"What baby?" she asked me.

"Well, your baby, my baby, our baby."

Oh boy, did that ever get her going: I braced myself for one of her teary-eyed diva tantrums: her body all tense and shaky, with salty tears, buggy eyes, puffy cheeks, runny nose, the whole nine yards. Right there on the church steps! Right in front of everybody. Like something out of an old movie where the star makes a big scene on the grand staircase.

Course, lemme tell ya, those McAracadies are an easy bunch to upset. It's in the genes I swear, this little quark showing up generation after generation. And what's more, they're as cliquish as they are highstrung; you'd swear they had blue blood.

So anyway there she was, throwing a tantrum of patrician proportions: insulted, indignant, incensed…. With the waterworks and the whole chain reaction like a nuclear bomb. And all that, just for a baby. That's it, just a baby.

If only I'd known that bloody little word was going to detonate a full tormented-diva tantrum…. How was I supposed to know she'd already been victimized by a fetus? But don't worry, my mother-in-law made sure I heard the whole story.

"I told her, 'Don't do it.' But Jane went ahead and let that other woman carry her baby for her, and y'know what, that ungrateful surrogate, that malicious witch of a mother, took off with the baby AND the 15,000 bucks Jane paid her. As usual, everyone had to get in on the act: the *Globe*, the *Sun*, the *Chronicle-Herald*, *Times & Transcript*, even the *Albert County Voice* and all the weeklies on the island… but no luck, not a word."

Poor Jane…. Poor baby! I tell ya, they're an awful greedy bunch these surrogate mothers. For nine months, if not more, they save on cigarettes, they save on booze, on drugs; they get fed like royalty with piles and piles of granola. And to top it off, they even get paid! Then they come around moaning about it being

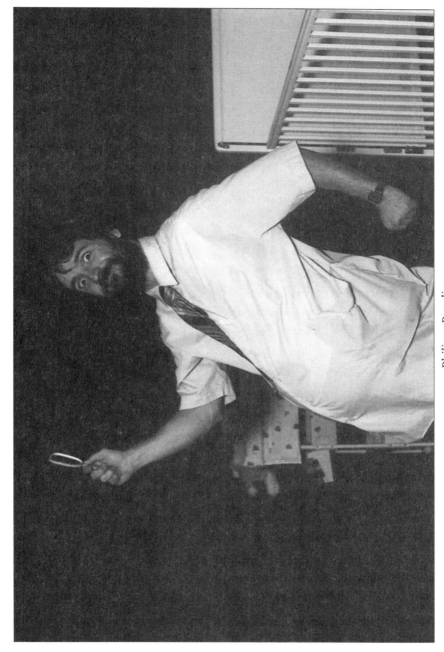

Philippe Beaulieu
Photo by Jean Berthélémie.

such a sacrifice and that they want the baby as well as the fifteen grand you've already given them. Oh yeah, they're quite a bunch, those counterfeit mothers…. But the worst thing is it was us men who put the idea in their heads… and who put this one in my belly. I think we've had enough to do carrying the weight of the world on our shoulders without havin' to carry the human race in our bellies too.

Yeah, I know it's not right to generalise like that, but, well, once bitten twice shy I s'pose. And I guess you have to understand, when it comes right out of your own insides like that, when you've been feeding it from arteries hooked up straight to your own heart, it's pretty tough just to let it go afterwards…. Well, let's not talk about it anymore; we got no claim on that baby.

No. We're just gonna make our own baby instead, our very own. And it's going to be even more wonderful than the other one. The proof: he's staying home…. (*touching his stomach*) Oh, and don't worry about me. You just have to understand. Jane is a career woman, an opera singer; and an hour at church dressed in white and one wedding dance isn't going change anything. She warned me; I accepted. She even threw another titanic tantrum too, just to remind me…. And you can bet your bottom dollar I haven't forgotten. I'm crazy about my Jane. So, if I wanna make sure I never lose her, I hafta cut her a bit'a slack… enough slack for her to go to Europe on that big European tour that was waitin' for her. Not a bad bit of slack, eh?

(*assembling a crib*) Sure could use a bit of slack with this box-spring though! The damned thing won't fit. OOOooOO…. There, that's it. Gotta be sure the contraption don't collapse the first time the kid sleeps in it. Later on, well there's no guarantee, but the first time…. Yep, amazing what a bit of slack can do for ya.

Course, psychologists like me always come up with these great theories that've never been tested, in practice. That's basically what happened the night I tried to patch things up with my tormented teary-eyed diva; to try calming her down, I said to her, "Look, it's okay dear, we'll just have to make a baby all by ourselves." But all that big idea produced was an even bigger display of waterworks which already threatened to drown her wedding bouquet.

In full European opera pitch she punctuated every word with tremolos and staccatos: "And just how do you propose we make a kid? You know very well, my darling Tarzan, that I cannot interrupt my career to have a baby right in the middle of a tour. And having a baby, being pregnant, you know how that wrinkles a woman's body! No. I can't do it. Oh but how I do love those little bundles of joy."

That's when I repeated my "It's okay dear" and then added, "We can still have a baby without you being pregnant y'know Jane…. No, no, I wouldn't subject you to the plots of a counterfeit mother again…. No, of course I don't mean adoption; that's no guarantee against product recalls either. No way." And then that's when I said it. I had to do something, make her feel better somehow. It was getting embarrassing with everyone watching, so I said, "Look, I'll carry the baby myself…"

"YOU!?!" Well, the torrent dried up quicker than you can say, "*in vitro.*" No more tears, she just closed her eyes, grabbed me, gave me a big kiss and said, "Tarzan, you're an angel." That's where the title comes from: "My Husband's an Angel."

Y'know I've never understood why she was so surprised. They've been talking about men getting pregnant for ages. And, well, it's been done. (*indicating his stomach*) Even in New Boomswick. Hard to believe, eh, but miracles don't only happen to folks from away…

So, that's how I got myself into this fix. After the baby was conceived, *in vitro*, Jane left for her big European opera tour to Europe. I went back to giving my psychology classes at the university and… well… baking buns. Ahh, but it was a moment that moved the earth! OOOOOO oooooOOOOOOO!! (*He starts to throw up, so he turns upstage away from the audience.*)

Scene Two

TARZAN recovers from his nausea and crosses back downstage.

'Scuse me, it was just a false alarm, but I wanted to be sure I didn't bring up in front of you. Despite appearances, I have been well brought up y'know: enlightened, understanding, in short, an angel. But the symptoms don't change just because motherhood has changed sex. A foreign body is still a foreign body. A speck of sand stings in a man's eye as much as in a woman's eye. Nope, it really doesn't change anything…. All the same I wish this nausea would stop. It does seem to be draggin' on a long time. Even hits me during class sometimes, and my students think I've been boozin' it up all night. It's so humiliating.

Like the other day it hit me right in the grocery store, at the meat counter. I was asking for a roast o' pork and just as the butcher was handing it to me I felt my stomach lurch, so I lurched for the door… I had to find a garbage can, or some sort of hole somewhere. The cashier yelled at me like I was some kinda thief. She pressed the alarm button and for once the police were right there and caught me in the act. They jumped me and ripped off my jacket. I was still feeling pretty nauseous, so when they made me open my mouth… I couldn't help it, I porked all over their shoes!! Boy were they ticked off! They made me take off my shirt; then one of 'em asked, "Hey buddy whaddaya got swallowed down there? Better spit it up!" Flabbergasted, I started to bawl like a woman… I mean like a baby! Damn! It was humiliating. "Look," I said, "I didn't eat it, they injected me with it, *in vitro*." The cops didn't believe me. So I had to show them the newspaper clipping from the Home and Garden section, the one with my picture on it.

They still weren't impressed, "What kinda man lets himself get knocked up like that?"

So I said, "Yeah well what's so manly about you wearing that funny yellow stripe down your leg?

"S'pose ya got a point, but what made ya do it, sweetheart?"

"I did it out of love. Love with a big 'L.'"

Oh and I do love my Jane; I'd do anything for her. That's what being a couple is all about. You have to learn not only to get along with each other, but also to give yourselves to each other. Especially giving yourselves. The reason is really very simple: there's more pleasure in giving than getting. Why? Because, well, what we give to others is always bigger and nicer than what they give us.

So that's why I decided to give my Jane a baby; it'll be more beautiful, and much bigger, than if she'd given it to me. And it'll be better for the baby too. I think I'm going to be pleased as punch to give Jane the baby when she gets back from her tour…. And she's going to be pretty pleased to see the baby too. I can just see her now… taking the bonnie bambino in her arms, singing a sweet opera lullaby, some charming classical chamber piece. She's going to love it so much that…. Oh my God! I hope she doesn't start bawling. Because that would make two of them for me to cheer up, and that's no small job. Psychologist or no psychologist, couch or no couch, cheering Jane up is no small job. Not that it's rocket science either: she just bawls as loudly as she sings, and she goes on for as long as a three-act opera.

No, but I know she's going to be pleased. (*He looks at a skeptical audience member.*) Look, if you'd seen how upset she was on our wedding day, buddy, you'd take my word for it without pulling such a sour face. She's gonna be happy because Jane loves children, no question. She turns into a grand tormented teary-eyed diva whenever she sees an unhappy kid. (*He looks at the same audience member.*) Do you take a fit when you see an unhappy kid? You try to be a tormented teary-eyed diva at the snap of your fingers just because there's a kid crying in your face… a kid you don't know from Adam…. Go ahead, try. It's not easy, eh! Well, my Jane can do it. And that's why I love her.

I can see her now, comin' through that door. I just know she'll even want to bring home a squeaky little plastic carrot, or a squacky little yellow duck or a screechy little toy car or something else that 'queaks, 'quacks, or 'creeches…. For sure something with a noise that'll drive us crazy. Thrilled to bits, she'll rock that baby to sleep singing some pretty little love song:

Hush, l'il baby, don't say a word
Mama's gonna buy you a mockin'bird.
If that mockin'bird don't sing
Mama's gonna buy you a diamond ring
If that diamond ring turns brass,

Mama's gonna buy you a looking glass.
If that looking glass gets broke
Mama's gonna buy you a billygoat. (*fade to humming a line or two*)

So, you can see how much she loves her baby; she's ready to buy 'im the world...

Hey, I'm gonna have to find a name for the little tyke, y'know, if I don't want them to start calling him Baby M like those others. So, what am I going to call him? It has to be a name that goes with Mazerolle... or with McAracadie? hmmm... McAracadie.... Talk about a name what sticks out like a sore thumb, eh. With a name like McAracadie the kid'll never get a real job. Y'know, I've never really liked the name McAracadie; it sounds so marginal. That's the only thing that bugs me about Jane, her family name. No, this little one's gonna go by the name of Mazerolle, and that's final.

Otherwise, Jane is perfect. That's why I love living with her. You should've seen her the day she left on her year-long European tour to Europe. She was radiant as a goddess. She kissed me and whispered hot sweet nothin's in my ear! Called me her angel, caressed my wings. (*sigh*) Then suddenly she turned to me with a dramatic flourish which I could never describe, a look in her eyes I didn't understand and said to me in Shakespearean tremolos I could never reproduce, "*Adieu*, Tarzan!" And that's how she left. Dramatically. Dramatically, as only a grand tragic opera star can leave. My God, she's beautiful when she gets dramatic.

I tell you though, a grand exit like that sure made me stop and think, "Is she leaving me for good?" But no, once I got hold of myself again, I knew that couldn't be true. It's just an idea I musta picked up from all those cheap novels, documentaries and news reports. They make women all look like tramps. It doesn't make sense anymore. Just old wive's tales.

Yep, she's gonna come back to me because I love her, my dear Jane, my darling tormented diva, with all her tearful goodbyes, her heart tearing apart for an unhappy child: I just know she's going to come back to me.

She'll be back with European airs, with perfumes that smell a mile away; and you can't miss the sleek Italian dresses and especially the Parisian accent. It's always like that. Ever since I've known her, every time she comes back from a tour, she's picked up a Parisian accent. Even when she's only coming back from Fredericton, she finds a way of picking up a Parisian accent. But I can assure you that after two weeks rubbing shoulders with Tarzan Mazerolle, she's back to her old Jane-self. Two weeks, that's all it takes. What's too bad is that she always takes off again not long afterwards. This time, she stayed a month. That's how we ended up married and... well... y'know (*He strokes his stomach tenderly with a knowing look.*)

Hey, now you mustn't think that just because I let myself get pregnant, *in vitro*, means I'm a pushover. No way. I'm still a real man. You don't erase a lifetime's education just like that… like magic, poof! Centuries of tradition have left their mark on men. And besides, weren't we the ones created in the image and likeness of God? (*looking at himself in his pocket mirror*) *Deus ressemblus malus.* God must be one good-lookin' dude, eh boys!

Scene Three

Whew! I'm gonna hafta take off my shoes; my back is killing me. Oh don't worry, I'm not going to do what I did a few minutes ago. No, no. That was just a passing upset. You women out there know all about these little upsets, eh. Some worse than others.

I know one woman who weighed 130 pounds when she got pregnant on November 26th. Five months later she had a beautiful little bun in the oven, but she didn't weigh more than 85 pounds, placenta, baby and all. She looked awful. But her husband didn't say a word; oh no, he was more diplomatic than that. I mean, you can't go and tell her she looks tired, ask about her limp lips, sunken cheeks and that greenish colour… no, no, not a word. Instead you bring her breakfast in bed, wipe away the toast crumbs from the sheets so they don't pick her, or tickle her if she is ticklish, and fluff up her pillows real puffy so she can rest peacefully while you do the dishes. It's just like being newlyweds again. Now that's diplomacy.

Anyway, I'm happy to have put on a little weight myself, because if I only weighed 85 pounds I'd never get the mother-in-law off my back. She still hasn't forgiven me for causing such a fracas in the great McAracadie family. Like I said, the McAracadies have been a nervous bunch for eons.

Everybody's gotta stick their oar in everyone else's business. Gotta have the last word about everything: weddings, divorces, funerals, birthdates, how many babies you're gonna have, how soon you should feed them solids, when they're gonna stop crapping their diapers. Get the idea? For them it's normal.

My mother-in-law also thinks it's normal that I'm the one carrying the baby. "Always a good sign when a man finally does some good with his life. But poor Jane. She's the one has to put bread on the table." So it's especially important she don't see me lookin' sick; she already treats me like a wimp because she only puked for the first month. She can't accept that my legs hurt, that my back is killing me…. She doesn't know my blood pressure's been high for a couple of weeks either and… and don't you dare go telling her…

Oh yeah, if men had known women weren't faking all their little "upsets," they probably would never even have tried to get us fellows pregnant. Scientists would more'n likely've been happy to stop at surrogate mothers. And with all the stories you hear, that sooner or later would've gone back to normal, back to nature's natural cycle: those who can have babies have them; and the rest don't try to fake it; just leave the baby booms to mother rabbits, I say.

But that's not how it happened. The scientists were all men; it should have turned out better. But I suppose they couldn't know everything, predict everything. At any rate, they sure didn't predict the ribbing a man has to put up with just because he lets himself get pregnant. Oh, it's easy to get it put in. Doesn't take longer than to grab a coffee in a drive-through. But when you go back to the restaurant you find the doughnuts are all a bit stale. Everyone wants to stroke your stomach like it was some kind of angora cat. Stroke, stroke, and stroke some more. All the way around, first one way, then the other.

"When's it due?"

"I bet you'd like a boy, but I just know it's gonna be a girl; you're carrying it too low for it to be a boy."

"What a lovely tummy."

"Oh! You have such a healthy glow."

Then they pet the pussy some more. Y'know I've never been fondled so much in my life, not even when we were makin' the little bugger. The other day there was a young lady who even slipped her hand inside my shirt to feel the baby move. She was pretty cute herself, blond, blue eyes… and she just parked those gorgeous blue eyes in my brown eyes and felt around a bit to catch the baby move. Then she felt a little farther down and, well, other things started to move…. She called me a creep! Clobbered me with her bag and left.

Nope, doesn't look like those men of science coulda predicted an outcome like that. Y'see, they were all freaked out by the sociologists who were getting worked up for nothing over the falling birthrate. They were worried there wouldn't be enough young people to pay for their old-age pensions. That's why they decided to try cultivating their own little pension funds, a few extra pension payers for down the road. Even if there aren't any more jobs that come with pensions. Now that was unpredictable too. Apparently.

Oh there are lots of things the scientists didn't think about. Must be a few women behind it all. So anyway here I am, pregnant, my belly like the back end of a bus, all alone, marooned with my real and physical upsets.

And I'm afraid. Not just your everyday sort of fear, real fear. What if my body rejects the artificial uterus they fitted me up with? What would I do with it, eh? Say one fine morning I wake up and find a rejected uterus in my bed, with a fetus inside struggling to survive… what do I do? Do I throw it in a bag of ice and run to the hospital? Do I call an ambulance? The police? My insurance company? A lawyer? S.O.S. Pro-life? Shelter for homeless children? Who do you call for a thing like that? And besides, would I even be conscious enough to call any of those guys there, eh? I mean, who's to say I wouldn't just pass out seeing a rejected uterus jumping around in my bed. So, don't you think I've got good reason to be scared? (*The baby moves.*)

Oh! He moved! Look! He moved! He's still alive! He moved! My own little Mazerolle; my own flesh and blood. There really wasn't any need for me to flip out like that. That's what my doctor told me. And she knows everything. She says that the scientists wouldn't have tried it on men if it hadn't worked on other animals first. And she says that I've got an even better chance because all the guys in my family are a real tough bunch of mothers. So if that's what the doctor says, who am I to doubt her, and I'm not going to worry. It's better for the baby too. So you see it's true, nothing's changed. Just the sex. The doctor's a woman and the mother-to-be is a man.

Oh shit! Maybe it worked on lab animals, but that's it; p'raps a few boars've borne litters, a few rams have lambed, but when it comes to men, there still aren't a lot of examples of guys growing their own wild oats, sowing the seeds of life in their own furrow, so to speak. (*He feels a cramp.*) And you can be sure that I've been plenty furrowed these days. I'm risking my life! This is no walk in the park here! There are women who have died from it; and it could happen to men just the same. When it comes to things like this we really aren't all that much tougher; we're just made of skin and bones too. Even though it doesn't always seem that way… Training and diplomacy, y'know.

Diplomacy, yeah right. I sure put both feet in it that time. I only said what I said to make her feel better. I never thought making her feel better would take nine months. At least, I hope it doesn't take any longer just because I'm a man. After all, we men are built bigger, stronger… that could mean more time. Elephants gestate longer than rabbits because they're bigger, right? (*He feels another cramp.*)

Oh my God, I'm not going into labour, am I? I hope not. I'll just sit down here for a minute. I'll rock the baby a bit; maybe he'll go back to sleep.

Rock-a-bye baby, in the tree tops
When the wind blows, the cradle will rock.
When the bough breaks, the cradle will fall
And down will come baby, cradle and all.

There I think he's quieter now. (*He strokes his stomach from top to bottom and all around. He addresses a man in the audience.*) What are you looking at me like that for? (*He squeezes his breasts.*) What?! Don't you think they're big enough? Well, there are miracles and then there are miracles! Hormones can only do so much y'know. But don't worry, I'll be able to feed my little Mazerolle just fine. It's not the size that counts, remember. I know women who've fed twins with breasts no bigger than shelled peanuts. You remember the woman who only weighed 85 pounds? That's right, sir, 85 pounds, no kidding, and she fed twins. You don't need double barrels to hold a shot of hormones. They pump millions of 'em in every little chicken ya buy. A hormone isn't all that big after all. A little squirt from the left, a little squirt from the right… and the squirt's all fed. And the more he suckles, the more the hormones build up. No problem, my milk will flow. I can feel it starting already. Have no fear, no Mazerolle has ever let his family starve.

And besides, if it doesn't work the first time, they sell pumps for just that purpose at the drugstore. It's like a bicycle pump except that it pumps stuff out instead of in. Well… out of me, but into the pump. And then you attach the baby to the end of the pump with this part that looks like a little oxygen mask; once you get it going, runs all by itself. I learned all that at the prenatal course I took.

Oh damn, was that ever funny, the first time I went to the class. The women all stared at me, their eyes popping out of their heads, their knees buckling at the sight. And the men…. Ohh. You could just feel the cold sweat break out between the legs of every Tom, Dick and Harry in that room! Now that is predictable I suppose. But what I really don't understand is the women. No matter how long they've been liberated and have been trying desperately to do the same to the rest of us, they still get all mushy and upset when you show up with a few months of liberation under your shirt. They look at your tummy, your breasts, then your face, trying to figure out who you are. Back down to your breasts, your tummy, and then a little lower to check out what'cha got down there. Then back up to your face, breasts, tummy, face, tummy, face, tummy… like a broken clock spring. They just can't get their heads around the idea that a beard could have a… oh heck, it's too embarrassing. What do you say? What do you do? Where do you look? Where do you start?… Lemme tell ya everyone there was completely discombobulated…. Faced with sweeping waves of public unrest, the leader tried to get us doing relaxation exercises. It didn't help. That evening a coupla first-time mothers went into labour two months early. Gimme a break!

Speaking of exercises, I'd better be doing mine. Let's do some exercises. I hope I don't wake up the baby though; he's sleeping so nicely. And a sleeping baby is outta sight. Yep, outta sight, and I don't mind. (*He gets himself in position to do his exercises.*)

Scene Four

TARZAN starts with his arm exercises. His arms are straight out to the side, parallel to the floor and he stretches them to the side and back.

I must increase my bust. I must increase my bust. I must increase my bust. I must increase my bust. I must…. (*He stops suddenly.*) Hey, why am I saying that? I just finished explaining that I don't have to be big. I don't WANT to get big. I mean, my skin isn't too likely to bounce back to the way it was before, is it? After 35, y'know, your skin starts to look like a government program: more and more wrinkles and less and less flexible. And I don't want to end up with two big shopping bags hanging there forever and ever amen after I have the baby. No way, I'm not doing those exercises anymore. They're for women. Like I told you before, just because I let myself get pregnant, doesn't mean I'm some kinda patsy pushover. Oh no, I got a few ideas of my own.

I know, I'll do my pelvic exercises. Takes a good solid rack to carry a baby. I have to strengthen my muscles, loosen up the pelvic cage. They say there's a heck of a pressure per square inch down there by the end. That's just like kids, eh: pushing on the door instead of opening it nicely. (*He sits on the ground, the bottoms of his feet together; he starts to count.*). One, two, three, four, stretch seal. Yep. You've gotta be solid yet flexible. Seven, eight, nine, ten, stretch seal. The baby will come out more easily and faster, especially faster.

Fourteen, fifteen, sixteen… the doctor… stretch seal… might not have to do any cutting. Oh! Cutting? Where? She didn't tell me which outlet they plugged that artificial uterus into. (*He touches his backside, his front; his eyes grow big.*) If you've ever passed a kidney stone, you wouldn't dare try to pass a full-size baby that way, with or without opening the door! And it's got to be one or the other; I haven't got one in between… stretch seal damn it!

Maybe they've got it in their heads to have me deliver by cesarean section. Bloody stretch seal, yeah right! What's that gonna make me look like in a bathing suit with a bright pink seam stitched all the way down my front. I'll have to get a big butterfly tattooed across my chest… a big fancy butterfly… all sorts of colours… hmmm when you think about it that way, it might be sorta sexy. Stretch seal, 35, 36, 37, 38, 39, 40, 40, 40… 40… 40…. (*Losing his enthusiasm.*) Oh, it's always so much easier getting into trouble then getting out of it.

I wonder if they're gonna leave that plastic bag in there after the baby's born? Because I have no intention of making more than one baby, just one little old-age pension payer thank you very much. I've got a pension from the university, and Jane, well, it's a waste of time worrying about a pension for her; she's an artist. That's why I'm making this one for her. So I won't need the plastic bag in there just taking up space for nothing. I'll have to ask the doctor 'bout that next time I see her. I'd better write it down though. So many things to think about I end up forgettin' some. (*He goes to write it down.*)

And Jane isn't here to remind me. Even if that long distance feeling is as good as being there, Jane doesn't have much to say about all this; well, she's never been pregnant, has she? She doesn't know what it's like. She knows what she likes for sure, but she doesn't have a clue what it's like. (*He goes back to his exercises: on all fours he rocks from front to back.*)

In any case, she wouldn't understand. How can you understand something you've never experienced? Huh? It's impossible. Don't feel bad about it, though. Even if some of you out there don't quite understand either, don't worry. It's just that not everyone is gifted to conceive the inner workings of life. And in particular, not everyone can be a perfect husband of immaculate conception.

Ah, heck. If they're going to make me have a cesarean, fuck the exercises. I'm hungry. I've had one helluva craving since this morning, and I'm damn near to losin' control. It's not just a craving anymore, it's a raging obsession. When they hit me really bad, I can't be held responsible for what I might do. Sometimes they get so bad the whole neighbourhood takes cover. Women are lucky. When they get pregnant and the cravings hit them, their husbands go running off at full tilt to get them a ketchup pizza or red pepper ice cream or cinnamon-flavoured frog's legs or fried eggs in maple butter… nothing is too difficult to find. But I haven't got anyone to run out after my cravings like that.

No, nothing's really changed, has it? A little one on the way is a little one on the way. As long as it's on the way to someone who really wants it. And somebody has to do it. If not women, then it'll have to be us men. And when men don't wanna do it anymore, women'll just have to take the job back, job or no job, career or no career. Whether they're flipping burgers or beaver skins, or singing "Toreador," somebody has to make these little ones; that is, if we want any old-age pensions.

So here I am, helpless to quench my cravings… I can't even have a cigarette without poisoning the baby and pissing off "smoke-free Canada." Can't break into a little Western tune, don't have a band…. Hardly have any scenery even. It's a lucky thing I made it into the world at all or I wouldn't even be sure I have a mother… that's how serious doubt can get.

Scene Five

As he crosses the stage, he knocks over his briefcase from university. He gives the briefcase an angry kick.

Damned briefcase! Damned courses! Damned job! I don't know what keeps me from just blowing my stack!

One day! Can you believe it? One day. Twenty-four hours of paternity leave. It was a waste of time trying to reason with the head of the department, the dean of the faculty, the vice-president in charge of teaching… I even went all the way up to the university president to explain that I needed a longer paternity leave. It seemed pretty obvious to me. But all he did was look at me with a patronizing smirk, his eyes all watery, sweat beading on his forehead. I even went to the union. That was worse.

I used every argument I could think of even though only one seemed valid to me: I'm pregnant, and my operation is going to cut me open from stem to stern. But nothing doing. The union can never agree to cuts; it's just not on the table. It took two months of negotiation, but I finally got an extension all right… three days.

I was trying to figure out how I was going to get back to work three days after having my belly dissected. And it wouldn't be any easier if I delivered naturally, passing it like a big kidney stone, the doctor having to slice things so they don't rip… I really couldn't see how I'd be able to go back to work three days after something like that. Just because we're made in the image of God doesn't mean we can patch everything up again in three days. I really wondered what I was going to do. But I didn't have to wonder for long. They gave me an immediate leave, indefinite and without pay. Instantly, just like that. An exquisite oh-so-polite thanks-but-no-thanks on fine university letterhead…. Bye-bye, Tarzan, good luck.

I'm not sleeping too well anymore. A little one costs money. And the smaller they are, the more they cost. This one's not even born yet and it's already starting to cost us money. And nerves. At any rate, it sure isn't the time to be losing my job. Polite letter or not, indefinite or permanent… what matters is that it's without pay and I need money. Nope, not getting much sleep these days, nights… weeks.

Maybe the rest of you don't quite get it. Y'see I can't take valium; I'm pregnant. I don't want the kid to get addicted. I think it's better if he chooses his own addiction. Whether it's drugs, religion, music, technology, psychology… whatever, I can understand that. Men are naturally addicted to somethin'. But I'll leave the choice to him. I think it's important for an angelic father like me to respect that. But it doesn't help me sleep any better.

Two or three sleepless nights later, I decided to go to the EI office. I'm not ashamed; I've paid enough into it after all. It's an insurance right, employment insurance. They turned me down.

"Not eligible for benefits because not available for work."

So I told her, "Yeah, but I'm workin' on my own homemade pension plan here."

"No question of touching a cent before the fifteenth week after giving birth." Which means four months of pablum and pampers on credit. What's more, I have to prove to them in fifteen weeks that I've "arranged a stand-by babysitter for the baby."

"It seems there have been a number of abuses of this sort in the past."

"There are women who say they are looking for work but who are really doing nothing but staying home and feeding their baby."

"It's beyond me how dishonest people could cheat the government like that. The poor government can hardly bring itself to make cuts and wears itself out trying to find ways to tighten our belts without our noticing. And still there are people, women with babies especially, who you'd think'd be honest, but no, all they do is look for ways to screw the government."

"They don't make themselves ministers of the crown just to live off the backs of the people, now do they?"

Could it be the laws still aren't strict enough for ordinary folk? Nevertheless, if men start having babies, I think the laws won't be long in changing. That's usually the way it goes, eh.

So anyway, I let a week go by, but nothing changed; I still needed money, so I went back to the EI office. And I said to them, "Hey, what about my rights in all this?" So he brought out the *Charter of Rights and Freedoms*, though there seem to be more freedoms than rights.... "Go ahead. See if there's an article in there on the rights of pregnant men to get EI benefits…" So I asked how many months it would take before getting my first family allowance cheque. As if 32 or 38 bucks would change much of anything. "That's in the office upstairs."

So I lug myself and my bulging cargo all the way up to the third floor, in full view of everyone because the elevator wasn't working. But the secretary at family allowances wasn't taking new applications. "In case the baby should die in delivery, or just before. We mustn't take any chances. Especially when the mother is a man; it's terribly risky don'tcha know." Imagine saying something like that to a man about to drop a litter!

I took out the *Charter* again to see if it had anything to say about this, but there wasn't a single article on family allowances for men about to give birth. That charter's not very useful, is it? Just like a diploma. Now that everyone's got one, it ain't worth a damn. It's worse than social assistance. You can't even make babies anymore without starving. So I came back here, all alone, the baby's room not ready, just waiting for the big operation.

Now you're going to say that a psychology professor should have known better than that. Well I'm not a political science professor, am I, who knows the *Charter* by heart. And I've never had a baby before, have I? And there aren't any role-models for pregnant men either. No stereotypes for us men to trust in. While for women there are thousands of case studies, precedents, stereotypes… and a clutch of examples for every stereotype: a whole gallery of antiquities. On top of that, they've got every book imaginable that men have written for them: *The Canadian Mother and her Child, Natural Health Before, During, and After Childbirth, The Active Mother, The Passive Mother, The Joy of Childbirth…* name it and we've written it for them.

But nothing for men. Not a single precedent whatsoever, not a paragraph, law, magazine article; not even a prayer. I can't even find myself any decent paternity clothes. Everyone's behind the times. And they call this "progress"? If it keeps up like this, it'll be Jane who'll have to console me for trying to console her.

And to think it all could have unfolded so differently. Oh yeah, for some time now they've been talking about a moratorium on all these breaches of science. If they'd put a moratorium in place nine months ago, they'd've saved me from my own idiocy; I would've simply found some other way to make Jane feel better. It was just the easy way out to suggest having the baby myself, the first thing that popped into my head. I mean, they'd been talking about almost nothing else on the news. After making yourself say "It's terrible. It's terrible" enough times, you end up trying it out yourself to see what's so terrible about it. That's what I did.

Plastic uteruses, cloning, genetic selection… the whole kit'n'caboodle. You don't know which method to choose anymore: Coke Classic, new Coke, old Coke,

Philippe Beaulieu
Photo by Jean Berthélémé.

Diet Coke… you name it. When the doctor started to ask me about green eyes or blue eyes, blond hair or red… blond has been very fashionable since the Second World War, y'know… about one, two or three infusions and how many months between them… well, whoa, I said, whoa right there. I only want one baby and I want him to look like me. You know what you can do with your kinds of coke. It's not a pizza I want here, it's a baby. A baby with all the fixin's and no parts missin'. There are limits to how far you can muck around with a person's body. Sure, I'm all for getting the piping installed here so they can put the baby in me and then flush it out again nine months later, but beyond that, to argue about the colour of toilet paper… take a pill!

I know I shouldn't talk about this, but, well, it's hard not to think about it. They've got themselves in a bit of a fix. I mean, there're piles and piles of sperm filling refrigerators so there's hardly room for any more, and no more money to buy more refrigerators. Yet guys with a taste for handiwork haven't stopped supplying it. Supply has simply outstripped demand. When someone comes along with a fistful of life, you can't just throw it out without feeling guilty of murder. The test tubes are full-up waiting for women whose husbands aren't angelic enough to pot-up their own seed. And they don't dare throw out the leftovers in case the first try doesn't take or in case they discover it could cure AIDS or the manic madness of those who can't get it up. Yep, in a situation like this, you'd better find a solution, and quick. If you don't find it, you stop everything. That's what a moratorium's for. Oh, why do I always go an' get myself so worked up like that? (*cramp*)

Scene Six

Maybe it's just fear… of giving birth, of the unknown waiting for me; the fear of having a baby, of not being up to it, of screaming when I'm supposed to breathe in or puff out, or just simply the fear of being afraid? Do you women really have the same kind of fears too? After all, I guess the first time, whether for a woman or a man, is still the first time, eh.

Damn, there's nothing more natural than baking buns, is there…. Whoooooofff!! (*completely relieved*) It just makes a whole new man out of you. It feels good to find yourself again, feet on the ground, head clear. (*He takes a banana out of his shirt pocket, peels it and begins to eat it.*) Yeah, I'd say that since I got pregnant I've felt closer to myself, to my real inner nature, my true self. And it's important to listen to your inner self, instead of always listening to the inner self of other people. Especially when you're the topic of conversation.

Tarzan, just shut up and rock. This might be the last time you get to rock him without him screaming his lungs out. Oh yeah, the big day's getting close. It could be anytime now. Oh but don't worry, you don't have to leave. I'm not going to pull a fast one on you and do it here or anything. No sirree, my mother-in-law gave me strict instructions to get to the hospital: "It's not far: two lights, a stop sign, two more corners… at a fast trot, a half-dozen OOOoooOOOOo's, and you're there: bing, bang… you're in a bed; a coupla flicks of a good sharp knife, the baby howls... that's it." So you see there really is no reason for me to make such a fuss.

On the other hand, it would be a beautiful thing to have a baby right out here in nature, in the most beautiful park in the province. I'd for sure get my picture on the front page of the *Times & Transcript* then: "Quite a Show: Tarzan Mazerolle Gives Birth at Fundy Park." (*change location to suit production*) Looking at it like that, it'd be a hoot to deliver a baby. After all, things always seem worse than they really are. Me, I always end up seeing the positive side of things. That must be why my Jane calls me her angel. It's true I am an angel. Don't you think so? I mean, how many of you guys would do what I've done to make your wife happy, hmm? Most would have just said she was crazy and thrown her out without a speck of alimony. That's one to nothing for me.

Okay, I suppose a pregnant man, a house husband, a liberated fella isn't maybe the most male-male guy around, but between you and me, is it really necessary to always be male-male with a big... "M"?

Just think, before 1975 nothing like this could have happened.... Oh let me tell you it feels good to know we're not the only intelligent ones around. In any case, me, I saw it coming and I supported women's liberation. A woman, too, has to get out of the house. Especially if she has a career that's really going somewhere.

Sure, there were lots who supported the movement. But I bet nobody ever thought it would go this far. Not even me. It's not just liberation anymore, it's become libertarianism, and that's an important nuance. They don't just want to get out of the house now, they don't want to go back home anymore. And they're mixed up in everything. Even in places where men have always been mixed up. So there, men.... Go fly a kite! Oh boys, I tell ya, when it gets to the point the only intelligence is feminine intelligence, it's enough to drive ya outta your tree. When you get right down to it, is female with a capital "F" really any better than male with a capital "M"? (*He feels a cramp.*)

I think this might be it. Now how many cramps per minute was it when I'm supposed to think about going to the hospital? Fifteen per minute?... ONE every fifteen minutes! Whew! I'm okay then; the last one was longer ago than that. I think. (*another smaller cramp*) Yep, today's the big day. I thought it'd show up at the next full moon. But maybe with men it doesn't work with the moon. I was told that with first-timers like me, it could be a week or two late. (*another little cramp*) Unless this is false labour. That happens sometimes. Women think they're going into labour and it's just their intestines labouring. (*cramp*) Anyway if this is false labour, then I'm in for a heck of a case of diarrhea. (*He touches the bottom of his shorts.*) My water hasn't broken; must be diarrhea. Course, I'm not really sure where the broken water's supposed to come out anyway.

Oh it's so much easier for women! Everybody knows where it goes in, everyone feels it, and everybody knows where it comes out... they feel it. Yeah, it's a lot simpler for women. Unless it's just a question of getting used to it. (*cramp*) I'm not sure anyone could get used to these cramps. It doesn't matter. It's almost show time and I'm ready and raring to go... all ready to see you little fella.

Y'know, I'm as happy to be having this baby as any woman would be. It must be natural, I suppose.... Nope, nothin's changed. Not since the world began. You come into the world, you grow up, you get married or not, depending on the times, you celebrate Christmas on December 25th, and after so many Christmases, that's it. (*cramp*) But this little one here, he's on his way into the world. No two ways about it, he wants out. This must be what they call the transition of power. Tarzan, it's time. (*cramp*)

Well I'd better go. It's now or never. OOOOoooO! (*He feels a cramp. He looks between his legs.*) Nope, nothing's changed, my angel, nothing's changed. (*as he leaves*) OOOOooOOOOOO!!

The end.

Twelve Strands of Wool

Ivan Vanhecke
translated by Glen Nichols

The original French play was inspired by the children's story
Le tapis de Grand-Pré by Réjean Aucoin and Jean-Claude Tremblay.

A native of Belgium, **Ivan Vanhecke** has worked in the theatre for thirty-five years, of which twenty have been spent in Acadie. His training in philology and theatre in Brussels have led him to explore almost every field of communications: radio, television, film, theatre, journalism... as a writer as well as an actor, technician, director, and teacher. In film, he can be seen in "Le violon d'Arthur," "Les années noires," "The Secret Life of Algernon," and "Cigarette" by Monique LeBlanc, among other films, as well as in an episode of "Histoires Max" produced by TFO. In radio, besides playing a wide range of roles, he has written a number of plays, one of which received first prize in the Radio-Canada words and sounds contest. He was also heard reciting the entire Longfellow poem "Évangéline" on the national network. Ivan was the first director of programming for Radio Beauséjour in Shediac.

He has tackled every aspect of his favourite field – theatre: writing for example *Promenade en haute mer* and the adaptation *Le tapis de Grand-Pré*, directing *Vol en piqué dans la salle*, *Pot pour rire*, and *Ent'Quat'Dieux*, and acting in *L'éducation de Rita*, *Évangéline Deusse*, and *L'Indifférent*, among others. He has more recently broken into a new career of writing screenplays and directing for film and television by co-writing "Cigarette" with Monique LeBlanc and "Joséphine" with Anne-Marie Sirois. Ivan has also written the screenplays and directed "Sur la piste d'Éole" and a documentary series entitled "Les voyelles enchantées."

INTRODUCTION TO *TWELVE STRANDS OF WOOL*

Inspired by the award-winning Nova Scotian story, "Le tapis de Grand-Pré" by Réjean Aucoin and Jean-Claude Tremblay, *Twelve Strands of Wool* is a children's play adapted by Ivan Vanhecke that combines aspects of traditional Acadian mythology with modern settings. It is Christmas Eve and the twins Rosy and Connor are inspired by their grandmother's storytelling to seek twelve special strands of wool which will complete the hooked rug hanging on their grandmother's wall. This is no ordinary hooked rug, though, but the very rug their ancestors were making as a gift for the Chapel at Grand-Pré when the Acadians were rounded up by the English in 1755 and deported from the territory. The story goes that the twelve strands of wool needed to complete the rug were scattered with the Acadians; however, if the pieces of wool could be brought together again and the rug finished, "the magic of our ancestors would be fulfilled." This idea inspires the exuberant twins who take on the task of finding the wool.

Through the action of the play, Johnny Longlegs, a magical mailman with the gift of flight, carries the twins across Nova Scotia as they solve the mystery of what happened to the twelve strands of wool. Along their travels they meet a loquacious historian, various talking animals, a helpful farmwife, a not-so-scary ghost, and finally the parish priest of Church-Point and his housekeeper. In the end, Rosy and Connor succeed in their quest: the rug is restored, the ancestors are able to celebrate the Christmas that was robbed from them in 1755, and the children give their grandmother "the best Christmas present ever."

Structurally the play is loosely episodic, opening with a *tableau vivant* of the 1755 events followed by three expositional sequences in which the twins hear about the rug of Grand-Pré, first from their grandmother then from Johnny Longlegs who later conspires with the children to take them on the magical quest. Several songs are used to mark transitions throughout the play as the twins travel and meet the various characters in locations around Nova Scotia. Finally the play closes with a wondrous transformation when, "at the stroke of midnight, the church of Grand-Pré appears onstage [and] from inside we can hear violins and guitars. A song is heard." The play makes considerable demands on the imagination of its young audience, engaging them in the magic of the theatre and of the story itself.

Although the story is not based on any particular Acadian folktale, the simple quest narrative draws on numerous conventional elements like the flying "helper," animals with the gift of speech on Christmas Eve, and the ubiquitous presentation of food packets to the weary travellers. The Aucoin/Tremblay story is set in the late nineteenth century, but Vanhecke updated it to the present time and introduced clever modern touches to the play's magic, like having the enchanted mailman appear to the twins through their television screen. The effect is a wonderful integration of traditional and contemporary elements which reinforce the importance of the children's quest to complete the cycle set in motion by their ancestors, not to bring them to life again, but to allow those old ghosts to rest and the lives of the new generation to go on, enriched by the past but no longer indebted to it.

Of the five plays in the collection, this one was the most fun to translate due to the variety of imaginative characters. In addition to the distinctive children's voices versus adult voices, there is also the cartoon-like historian, ghostly sea captain and a somewhat pompous parish priest, not to mention the chicken, horse, sheep, and Canada Goose! The playwright expressed to me in conversation his sense that the language of the original play was perhaps "too standard" and he encouraged me to broaden and particularize the characters. Using linguistic cues embedded in the source text, such as the subtle dialect of Johnny's speeches, the repetitions between the speeches of the two sheep, the lexical register of Mrs. Goose and so on, I attempted to draw out these characteristics.

The play emphasizes the rug's origins at Grand-Pré, a site loaded with mythic significance for Acadians: it was an important settlement at the time of the deportation and has been featured in various literary narratives about the Acadian story, such as the infamous *Evangeline* by Longfellow. Consequently, I have maintained the Nova Scotian settings and place-names. On the advice of the playwright, who felt the original character names too "French" for an English play, I have changed the twins' names, Rose-Marie and Constant to Rosy and Connor. He also suggested Johnny à Minou [literally, Johnny son of a cat] be called Johnny Longlegs.

I have also changed the title of the play in translation, a decision not taken lightly; however, the various combinations of rug/carpet/ with "Grand-Pré" just didn't have the imaginative pull or attractive sound of "Twelve Strands of Wool." Although the new title relocates the play's attention to the object of the children's quest rather than the end result, I think this is a justifiable compromise given the rather clumsy or distracting alternatives.

A significant component of the contemporary theatre repertoire in Acadie is devoted to theatre for young audiences, represented by two of the five plays in this collection. *Twelve Strands of Wool* is a well-known and widely acclaimed piece in which the integration of past and present, of magic and story-telling, of geography and history, of myth and action underscores a play written with a highly developed sense of the theatrical.

—GN

Twelve Strands of Wool by Ivan Vanhecke

Le tapis de Grand-Pré was performed in 1989 at Théâtre l'Escaouette in Moncton with the following cast:

Roxanne Boulianne
Daniel Chiasson
Mance Émond
Jean-René Paulin

Directed by Louis-Dominique Lavigne
Designed by Daniel Castonguay
Music by Jac Gautreau

This translation of *Twelve Strands of Wool* was workshopped and given a public reading in Moncton (December 2001) with the following cast: Evie Carnat, Kate Doucet, Cindy Fifield, Gerry Grandbois, Peggy Humby, Sarah Julien, Annie LaPlante, Claudia MacLean, Glen Munro, Joan Sichel, and Shannon Wetmore.

CHARACTERS

Rosy
Connor
Grandma
Johnny Longlegs
Gaby, the historian
Mrs. Goose
Theresa, a farmer
Mrs. Chicken
Mr. Horse
Sheep #1 & #2
Captain Broussard's ghost
Lucille
Father Sigogne

Twelve Strands of Wool

by Ivan Vanhecke

The scene opens with four women seated in an Acadian-style kitchen in the middle of the 18th century. They are hooking a rug which is nearly finished. Suddenly we hear the loud noises of a battle, shouts of English soldiers, cries of distress. There's a burst of stage lighting, flames. The four characters quickly fold up the rug, dropping a few strands of wool on the floor; one of the characters picks them up and gives three strands to each of the others. Blackout. The noise of battle and the firelight continue outside and gradually fade away.

Lights come up on an interior similar to the one above, but with modern details. An older lady, GRANDMA Henriette, is cooking; two children, the twins ROSY and CONNOR, are decorating a Christmas tree. The rug seen earlier is hanging on the wall. ROSY looks at the rug and asks:

ROSY

Hey Grandma, when are you gonna finish your rug?

CONNOR

That's right, Grandma! Isn't there supposed to be a cross on the steeple of the church?

ROSY

We could help you finish it if you like.

CONNOR

Yeah! Just give us some wool and we could do it right now. It wouldn't take long…

ROSY

It'd look nicer if it was finished…

> *GRANDMA Henriette has been trying to get a word in, but the children don't give her a chance.*

ROSY

Tell us where you keep your wool! Then when we finish decorating the Christmas tree…

CONNOR

We can finish your rug for you. Me and Rosy, we're big enough you know.

ROSY

Connor's right. Come on, Grandma, why don't you tell us where you keep your wool?

GRANDMA

Settle down, kids, settle down. It's not quite as simple as that. It's a long story. But tell you what; you finish decorating the tree while I finish the Christmas treats, and afterwards I'll tell you the story of the rug. Now go on! Hurry up, or we'll never be ready in time.

The twins go back to decorating the tree, but this time with much more enthusiasm and speed while GRANDMA goes back to her stove. In a few minutes the tree is finished; all that's left is to put the star on top. CONNOR quickly drags over the table GRANDMA was working at; ROSY puts a chair on top of it; CONNOR climbs up on the table and then on the chair. ROSY hands him the star and CONNOR fixes it to the top of the tree. GRANDMA and ROSY applaud. CONNOR climbs back down quickly, bringing the chair with him; he places it beside the table and sits down. ROSY does the same and sits beside him.

CONNOR

There. We're all done, Grandma; we're listening…

ROSY

Tell us your story now.

GRANDMA

Okay, okay. Very well. I'll tell you the story, but you have to give me a hand peeling them spuds what's on the table. This rug came from my great-great grandmama who made it a very very long time ago with the help of some of her friends in the village. On it is a picture of…

ROSY

The church at Grand-Pré!

CONNOR

'Cept the church at Grand-Pré has a cross on top.

ROSY

I bet the church wasn't finished yet back when your great-great grandma was alive, eh Grandma?

GRANDMA

Of course it was finished. But stop interrupting me or I'll never be able to finish the story. My great-great grandmama and her friends decided to give the parish a hooked rug as a Christmas present. It was supposed to be hung at the very front of the church, right behind the altar where everybody could see it. And everybody would've been so proud of it. My great-great grandmama and her friends made a good start on the rug, but sadly that was the year of the Great Deportation…

CONNOR

1755.

ROSY
> 1755?

GRANDMA
> Ahh yes, children, the year the Acadians were sent away from their own country, a very sad year with no Christmas because the settlers of Grand-Pré had been scattered far and wide.

ROSY
> So then how did we end up here in Cape Breton...

CONNOR
> And what's the rug doing hanging on your wall?

GRANDMA
> Some of the Acadians were able to avoid the deportation. My ancestor was one of the lucky ones; she was able to escape with the rug which protected her family from winter cold, fall winds, spring rains and sometimes the summer heat. For all these years the rug has remained in our family.

CONNOR
> Wow! But you still haven't told us why we can't finish your rug!

ROSY
> It just needs a coupla pieces of wool...

GRANDMA
> Twelve strands of wool.

ROSY
> Twelve! That can't be too hard to find.

GRANDMA
> Twelve strands of wool, scattered and lost...

> *Just at that moment there's a knock at the door. CONNOR runs over and opens the door; it's JOHNNY Longlegs, the mailman, with a big package under his arm.*

JOHNNY
> Merry Christmas everybody. Oh boy, does it ever smell good 'round here. Hey, Grandma, I got a package here for ya.

GRANDMA
> Well, whaddya know! Maybe it's the missing wool!

JOHNNY
> Well, well, Grandma, you still believe in Santa Claus!

ROSY

Hey, Johnny, do you know the story of Grandma Henriette's rug?

JOHNNY

Oh yeah, for sure I know it. Everybody in Chéticamp knows that story.

GRANDMA

Come on in and sit yourself down, Johnny. It's awful cold out there; you'd better have a glass of Christmas cheer. It'll warm you up and loosen your tongue so you can tell these two some stories to keep 'em quiet while I finish up in the kitchen.

> *JOHNNY Longlegs doesn't have to be asked twice; he sits at the table. GRANDMA pours a glass which ROSY brings over to JOHNNY. GRANDMA goes back to her stove. JOHNNY takes a drink, stands up and goes over to the rug on the wall. ROSY interrupts his daydream.*

ROSY

Hey, Connor, let's go look in the attic. See if we can find twelve strands of wool.

JOHNNY

Won't do ya any good kids; ya won't find anything in the attic.

CONNOR

Why not, Johnny?

JOHNNY

'Cause the twelve strands of wool you're looking for were scattered far and wide at the same time as the Acadians, and... and...

TWINS

And what?

JOHNNY

And them strands are the only ones ya can use to finish the rug 'cause...

CONNOR

What? What? Tell us!

GRANDMA

Johnny! Stop telling them those old stories. I'll never get them to sleep tonight.

JOHNNY

Now go on Grandma, ya know as well as I do it's the honest truth that them's the only twelve strands of wool, an' them alone, that can bring back to life the magic of our ancestors...

ROSY

The magic of our ancestors?

Roxanne Boulianne, Daniel Chiasson & Jean-René Paulin.
Photo courtesy of Théâtre l'Escaouette.

CONNOR
> Oh Johnny, hurry up and tell us how we can find the wool. You gotta know…

JOHNNY
> Sorry, Connor. Now, if things were the way they used to be, like in the olden days… if mailmen still knew how to fly…

ROSY
> Mailmen used to fly?

CONNOR
> Did they have wings?

ROSY
> Could they see angels?

CONNOR
> Did they use rocket boosters?

JOHNNY
> Calm yourselfs, now, kids, calm yourselfs. It was just a kinda magic spell…. The night b'fore Christmas, Santa Claus had so much work to do he used to call on a few mailmen in far away places to give 'im a hand deliverin' presents.

CONNOR
> Did you ever do it, eh Johnny ?

JOHNNY
> No, unfortunately. I'm still waitin' my turn. Ya see, kids, it's not always the same ones goes out. Every year Santa Claus has a sorta lott'ry to choose the ones he needs from all the mailmen in the world.
>
> Well, there now. I've told ya enough stories for one night. I hafta finish me route and you two, ya'd better get some sleep if ya wanna be ready for Midnight Mass.

GRANDMA
> That's a real good idea there Johnny. Go on now, kids. Go upstairs. You can watch a bit of television and get some rest.

> *The children go upstairs after saying goodnight to JOHNNY Longlegs who gives them a hug and a sort of conspiratorial wink.*

GRANDMA
> Now why'dya hafta go an' tell them those old stories?

JOHNNY
> Oh Grandma, it's Christmas Eve. It's the night made for sweet dreamin'. Didn't you ever dream on Christmas Eve yourself that some day the rug'd be finished? Well, so long Grandma and Merry Christmas to ya.

GRANDMA

Good night, Johnny. Take care o' yourself. And Merry Christmas to you too.

JOHNNY goes out, leaving GRANDMA Henriette alone with her dreams. She goes over and looks at the rug on the wall, taking it and caressing it tenderly. ROSY and CONNOR are in their room watching TV on a giant screen which is showing a Christmas special such as "Alice in Wonderland" or "The Wizard of Oz."

CONNOR

Hey Rosy, do you believe those old stories Grandma and Johnny Longlegs were tellin' us?

ROSY

Course I believe them. Don't you?

CONNOR

Well, I dunno; I never seen a flying mailman helping Santa Claus, 'cept on TV.

ROSY

Oh brother! You only believe what you see, don'tcha. Look, Grandma's rug is really there, isn't it? And it's missing the cross from the steeple of the church, right? So, all we need to do is find the twelve strands of wool to fill in the missing parts. And then we'd be able to make the best Christmas present anyone could ever give to Grandma, and then…

CONNOR

All right! All right! I get the point. So do you have any ideas how we can find the strands of wool?

ROSY

Well, no. I was hoping you might have one.

CONNOR

No. I don't know any more than you. I guess we might as well just forget the whole thing. Besides, I want to watch some TV.

ROSY

Connor, you put all your dreams in that TV screen. Sometimes I even think you believe that one day Santa Claus will show up there wearin' a big smile ready to give you the best present you ever wanted, just like that.

CONNOR

Be quiet, Rosy, let me think.

JOHNNY

(off) If you was thinkin' with your heart, Connor, maybe I could help you and Rosy.

CONNOR
Who's that?

JOHNNY
(off) It's me, Connor, Johnny Longlegs.

CONNOR
Where are you? Stop hiding.

JOHNNY
(off) I ain't hidin', I'm everywhere: I can fly, I can appear and disappear as quick as lightning.

CONNOR starts to look everywhere in the room: under the bed, in the drawers.... ROSY watches him, surprised.

ROSY
Hey, what's up Connor? Did you lose something? What are you looking for?

CONNOR
Nothing.... Nothing...

JOHNNY
(off) You won't find me that way, Connor. I'm in a magical land; only those who believe in elves and fairies can see me.

CONNOR
Rosy, do you believe in elves and fairies?

ROSY
Sure thing. Without them there wouldn't be any magic. Obviously you don't believe in them.

CONNOR
Yeah.... Yeah, I believe in them.... Hey, tell me Rosy, do you hear Johnny Longlegs?

ROSY
Yeah. Course I hear him.

CONNOR
Then where is he?

ROSY
He told me to tell you that you'll find him where you most truly believe him to be.

JOHNNY
(off) You can have three guesses, Connor.

CONNOR
Gee! I don't know…. In the closet?

ROSY
Wrong!

JOHNNY
(off) Wrong! Two more chances. Think, Connor, think with your heart.

CONNOR
In the attic. Yeah, that's it. I bet you're hiding in the attic.

JOHNNY
(off) Missed again, Connor. Rosy just told you where you put all your dreams.

CONNOR
…In the television…

> *JOHNNY Longlegs appears on the television screen; he's a little different from his earlier appearance. He is more handsome, taller; perched on stilts, he looks like a heron; he seems to be floating in the air.*

JOHNNY
(on the screen) You see, Connor, Santa Claus drew my name this year, so I have to go find him at the North Pole. But he promised me that b'fore I do that I could help make someone's dream come true. When I told him I had to find twelve strands of wool, he laughed at me.

ROSY
He laughed at you?

CONNOR
He laughed at you!

JOHNNY
But when I explained to him that two kids were lookin' for twelve special strands of wool to make a Christmas present for their great-great-great grandma, he started to cry and he said "Okay."

CONNOR
You mean it's true! We're really going to go look for Grandma Henriette's wool?

JOHNNY
Let's go!

ROSY
Wow! But where do we start?

JOHNNY
Grandma is sleeping. Rosy, go get the rug. Connor, go put on your astronaut suit. When you're both ready, open your bedroom window and I'll be waitin' for you out there.

> ROSY *sneaks down the stairs quietly and takes the rug from the wall.* CONNOR *quickly puts on his astronaut suit. Back in the bedroom they open the window.*

JOHNNY
Don't be afraid, kids. Just jump into my pack.

> ROSY *and* CONNOR *jump out the window. We find them both in JOHNNY Longlegs' pack, floating among the stars outside.*

CONNOR
Wow! Johnny, what keeps you up in the air like this and…?

ROSY
This is amazing! We can almost touch the stars.

JOHNNY
Y'know, kids, I have a reputation for being able to run pretty fast, eh; the folks in the village musta tol' ya. Well, it was the wind fairies who made me a magical mailman by giving me enchanted boots, which I only use for doing good deeds. And then this evening Santa Claus gave me the gentle wings of a Zephyr.

JOHNNY LONGLEGS' SONG
My name is Johnny Longlegs
The magical mailman,
And one special Christmas
I learned how to fly,
Oh so high in the sky
Like a bird, like a plane, like a magical mailman.

My name is Johnny Longlegs
The cosmical mailman,
A friend of the fairies,
With magic and love
Just like butterfly wings,
Special boots, great big heart, make a cosmical mailman.

My name is Johnny Longlegs
I'm bringing you good news
And presents for Christmas,
So wishes come true,
Put a smile on your face,
A magical mailman makes everyone happy.

ROSY

Oh! Look Connor, the big dipper… and over there is the north star…

CONNOR

Wow! We just went over the top of the church. I wonder what the priest would say if he could see us now…

ROSY

Johnny, aren't you afraid of crashing into the moon?

JOHNNY

Don't fret, Rosy, the moon is still a long ways away.

CONNOR

Hey Johnny, what's that down there?

JOHNNY

There? We just went over Plateau; and down there is Saint-Joseph du Moine, and over there a little further is Margar…

CONNOR

Oh look, Rosy, look down there, you can see the whole island of Cape Breton.

ROSY

Johnny, where are we going anyway?

CONNOR

Yeah, Johnny, what's your plan?

JOHNNY

We're headin' for Isle Madame, kids.

ROSY

Wow! Is that where we'll find Grandma's strands of wool?

JOHNNY

No. But what I heard, we should be able to pick up the trail there.

CONNOR

Lookit the big river down there, Johnny…

ROSY

Aren't you afraid of falling in?

JOHNNY

No, no, don't worry, Rosy, neither the wind fairies nor Santa Claus will let me down tonight. And that's not a river, Connor, that's the Strait of Canso you're lookin' at. So that means we're almost there. Hang on tight, kids; we're about to land.

ROSY

In the water?

JOHNNY

No, of course not, Rosy; over there, on the island. Don'tcha see it?

ROSY

Oh okay, yeah I see it.

CONNOR

Are you sure you know where you're going, Johnny? Will you be able to land okay on that island?

JOHNNY

Johnny Longlegs has never missed a mailbox b'fore, and he's not about to start on Christmas Eve.

ROSY

Now look what you've done; you've hurt his feelings…

CONNOR

…Uhh…. No. I was just asking for you. 'Cause me, I got my astronaut suit on, eh.

ROSY

Well, say you're sorry anyway…

JOHNNY

Look kids, this ain't a good time to start scrappin'. We're gettin' really close now. And besides, my feelings aren't hurt anyways. Magic is just a little scary sometimes, that's all.

> *JOHNNY and the twins land on the stage. Behind them people pass in silhouette. We can see Christmas lights, hear Christmas music. There's some snow on the ground.*

CONNOR

Who are we gonna see here, Johnny?

JOHNNY

The historian of Isle Madame. His name is Gabriel, but everyone 'round here just calls him Gaby. He's the only one who can help us.

ROSY

Why's that?

JOHNNY

He has a great big pile o' books and it'd be a shame if he didn't have at least one that talked about Grandma Henriette's rug.

CONNOR
Where's he live?

JOHNNY
See that house over there, at the end of the village? That's his house. Go on now. You go ahead, kids. While you're there, I'll go find us some food for the rest of the trip.

> *CONNOR and ROSY head in one direction, while JOHNNY Longlegs disappears rapidly on the other side. The children sing and move slowly towards GABY's house.*

SONG OF THE TWINS #1
We're off to find
Twelve strands of wool;
Twelve strands of wool
We're off to find.
Twelve strands of wool
To finish the cross
On the roof overtop
Of the Church of Grand-Pré
On Grandma's old hooked rug.
Twelve lost strands of wool,
Twelve lost strands of wool
Now we're off to find;
So Christmas this year
Will brighten forever
The Church of Grand-Pré,
The church of our people,
Our ancestors of Grand-Pré.

> *They finally get to the door which looks like the cover of a book with gold-coloured decorations.*

CONNOR
Go on, Rosy, go knock on the door.

ROSY
No. You knock.

CONNOR
Are you scared?

ROSY
I dunno. I just dunno what to say if the door opens. Besides, I never knocked on a book before.

CONNOR

Oh go on! And I'll stay right behind you so I can protect you if anything happens.

> *ROSY goes to the door. She knocks timidly and rushes back to CONNOR. Nothing happens.*

CONNOR

Maybe he's not there?

ROSY

Maybe he can't hear very well?

CONNOR

You didn't knock hard enough. Go back and try again.

ROSY

No way! This time we'll go together. The two of us can knock louder.

CONNOR

Ok! Let's go.

> *They both go to the door and after a hesitation they knock on the door together. In a moment they hear a voice coming from behind the door.*

GABY

Who's that out there come to bother me on Christmas Eve?

ROSY

It's Connor.

CONNOR

And Rosy. The two… the twins…

GABY

Ah! The twins. Well, well, well. Come in. Come in. The door's open. I was waiting for you.

> *ROSY and CONNOR look at each other in surprise. Slowly they open the door. The lights come up revealing a room full of big books. In the middle of the room on a stand is an open book as big as a grown-up. They see no one. The twins are very intimidated.*

TWINS

You… you were waiting for us?

> *GABY appears from behind the big book. We can only see his head.*

GABY

Of course. Of course. It was written in my book. See, December 24, 1989. Two twins will be delivered to Isle Madame by a flying mailman and will come to see the historian Gabriel with a hooked rug. So…. So… where is this famous rug?

ROSY loses no time showing him the rug.

ROSY

You see. It's missing a few…

GABY

I know. I know. This is the rug of Grand-Pré and you are looking for the lost strands of wool needed to finish it. Let's see what it says in my book about this… let's see… let's see… have to go all the way back to 1755… *(All three go behind the big book and GABY starts to turn the pages.)* 1940… 1850… 1810… 1760…. Here we are, 1755. Look, look, isn't that odd, the page has been marked. *(In fact, a bookmark of red wool hangs over the top.)* Let's see…. Let's see… what story does that first historian have to tell us…. *(While GABY reads, CONNOR comes out from behind the book and takes a close look at the strands of wool hanging out of the book. He looks from the book to the rug several times.)* "The wool chosen to make the rug was the purest and silkiest. It came from a flock of sheep that were the pride and joy of the Acadians at Grand-Pré. A young farm girl of the time managed to save two of the sheep and took them with her on one of the boats commanded by Captain Beausoleil Broussard who landed them at a place called Goose Lake. The name of the farm girl was Theresa and…"

CONNOR

Hey, Gaby, don't you think the strands of wool in your book look a lot like those in the rug?

GABY and ROSY poke their heads out over the book and look at CONNOR in surprise, then at the strands of wool. ROSY takes the strands of wool, comes out from behind the book and lays them on the rug.

ROSY

He's right, Gaby, they're really silky and the same colour as those in the rug.

CONNOR

Look in your book and see what else it says.

GABY

Let's see… let's see…. "My mother…" the historian must be talking about his own mother; "My mother gave me three strands of wool and I put them in this book for safekeeping until someone finds the rug."

The twins jump for joy and shout.

TWINS

We just found three strands of wool for Grandma's rug; we just found three strands of wool...

They start to dance around the room dragging GABY into it. Suddenly ROSY breaks off.

ROSY

Hurry up. Let's go get Johnny. We have to get to Goose Lake and find the other strands. *(She runs towards the door, stops, turns around and asks:)* But Gaby, where's Goose Lake?

GABY

Well, well now, I haven't a clue, my dear little Rosy.

CONNOR

But what about your book? Doesn't it say anything?

GABY

Sorry, kids; I'm just an historian you know, not a geographer.

CONNOR

But how are we going to find out where it is?

GABY

Let's see, let's see.... Maybe your friend the mailman will know.

ROSY

That's it! Let's go ask Johnny.

CONNOR

Aren't you coming with us, Gaby?

GABY

No, kids, no...

ROSY

But why not, Gaby?

GABY

Because I have to write down in my book what happened this evening; besides, I'm too heavy for the mailman and I'd just slow you all down...

ROSY

If we find the other strands of wool, we'll come back and tell you all about it so you can write the story down in your book.

ROSY jumps into GABY's arms and gives him a hug; CONNOR does the same. Then they head for the door, but both of them turn around just before leaving.

TWINS
Merry Christmas, Gaby.

The children exit leaving GABY very emotional. The lights go down. The children are outside and sing.

SONG OF THE TWINS #2
And now we've found
Three strands of wool;
Three strands of wool
We now have found.
Three strands of wool
To finish the cross
On the roof overtop
Of the Church of Grand-Pré
On Grandma's old hooked rug.
Lookin' over here,
Lookin' over there,
Lookin' everywhere,
For nine more strands of wool
To finish the rug
And bring back to life
The magic and joy of
Our ancestors of Grand-Pré.

The children continue to sing until they notice JOHNNY, his arms full of supplies.

JOHNNY
Well, what are you two so happy about?

ROSY
We just found three strands of wool.

CONNOR
And it was me that found them first.

ROSY
It was really easy. They were right there in this big book.

CONNOR
Yeah but it was me who saw them first.

JOHNNY
Three. That's good, but it means we still have nine more to find.

CONNOR
Yes, but we know where to find them.

JOHNNY
Well, okay then. Jump into my pack and tell me what direction to go in.

TWINS
Direction?

ROSY
But we don't know.

JOHNNY
You just told me you knew where to go.

ROSY
We do know where to go; we just don't know where it is.

JOHNNY
Ahh, well Rosy, that's a little like having a letter with no address.

CONNOR
Address! Oh, we got that Johnny: Goose Lake.

ROSY
And we figured you'd know where to find it.

JOHNNY
Goose Lake? Hmmm…. No, I don't know any place by that name.

CONNOR
Oh come on, Johnny, you told us you delivered mail everywhere. Try to remember.

JOHNNY
Connor, I deliver mail to people, not birds. Didn't Gaby know where it was either?

ROSY
No. *(ROSY and CONNOR sit on the ground, frustrated.)* So that's it then. We'll never be able to finish the rug for Grandma's present.

CONNOR
And the magic of our ancestors will never come back.

JOHNNY
Come on, kids, c'mon. Don't give up so quickly. There must be a solution. We just have to think a little bit. Here. Have a bite to eat. It'll help give you the strength to figure things out.

ROSY

    I'm not hungry.

CONNOR

    I am!

JOHNNY

    Did Gaby tell you anything else?

CONNOR

    Ah! He said that we should find a farmer there whose great-great grandmother's name was Theresa.

ROSY

    Hey Johnny, do you know any farmers by the name of Theresa?

JOHNNY

    Unfortunately I know lots of Theresa's. Besides, the one we're looking for might be called Hortense or Joséphine or Carmen or…

ROSY

    Oh. We'll never figure it out.

CONNOR

    There's nothing else to do but go home.

JOHNNY

    No, no, climb into my pack. We'll fly around some more and keep on thinking. I'm sure we'll find something.

    CONNOR and ROSY climb onto JOHNNY's back, the lights go down on the stage. We hear the children singing, but with less joy.

SONG OF THE TWINS #3

    We have to find
    Nine strands of wool;
    Nine strands of wool
    We have to find.
    Nine strands of wool
    To finish the cross
    On the roof overtop
    Of the Church of Grand-Pré
    On Grandma's old hooked rug.
    Lookin' over here,
    Lookin' over there,
    Lookin' everywhere,
    For nine more strands of wool
    To finish the rug
    And bring back to life

The magic and joy of
Our ancestors of Grand-Pré.

> *JOHNNY flies along among the stars, carrying the twins while the countryside slides by below them.*

ROSY
I'm cold, Johnny.

JOHNNY
Wrap yourself in the rug, Rosy; it'll keep you warm.

CONNOR
What are you thinking about, Johnny?

ROSY
Have you figured out where we're going?

JOHNNY
Not yet...

CONNOR
I know! I just remembered something else. Gaby said that farmer Theresa got there by boat.

JOHNNY
So then we'd best follow along the coast. We're lucky; the sky is clear tonight. We can even see birds flying along in a hurry to find shelter for the night.

ROSY
Oh look, Johnny, down there! There's a whole bunch of 'em. Let's go closer so we can get a better look.

JOHNNY
I wouldn't want to get too close. We might scare them...

CONNOR
Maybe if I threw them some crumbs from my snack...

ROSY
Oh come on, Connor, what if they fell on someone's head...

CONNOR
A little crumb isn't going to hurt anything...

JOHNNY
Rosy is right, Connor, you shouldn't be throwin' stuff overboard.

> *JOHNNY and the twins fly closer to the birds which grow bigger below them.*

CONNOR
Fine then, since you don't want to listen to my ideas. I just wanted to do something so we wouldn't scare the ducks.

One of the birds approaches, turns her head towards them.

MRS. GOOSE
Excuse me young man, but we are not ducks. We are Canada Geese.

JOHNNY and the twins cry in surprise and fear.

ROSY
G... G... Geese?

CONNOR
Geese?

MRS. GOOSE
Yes. Canada Geese. And what, pray tell, is so strange about that?

ROSY
Oh! Nothing, nothing...

CONNOR
It's just that you can talk...

MRS. GOOSE
But of course. There's no law against talking, is there?

CONNOR
No, no, not at all. Not at all. It's just that...

ROSY
You see, Mrs. Goose, we just happen to be looking for...

CONNOR
A place...

JOHNNY
A place named after you.

MRS. GOOSE
Me?

CONNOR
Yes.... Goose.

ROSY
Goose Lake.

MRS. GOOSE
My! That is a pretty name. But I must say I've never heard tell of any such a place. Pity…

ROSY
Are you sure?

MRS. GOOSE
But of course!

JOHNNY
Pity.

MRS. GOOSE
However, we are actually on the way to our favourite spot where we always make a stopover on Christmas Eve. It is sheltered from the wind and we can find lots of food there.

JOHNNY
And is there water where you're going?

MRS. GOOSE
Of course…

CONNOR
And is there a farm nearby?

MRS. GOOSE
Yes, but I don't think…

ROSY
That must be it, Johnny, that must be Goose Lake!

JOHNNY
Would you permit us to accompany you as far as your favourite resting place? And along the way you can tell us why you are still here at this time of year.

ROSY
Oh yes! Please, pretty please, Mrs. Goose.

MRS. GOOSE
It would be a pleasure to welcome you among us.

CONNOR
Oh thank you, thank you so much. And now tell us your story.

MRS. GOOSE
My sisters and brothers and I will tell you our story together.

CHORUS OF THE GEESE
> We are Canada geese
> Stopping on our way
> At ponds along the coast
> And on the edge of frozen lakes.
> Raising little baby geese
> And feasting in fields of corn.
> We are Canada geese
> Honking fills the sky;
> The calling marks our flight
> Across the stars both day and night.
> Making happy every sad
> Or weary soul who hears.
> We are geese of the north
> Grey and white and black;
> We cross and cross again
> Without a care the land we love.

> *While they are talking, flying and singing, the landscape from Canso to Pomquet slides beneath them. Soon a blue patch appears in the form of a goose with outstretched wings.*

ROSY
> Oh! Look, Johnny, look! That must be it.

JOHNNY
> Where?

ROSY
> Down there. See! Look at the shape. It looks like a goose.

CONNOR
> I dunno, I think it looks more like a butterfly.

MRS. GOOSE
> My dear boy, perhaps if you cleaned off that little window in your… swimming… thing, you could see this shape clearly looks just like me when I unfold my gracious wings.

ROSY
> Goodness, Connor, you do seem to have a special talent for offending everyone tonight.

CONNOR
> Well, first of all it's not a swimming "thing" I'm wearing, it's an astronaut helmet…

ROSY
> Do you know this place Mrs. Goose?

MRS. GOOSE
But of course. This is where we come every year to spend Christmas Eve.

JOHNNY
I see a light. I'm going to fly around a bit to try and find a spot to land where we won't get our feet wet.

CONNOR
Hey tell me, Mrs. Goose, do you always talk like this?

MRS. GOOSE
Oh, no, my dear boy, only on Christmas Eve.

ROSY
And the other animals, can they talk too?

MRS. GOOSE
Oh yes, this is the magical night when all secrets are told. But be careful; there is one place you must not go to listen to the animals tonight: the stable.

CONNOR
A table?

ROSY
What kinda table?

MRS. GOOSE
No, no. A stable.

TWINS
Oh.

JOHNNY
Excuse me Mrs. Goose, but it's getting late and we're in a bit of a hurry.

MRS. GOOSE
Don't forget, children, not in the stable.

CONNOR
She's gone.

JOHNNY
Hang on, twins, we're landing.

CONNOR
Be careful, Johnny, I don't know how to swim very well.

ROSY
And I really don't want to get wet.

JOHNNY

Don't you worry, I think… oops! I think I'm going a bit too fast…

CONNOR

Put on your brakes or…

> *JOHNNY has trouble stopping and they all smack into the door of the house. The porch light comes on and the door opens.*

THERESA

Well, well what have we here! Are you completely out of your minds, or did you just fall from the sky?

ROSY

Well… we just fell…

CONNOR

No. No. We're just a little…

JOHNNY

It was all my fault…

ROSY

You see, it's only the second time. You see…

THERESA

Right now, I don't see anything that makes sense. Pick yourselves up, for heaven's sake. You there, the one who looks like a mailman, what did you take my house for? A mailbox?

ROSY

We don't mean any harm…

JOHNNY

We're just looking for…

ROSY

Some wool for a rug…

CONNOR

And a certain Hortense or Joséphine or…

THERESA

Well, if my name ain't Theresa, I don't understand a blessed thing you're saying.

ROSY

Theresa?

CONNOR
> Your name is Theresa?

THERESA
> Well, yes kids. As far as I know there's nothing unusual about that, is there?

JOHNNY
> No, no. It's just that, well, we're actually looking for someone by the name of Theresa.

THERESA
> Do you have a present for her, Mr. Mailman?

ROSY
> If you are the right Theresa, we do have something to show you.

THERESA
> What's that, little girl? The right Theresa? At Goose Lake, there is only one Theresa and that's me.

ROSY
> Goose Lake!

CONNOR
> Rosy! Show her the rug. Then we'll know for sure.

THERESA
> So what do you have to show Theresa who has to be the right one.

ROSY
> It's a hooked rug that belongs to our Grandma Henriette which came down to her from her great-great grandma.

> *CONNOR shows the rug to THERESA.*

THERESA
> And her great-great-grandma lived at Grand-Pré?

CONNOR
> Yes!

THERESA
> And the church sewn on the rug is the Church at Grand-Pré?

ROSY
> Yes!

THERESA

I can't tell you how long I've been waiting for this. I've heard so many stories about it I no longer believed it really existed. Oh my! Oh my! So this is the famous rug of Grand-Pré. We've been waiting for you for a very long time. Come in. Come in. You must have a little something to eat. I just happen to have a rapi pie in the oven.

ROSY

I'm sorry. We don't have time. All we want to know is where the strands of wool are?

THERESA

What strands of wool?

CONNOR

You know, the strands of wool.

ROSY

The strands of wool we need to finish the rug.

THERESA

Well to tell you the truth, I haven't a clue.

ROSY

But Gaby told us we could find them here.

CONNOR

Because of the sheep your ancestor brought with her on Captain Broussard's boat.

THERESA

Funny you should mention sheep; I actually have two sheep who, every Christmas Eve, set to work the spinning wool off their own backs.

ROSY

Where are they Miss Theresa?

THERESA

You'll find them out in the stable, dear.

ROSY

In the stable?

CONNOR

Oh. It's just that…

ROSY

We can't go in the stable tonight.

CONNOR
  It's too dangerous.

ROSY
  Mrs. Goose told us that…

THERESA
  Ha! Ha! Ha! I don't know who this Mrs. Moose is, but she must know about the evil spell.

ROSY
  Evil spell?

THERESA
  Oh yes, my dear. In the stable tonight there are things that must not be said, 'cause if you are unlucky enough to say them you will instantly be turned into a chicken.

ROSY
  A chi… chi… chicken?

CONNOR
  I don't want to be turned into a chicken.

THERESA
  Then listen closely to me. You must never answer with a "yes" or a "no" to any animal who asks you a question. And you must never call any animal by their real name either.

CONNOR
  Oh I know this game. I've played it before.

ROSY
  Well let's go then. Are you coming?

THERESA
  Oh! No! I'm much too old to play those games anymore.

CONNOR
  Have you ever gone to the stable on Christmas Eve, Miss Theresa?

THERESA
  Sure.

ROSY
  How did you keep from being turned into a chicken?

THERESA
  I didn't say a thing.

JOHNNY

Well you better hurry along twins. It's getting late.

ROSY

You're not coming with us, Johnny ?

JOHNNY

No… Rosy, no. I'm a bit chilly… I think I'll go warm up inside.

THERESA

And while you're out there, I'll fix you up some little treats to eat. Oh, and another thing I'd better tell you. Because you're twins, if either one of you makes a mistake, you'll both be turned into chickens.

> *JOHNNY and THERESA disappear into the house and the children head towards the stable. As they get closer the sound of conversations coming from the stable gets clearer and louder.*

ROSY

You said you already played this game. Did you win?

CONNOR

No. Never. You're not scared are you?

ROSY

What I'm more scared of is the idea of having to scratch around for seeds the rest of my life.

CONNOR

Me, I don't like the idea of ending up in a casserole some day.

ROSY

Maybe if we practiced a bit before going in.

CONNOR

Good idea. Ask me some questions.

ROSY

Do you remember what you're not supposed to say?

CONNOR

Yes.

ROSY

I think I see you growing some feathers already.

CONNOR

Huh!

ROSY

Okay. Look, I think we better just stick together and say as little as possible. *(ROSY heads to the door of the stable; CONNOR stays where he is.)* Well… are you coming?

CONNOR

Maybe you'd better go in by yourself.

ROSY

Oh no you don't!… Together we can watch out for each other. Wait here a sec. *(ROSY goes back to the door and suddenly shouts.)* Be quiet in there all of you! D'ya hear? Okay let's go! Come on. Put your hand over your mouth.

> *The stable goes silent. ROSY and CONNOR put their hands over their mouths and go in. A number of animals appear, watching the children.*

MRS. CHICKEN

And j-just who do you think you aahre c-coming in here interrupting our c-c-caahnversation?

MR. HORSE

Especially given that we have so many profoundly interesting things to talk about.

MRS. CHICKEN

And we have to k-keep q-q-quiihet a whole year between ch-ch-chaahts!

MR. HORSE

Well, I'll be! I do believe they are unable to speak.

MRS. CHICKEN

Who aahre you, k-k-kids?

ROSY

Rosy and…

CONNOR

Connor, Mrs. Chi…

> *ROSY quickly puts her hand over CONNOR's mouth.*

MR. HORSE

And what, may I ask, are you doing here?

ROSY

We are looking for a couple of she…

> *This time, CONNOR covers ROSY's mouth.*

MRS. CHICKEN
A c-c-caaupla what?

CONNOR
Umm well, two of your friends...

ROSY
Who are spinning some wool off their own backs.

MR. HORSE
Ah! That'd be the sheep. You will find them back there in the corner.

Right away, the conversations pick up again even more loudly. ROSY goes towards the corner of the stable as indicated by the horse.

SHEEP 1
How awful! Another Christmas spent spinning our wool for nothing.

SHEEP 2
Oh yes, my dear. How awful! It doesn't look like we'll see our saviours come tonight either.

SHEEP 1
Another sad Christmas for our ancestors.

SHEEP 2
Another sad Christmas for the rug.

ROSY
Excuse me ladies, but you wouldn't by any chance be talking about the legend of the rug of Grand-Pré, would you?

SHEEP 1
Legend?

SHEEP 2
Legend? Did you say legend?

SHEEP 1
But it's not a legend, my little lamb. Oh no. It is the pure and simple truth...

SHEEP 2
The truth pure and simple...

SHEEP 1
We're spinning wool...

SHEEP 2
The wool we're spinning...

SHEEP 1
'Til one Christmas…

SHEEP 2
Two twins will come…

SHEEP 1
Who will ask us for some…

ROSY
That's it, my brother and I, we're twins, and we've come…

SHEEP 2
Your brother and you are twins?

ROSY
Ye…. Haaaa…

CONNOR
Haaaa… I think I just felt a feather shiver down my back.

ROSY
Of course we're twins.

CONNOR
That's right. Ever since we were born.

SHEEP 1
What proof do you have?

SHEEP 2
I don't see any resemblance.

SHEEP 1
No resemblance at all.

ROSY
Just that we were born on the same day.

CONNOR
At the same time.

SHEEP 2
Hmmm, that pretty much proves it.

SHEEP 1
Yep, proves it pretty much.

ROSY

So then you can give us some wool?

SHEEP 1

Bah! Now… just a minute.

SHEEP 2

Now you have to prove to us you have the right rug.

CONNOR

Show them the rug, Rosy.

ROSY takes out the rug and shows it to the two sheep who examine it closely.

SHEEP 1

It surely does look like it.

ROSY

In that case we have fulfilled all the conditions so now you can give us your wool.

SHEEP 2

Not yet…

SHEEP 1

Not so fast…

CONNOR

Now what?

SHEEP 2

If you really are the twins we've been waiting for…

SHEEP 1

Then you should have in your possession three strands…

ROSY

Ye…. Haaaa…

CONNOR

Haaaa… Rosy, please! Stop scaring me like that.

ROSY

We have the three strands of wool we found at Mr. Gaby's house. Here. Look at these.

SHEEP 1

Well, my lambs, this'll be the most beautiful Christmas we've ever seen.

SHEEP 2

    Here are three more strands of wool for your rug.

ROSY

    Three? Only three? Don't you have any more to give us?

CONNOR

    You've got lots of it on your back.

SHEEP 1

    Three, that's all.

SHEEP 2

    Not one more.

SHEEP 1

    Not one less.

SHEEP 2

    Now we can finally rest knowing that our ancestors will also be able to celebrate Christmas tonight.

CONNOR

    Only if we can find the six more strands of wool that are still missing.

ROSY

    And time is running out if we want to get there before midnight. Come on. Goodbye Mrs. Sheep…

        CONNOR and ROSY look at each other frozen for a second. Then they run out of the stable, crying. Once outside they stop and look at each other again.

ROSY

    I think your mouth is starting to take the shape of a beak…

CONNOR

    What!?

ROSY

    (laughing) It's not true…. It's not true…

CONNOR

    So the evil spell doesn't exist?

ROSY

    Guess not. But let's not tell anybody.

CONNOR

    It'll be our secret.

SONG OF THE TWINS #4
>We have to find
>Six strands of wool;
>Six strands of wool
>We have to find.
>Six strands of wool
>To finish the cross
>On the roof overtop
>Of the Church of Grand-Pré
>On Grandma's old hooked rug.
>Lookin' over here,
>Lookin' over there,
>Lookin' everywhere,
>For six more strands of wool
>To finish the rug
>And bring back to life
>The magic and joy of
>Our ancestors of Grand-Pré.

>*ROSY and CONNOR sing merrily as they go to the porch steps where THERESA and JOHNNY are waiting for them.*

JOHNNY
Well, kids, by the sound o' your happy voices, I take it your hunt was successful.

ROSY
Three more strands, Johnny, three more strands.

JOHNNY
Only three. But why only three?

ROSY
Nobody told us.

THERESA
And you managed to avoid the evil spell! How did you do that?

CONNOR
Well, I'll tell you…

ROSY
Ssshh! It's a secret.

JOHNNY
Ah, okay. Well, let's get a move on kids.

CONNOR
Do you know where we're going?

JOHNNY

Theresa explained a few things. Gave me an idea of what direction to try. So, let's put the pedal to the metal.

CONNOR

We're not flying anymore?

ROSY

Oh boy, now he thinks he's a car.

JOHNNY

No, no, kids, it's just an expression.

THERESA

Hold on! Wait a minute! I'll give you some rapi pie for the road. It's still warm. There you go. Good luck and bon voyage.

ROSY

All I hope is that the take-off will be smoother than the landing.

JOHNNY and the children are back in the air and the coast slides along under them. Nobody says anything for a minute.

CONNOR

Hey Johnny, where are we going?

JOHNNY

South.

CONNOR

Where's south?

ROSY

Opposite the north, geez!

CONNOR

Oh smarty-pants. I wanted to know how Johnny knew which direction was south.

JOHNNY

By watching the stars, Connor. Look at that one over there, the brightest one. That's the north star.

ROSY

Aren't you afraid the south might be a bit too big?

JOHNNY

Don't worry, kids, we're heading for Pombcoup.

CONNOR
Pom... what?

ROSY
Is that where pompoms come from?

JOHNNY
Pombcoup has nothing to do with pompoms. It's the village where Captain Broussard stopped after he dropped Theresa off.

Suddenly they find themselves in a thick fog. They can hardly see anything. They can hear a sort of boat bell.

ROSY
Oops! I think we've just lost the north and the south.

CONNOR
I can't even see the end of Johnny's nose anymore.

ROSY
Johnny! Are you still there?

CONNOR
Listen! Do you hear that funny noise?

JOHNNY
That's a fog bell. That's how boats call out when they can't see anything anymore, like now.

ROSY
Do they call up the stars?

CONNOR
Don't they have radar?

JOHNNY
I doubt that one does, and I think it's lost. Let's go down and see.

ROSY
No, I'd rather go up higher so we can look for a star to guide him.

CONNOR
Listen, the sound is getting louder.

JOHNNY
It must be right beneath us.

ROSY
Well, let's go down and see.

CONNOR
See? How can you see anything? I can hardly make out the ends of my feet.

The sound of the bell gets louder and louder. Suddenly a dull light appears.

CONNOR
Look, Johnny, a light.

JOHNNY
Let's go in that direction. Don't take your eyes off it. We don't want to lose it.

JOHNNY and the twins continue their descent, the light grows bigger and the sound of the bell gets louder, somewhat spooky. Soon we can make out the shape of an old-fashioned sailing ship. JOHNNY gets a bit closer and lands on the deck; everything is deserted. There doesn't seem to be a living soul on the boat. The children climb carefully out of the sack.

ROSY
Yooohoo! Is anyone here?

CONNOR
Johnny, I think I'm getting scared.

JOHNNY
It looks like a ghost ship.

ROSY
(huddling up against JOHNNY) Ghosts? Where?

JOHNNY
It's okay, Rosy, ghosts don't really exist.

A sudden voice.

GHOST VOICE
Whooooo says ghosts don't exist?

CONNOR jumps head first into the sack.

Soooo? Who dares suggest I don't exist?

ROSY
Is that a real ghost, eh Johnny?

CONNOR
Let's get out of here!

GHOST VOICE
Nooot soooo fast. Since you have landed here, you must have a reason.

JOHNNY

Maybe, Mr. Ghost. But we don't know who you are. If we could see you at least…

GHOST VOICE

Humbug! You can never see me.

ROSY

Then you don't exist!

GHOST VOICE

What's this? I don't exist? You are rather pretentious for someone your age. I am a ghost; you can't see me but I'm here just the same. Watch!

The bell starts to ring faster.

ROSY

Tough, I say you don't exist.

Objects start to fly around them. They get scared again.

GHOST VOICE

Ha! Ha! Ha!…

JOHNNY

Okay! Okay! We believe you, we believe you…. But who are you, Mr. Ghost?

GHOST VOICE

I am the ghost of an old sea captain condemned to wander forever and only appear on Christmas eve.

ROSY

If you've been condemned, it must be because you were mean like you are now.

CONNOR

Will you be quiet! You're gonna make him mad!

GHOST VOICE

(nearly in tears) I'm not mean. I thought I was doing a good deed, and the cargo I delivered was very precious.

ROSY

If you aren't mean, then come out of your hiding place.

GHOST VOICE

I'm not in a hiding place. I am a ghost condemned not to celebrate Christmas now for more than 200 years.

JOHNNY

Excuse me, sir, but you wouldn't happen to be the ghost of…

GHOST VOICE

234 Christmases to be exact; I've missed celebrating 234 Christmases.

ROSY

234?

CONNOR

234 Christmases would take us back to… ah…

JOHNNY

You… you wouldn't be Captain… ahhh… Buzzard by any chance?

GHOST VOICE

Broussard… Captain BROUSSARD…. Yes, I am Captain Broussard. But how did you know that?

JOHNNY

It's a rather long story…

ROSY

And we are in a rather big hurry.

GHOST VOICE

What's the point of being in such a hurry when all eternity stretches before us. And eternal rest can never be found until the precious treasure I delivered is finally brought back together again.

JOHNNY

Captain, ahhh… let's just say, we might be able to help you find that rest.

GHOST VOICE

How could you help me?

ROSY

The treasure you speak of wouldn't be a rug, would it?

CONNOR

And what you delivered wouldn't be the strands of wool needed to finish it, would they?

GHOST VOICE

And you wouldn't be the twins I've been waiting so long for, would you?

JOHNNY

No doubt about it, Captain, these are the twins Rosy and Connor, grandchildren of Grandma Henriette, heir of the rug of Grand-Pré.

GHOST VOICE
And you? Who are you?

JOHNNY
Me, I'm Johnny Longlegs, the mailman.

GHOST VOICE
Well, mailman, for once you have brought good news.

ROSY
But tell us, Captain Broussard, tell us where we can find the strands of wool we're still missing?

CONNOR
Are they far?

GHOST VOICE
Not far at all, my friends. For here they are.

> *Three strands of red wool arrive out of the air like the objects we saw earlier. ROSY and CONNOR run around everywhere trying to catch them. Finally it's JOHNNY who snatches them.*

JOHNNY
Here you go, kids, three more strands.

CONNOR
Three plus six… that makes nine.

ROSY
We still have three more to find.

GHOST VOICE
Children, you will find those three strands on the shore of Baie Sainte-Marie, the last place I stopped.

JOHNNY
Isn't the bay rather large though?

GHOST VOICE
Go to Church Point, and there you should look for three bright red strands of wool on the back of a sacred lamb.

ROSY
A sacred lamb?

CONNOR
A bright red sacred lamb?

ROSY
It's not very nice, Captain Broussard, to make fun of us like that.

CONNOR
My sister's right. You're not very nice.

GHOST VOICE
Now, now, children, do you really think I'd be making fun of you. After all, I want you to find the strands of wool as much as you do.

JOHNNY
The Captain's right y'know, kids.

CONNOR
Well, okay, but where are we going to find a bright red sacred lamb at this hour?

GHOST VOICE
The family I brought there told me I would find their three strands of wool on the back of a lamb. Perhaps it was a kind of secret place where they wanted to hide the wool to keep it safe. Hurry. If you are successful, don't worry, I will know. And here, take a few smoked herrings out of my barrel; they'll help contain your hunger on the journey. Go now, on your way, and may this Christmas Eve bring you good luck.

ALL
So long, Captain Broussard and Merry Christmas.

JOHNNY and the children take off again for the sky. The children sing.

SONG OF THE TWINS #5
We have to find
Three strands of wool;
Three strands of wool
We have to find.
Three strands of wool
To finish the cross
On the roof overtop
Of the Church of Grand-Pré
On Grandma's old hooked rug.
Three lost strands of wool,
Three lost strands of wool
We just got to find;
So Christmas this year
Will brighten forever
The Church of Grand-Pré,
The church of our people,
Our ancestors of Grand-Pré.

SONG OF THE TWINS #5A

VOICE OF THE GHOST
They have to find
Three strands of wool;
Three strands of wool
They have to find.
Three strands of wool
To bring to an end
Oh a terrible fate
And reward my good deeds,
Bring peace to you and to me.
Three lost strands of wool,
Three lost strands of wool
They just got to find;
So Christmas this year
Will bring me the peace
And joy of our people,
The Church of Grand-Pré,
Our ancestors of Grand-Pré.

ROSY
Johnny, do you have any idea what we're going to do when we get to Church Point?

CONNOR
That's right, Johnny, do you know where to find our lamb?

ROSY
A lamb with bright red wool.

JOHNNY
The best thing to do is go see the parish priest. He should be able to tell us about everything sacred.

ROSY
But where will we find the priest at this hour?

JOHNNY
We'll head for the church and then we'll find the rectory, it's never far away.

Below them the countryside passes lit up with thousands of little Christmas lights. A very tall bell tower appears.

JOHNNY
There it is, kids, I think we're here. Prepare for landing.

JOHNNY lands in front of the church. They see a house to one side.

JOHNNY
There's a light on in that house. Let's go ask.

> *All three move towards the house. CONNOR knocks on the door. It opens and LUCILLE appears in the doorway dressed in a white apron.*

LUCILLE
Well merciful heavens! What have we here? Are you lost?

CONNOR
No, no...

ROSY
Well, not completely anyway. We're looking for the rectory.

LUCILLE
The rectory! This is it! But what do you want here?

CONNOR
Well, it's not the rectory we want to see exactly, but the priest.

LUCILLE
Father Sigogne? He's over in the church getting ready for midnight mass...

ROSY
In the church! Come on, let's go. Thanks lady.

LUCILLE
Oh! Wait a minute, kids, I'll go with you. I was actually just going over with a jug of water for Father before mass. *(turning to JOHNNY)* And you my good man, are you coming with us? You look kinda tuckered out! Whad'cha do? Fly across the province?

JOHNNY
Yeah, something like that.

LUCILLE
Well, go on inside and rest a bit. You'll find some coffee on the stove. Wait here, kids.

> *LUCILLE and JOHNNY go into the house. LUCILLE comes back out in a minute dressed for the cold and carrying a jug of water. LUCILLE and the children head to the church and go inside.*

LUCILLE
You still haven't told me what you want to see Father Sigogne about.

CONNOR
It's a long story.

ROSY
And we haven't much time.

CONNOR
We have to find a sacred lamb.

ROSY
And we were told we could find it here.

LUCILLE
A sacred lamb? Here? Wait for me, kids, I'll go see if Father Sigogne can talk to you now. A sacred lamb! In Church Point! Never heard tell of such a thing.

LUCILLE comes back in a minute with FATHER SIGOGNE who is all dressed ready for midnight mass.

FATHER SIGOGNE
So, my children, my housekeeper, Lucille here has been telling me a very strange story indeed. I'm not sure I quite understand.

ROSY
Here. It's for Grandma Henriette's rug.

CONNOR
We're looking for some wool.

ROSY
So we can finish it for her.

CONNOR
And the ghost told us that...

ROSY
That we would find some here.

FATHER SIGOGNE
A ghost told you that I sold wool?

CONNOR
No, no, not that you sold wool.

ROSY
But that maybe you had a sacred lamb.

CONNOR
Or that maybe you'd blessed one recently.

FATHER SIGOGNE
Oh, it's been quite awhile since I blessed a lamb, hasn't it, Lucille.

LUCILLE
Oh yes, Father.

FATHER SIGOGNE
In my opinion, your ghost must have gotten his story mixed up. Excuse me, my children, but I have to finish getting ready for mass. Lucille will take you back.

FATHER SIGOGNE turns to leave. That's when CONNOR notices the beautiful embroidery on his robe: in the very centre of the cross is a lamb done in bright red wool.

CONNOR
Father, wait.

FATHER SIGOGNE
What is it now?

CONNOR
Tell me, Father, have you had this robe for a long time?

LUCILLE
This robe has belonged to the parish for more than 200 years.

CONNOR
And where did it come from?

FATHER SIGOGNE
They say that the refugees from Grand-Pré embroidered it.

ROSY
That's it! That's it! The sacred lamb. Quick. Do you have anything that'll cut three strands of wool?

LUCILLE
Yes, I just happen to have a pair of scissors with me.

CONNOR
Turn around, Father, please.

FATHER SIGOGNE
But, Lucille, you're not going to let them do it?

ROSY has already grabbed the scissors and runs around the priest cutting a few strands of wool from the lamb on the chasuble.

FATHER SIGOGNE
They're crazy!

ROSY

No, it's for a miracle. Thanks, Father. You couldn't have given a more wonderful Christmas present.

ROSY and CONNOR run out of the church and head to the house.

TWINS

Johnny, Johnny, come quick!

ROSY

We got them all.

CONNOR

Hurry up! We have to get home.

JOHNNY appears at the door.

JOHNNY

Is it true, kids? Did you really find them?

ROSY

Yes, Johnny, yes. Look.

JOHNNY

Okay then. Let's go. Immediate departure for Cape Breton.

We find ourselves again in GRANDMA Henriette's house.

GRANDMA

Rosy, Connor, wake up! It's almost Christmas. It'll be midnight in a few minutes.

CONNOR and ROSY rush down the stairs. In the kitchen the rug is hanging on the wall again, complete. At the stroke of midnight the church of Grand-Pré appears onstage; from inside we can hear violins and guitars. A song is heard.

SONG OF THE TWINS #6
We found them all
Twelve strands of wool;
Twelve strands of wool
We found them all.
Twelve strands of wool
To finish the cross
On the roof overtop
Of the Church of Grand-Pré
On the rug that went astray.
Grandma's favourite twins,
Rosy and Connor,
Finally found them all;

So Christmas each year
Will brighten forever
The Church of Grand-Pré,
The church of our people,
Our ancestors of Grand-Pré.

GRANDMA
It seems to me that Christmas this year feels a little different from all the rest.

ROSY and CONNOR look at each other and smile.

The end.

Cape Enrage

Herménégilde Chiasson
translated by Glen Nichols

Born in St. Simon, New Brunswick, in 1946, Herménégilde Chiasson has become one of the leading artists of modern Acadie. He holds several degrees, including a doctorate from the Sorbonne and a Masters of Fine Arts from the University of New York. He taught at the Université de Moncton, and worked as a researcher, journalist and producer for Radio-Canada before trying his hand at film production in 1985.

In the theatre he is the author of some thirty plays including *Cap enragé* (*Cape Enrage*), *L'exil d'Alexa, La vie est un rêve, Aliénor,* and *Laurie, ou la vie de galerie.* His work as a playwright, through which he addresses a wide range of audiences, has always been closely associated with Théâtre l'Escaouette, the Moncton-based company that has produced the majority of his plays. Among the seventeen books he has published as a writer we find *Mourir à Scoudouc, Vous, Miniatures, Climats* and *Conversations,* which won a Governor General's award in 1999. He has directed seventeen films including "Toutes les photos finissent par se ressembler," "Le Grand Jack," "Robichaud," "Épopée," "Photographies" and "Ceux qui attendent." In the visual arts Herménégilde has put together twenty-five individual expositions a n d participated in a hundred other group expositions. He has also chaired several artistic organizations and has participated in setting up a number of others.

INTRODUCTION TO *CAPE ENRAGE*

Suicide, authoritarian and perhaps abusive parents, school gangs, co-dependency, death of a young friend, and an alienating justice system are some of the topics dealt with in Herménégilde Chiasson's *Cape Enrage*, a play with tough themes for teens growing up in a world full of difficult decisions. Reminiscent of *Being at Home with Claude* in form, *Cape Enrage* is the story of Patrick Leger, a teen with a troubled past who has been accused of murdering a buddy from school and must spend several days in jail while the detective assigned to his case, Victor, interrogates him and his girlfriend, Veronica McLaughlin. In addition to being a metaphor for the main character's inner turmoil, the title actually comes from the name of a popular tourist spot on the southern coast of New Brunswick where high cliffs afford panoramic views of the Bay of Fundy. The dead boy, Martin, was found at the bottom of the cliff and since Patrick had been the last of the group of teens picnicking that day at the cliffs to see Martin alive, he is fingered as the one guilty of pushing him. In the end it is revealed that Martin in fact committed suicide, but the prolonged interrogations effect important changes in the way Patrick sees himself and the people around him.

Patrick usually resists authority figures whom he feels do not treat him well: he gets himself moved out of his family home and away from his alcoholic father, he damages a teacher's car, and vandalizes school property; however, in Victor he finds a force he can't avoid or attack, a force who actually makes him think about how he is living his life. He is strangely empowered by the confrontation and is able to transform the rage he feels. As a result he moves from feeling helpless in the face of an unsympathetic world, to being willing to try to change things, such as attempting a reconciliation with his father.

The intense realism of the piece is relieved by an episodic structure interrupted by two surreal dream sequences which use a kind of telephone motif as a vehicle for Patrick's monologues to his absent parents, revealing some of his feelings about them. Despite the power of the characterization and the intensity of the situation, the play's dramatic potential is slightly weakened by the *deus ex machina* revelation of the suicide in the second last scene. This weakness is exacerbated in the 1999 version of the play which, as David Lonergan explains in his introduction to this collection, was watered down to accommodate public sensitivities following a number of suicides in a local high school. Because of the important relationship between these textual changes and the play's production history, I have included both versions of the ending in the translation here.

Thematically the play adds little to the understanding of adolescent suicide, but performs a significant role in dramatizing the phenomenon without glorifying it. This is accomplished by not portraying the victim directly, but only the survivors, the ones who must deal with the aftermath. It also decentres the suicide by focusing on Patrick, first as a possible murderer and then as someone who must deal with a host of other demons. The suicide is not the catalyst for Patrick's growth; rather the catalyst is his having to come to terms with an unwarranted accusation. Veronica repeatedly calls both Martin and Patrick, "fragile." Patrick clearly struggles with portraying a "tough-guy" image of himself and what he learns through his encounter with Victor, who inadvertently forces him to face the futility of disguising his inner pain, is that fragility becomes a kind of strength when it means reaching out to others. The play is about survival and change, about learning to find one's place in the world, a play honest enough to admit that suicide is a reality, but clear-headed enough to show that it is an option with no answers.

The translation of the play posed few serious difficulties despite the significant variety of voices: youth versus age, police officers interrogating an accused versus chatting among themselves, Patrick with his nemesis Victor versus with his father, his mother, his girlfriend. There was also the need for a slight adaptation of the overall language from the source text. Because the original play was prepared for presentation in regional schools, it had to reflect the kind of standard French local school authorities want to hear students exposed to, rather than the kind of French the young people actually speak. To help close the gaps between the situation, the characters and the language they use, I have allowed the English version more latitude in expression and tone. Part of the workshop process also involved students familiar with the sociolect of the younger characters who commented on the expressions and lexicon. The result is still a compromise because presumably an English production of this play intended for youth would encounter similar reservations from school boards and officials; however, the translation reinforces the situational language of the source play, allowing the language to underscore the conflicts between the various characters.

Another translation issue for which there is no real solution was the use of English in the original opening voiceover sequence depicting the police on their walkie-talkies tidying up their investigation at the cliffs the night Martin was found and Patrick arrested. I have left this sequence in English in the translation thus unfortunately erasing the contrast with the rest of the play and diminishing the underlying conflicts of language and power. The presence of target language elements in a source text is a perennial issue in translation studies for which there is of course no single solution. Indeed, in *Dark Owl*, the first play in this collection, I chose a very different approach to a parallel language situation. Here, however, due to the differing sociolinguistic implications of English and French in the community, simply reversing the language (using French for the voiceovers) would not satisfactorily address the underlying questions of cultural authority and resentment. The result of leaving the scene in English means a central conflict of the play, that of the police versus youth, takes an even more dominant position in the translation because the inter-linguistic conflict is masked.

Ironically, the need for compromise in the translation actually reflects a significant theme of the play. The hard-nosed Patrick learns to compromise his resentment in order to find hope, Veronica must compromise her altruism in order to find true love, and Victor compromises his own feelings in order to perform his sometimes cruel task of "cleaning up the world so others can feel safe at night." Although built on the traditional conflicts of youth versus age, personal desires versus public behaviour, and taking action versus passive acceptance, the play resists simple answers; the compromises of the characters are not rooted in fatalism, but rather are expressions of forward growth, evidence of the complexities of life and the multiple responses to the difficult choices facing youth.

—GN

Cape Enrage by Herménégilde Chiasson

Cap enragé was performed in Moncton at Théâtre l'Escaouette in 1992 with the following cast:

Eloi Savoie   Patrice
Jocelyn St.Pierre Victor
Hélène Paulin   Véronique
Direction by Marcia Babineau, design by Pierre Perreault, lighting by Guy Babineau, music by Claude Guy Gallant, and sound effects by Jean-Marie Morin

---

Cap enragé was remounted with a revised text in Moncton at Théâtre l'Escaouette in 1998 with the following cast:

Hughes Paulin   Patrice
Yves Turbides   Victor
Karène Chiasson Véronique
Direction by Marcia Babineau.

This translation of *Cape Enrage* was workshopped and given a public reading in Moncton in April 2002 with the following cast: Will Ellis, Scott Mealey, and Whitney Morrison. Scott Mealey directed the workshop and reading.

CHARACTERS

Patrick Leger
Victor Blanchard
Veronica McLaughlin

Cape Enrage

by Herménégilde Chiasson

The play begins with a sort of movie credit sequence projected on some kind of screen, with an electric guitar solo playing in the background. This guitar music reoccurs throughout the play. The opening scene is lit by a police-car flasher spinning red and blue light around the room. The sound of waves crashing on a rocky beach, the occasional barking of a police dog, finally the following conversation is overheard on the police radio…

VOICE 1

Yeah, we just found him. Well the dog did. Good thing too, 'cause another hour with the tide comin' in, well, it woulda been a whole different ball game.

VOICE 2

Right. We sent everybody home. Just kept Patrick Leger. I guess they'll let him cool his heels overnight at the station. Question him tomorrow I s'pose.

VOICE 1

Yeah, well, it's about time to call it a day…

VOICE 2

Lucky you. We still got a coupla hours ahead of us. I hate these long weekends. And besides, the Expos were playin' the Cards tonight. Hear the score?

VOICE 1

Not a fan. Sorry. (*sound of a siren*) Oh, they're here now; I'll have to direct them over your way. Can you shine a flashlight or put up a flare if you got one? See you in a minute. Over.

VOICE 2

Over.

Prologue

PATRICK is lying on a cot in his cell as the lights come up. The scene is a sort of waking dream. VICTOR's voice, electronically altered, is heard frequently, followed by the sound of metal doors opening. The image of a man in his fifties is projected on a screen. A series of images linked by quick fades gives the impression the image is moving.

VOICE

Patrick Leger.

PATRICK

What.

VOICE

Your father's on the phone.

PATRICK

What are you calling me here for? Where were you when I wanted to talk to you?… When I wanted you to hold me?

VOICE

Patrick Leger.

PATRICK

What. What! WHAT!!

VOICE

Your father's on the phone.

PATRICK

I'm not here.

VOICE

Your father's on the phone.

PATRICK

I'm not here anymore. You can call me all you want. I don't remember what I wanted to tell you. I don't want to talk to you anymore. I don't want to talk to you anymore. You stir up things in me that hurt so much I don't know how to make sense of them anymore. You work all day long without ever getting ahead, just so you can hang out down in your basement and pretend everything is fine. Well everything is not fine. Everything is not okay. You're wrong. There's stuff gotta change but you've never had the courage to stand up and question things. I saw you. I saw you grovel in front of your boss. I saw you grovel in front of the strong person you could have been. And it hurt me to see you do that. It made me feel ashamed. And that's when I swore I would never grovel in front of anyone… ever.

VOICE

Patrick Leger. (*pause*) Your father's on the phone.

PATRICK

But when you'd get home you'd play the big boss. Everyone knew it. You'd throw stuff around. Yell like a wounded animal. You used to hit us, humiliate us. You made sure we kept our mouths shut. You didn't want us to see how much you hurt inside. You were afraid we'd see you for what you were. But now I don't feel like making excuses for you anymore. I don't feel like taking any more of your misery, any more of your beatings. You can yell all you want. I'm not afraid of you anymore. I know it's nothing but the brave bark of a very small man. A very small man with a terrible wound. Don't be surprised if I don't answer anymore. I don't have the strength to answer anymore. I just want to rest. Even if I have to sleep here my whole life, at least I will sleep peacefully because I'll never have to hang my head in shame; I'll never have to say I'm sorry for being alive.

VOICE
Patrick Leger.

PATRICK
What…

VOICE
Your father's on the phone.

> *PATRICK exits from the circle of dream lighting as if he has awakened back to reality. The lights go down on him and come up on the constable.*

Scene One

Monday, 10:13 AM. VICTOR's office.

VICTOR
Good morning. My name is Corporal Victor Blanchard. (*He reaches forward to shake PATRICK's hand, but PATRICK does not move or respond.*) Patrick Leger. That's right isn't it? (*pause*) Look, I'm talking to you, buddy! And when I ask you a question, you answer me, okay? That's how things work around here. You got that?

PATRICK
Guess you already know that's my name though eh. Don't see anyone else in here, do ya? Shouldn't be too…

VICTOR
Let me give you a word of advice, boy: you better start giving me some straight answers; 'cause if you don't, things can get pretty ugly for a pup like you.

PATRICK
In that case you can call me Mutt-face or any other goddamned name you like if it'll make you happy.

VICTOR
Yesterday, Sunday October 11 about 6:00 o'clock in the afternoon, you were at Cape Enrage, right?

PATRICK
If you say so, it must be true…

VICTOR

(*restraining himself*) Listen to me Patrick; I got a job to do here, okay? Maybe we could've met in a more congenial place, but you know as well as I do we don't always get to choose where we meet people. So it's up to me to take your statement. If you don't want to give it to me, I don't give a shit, all right? But you're not going to keep screwing me around like this 'cause that'll mean we just gotta get a bit tougher with you. So, now you're gonna start telling me what I want to know and the faster you tell me, the faster we can get on to other things...

PATRICK

Yeah, like what...

VICTOR

Like your trial. You're gonna have to get ready for your trial...

PATRICK

But I'm innocent. Why should I be accused? What are you charging me with anyway?

VICTOR

No charges have been laid. Not yet at least. That's why it'd be helpful to me if you'd start helping yourself out here a bit. Do you have a lawyer?

PATRICK

No. Everything's already decided in your mind, right? You've already judged me. There were eight of us at Cape Enrage. Why am I the only one in here? How many years will I get anyway?

VICTOR

Look, it's not up to me, okay? Just stop screwin' around and talk to me, will ya! Sit down... I said, sit down! (*threatening*) Do I have to help you? (*The telephone rings.*) Don't push me, buddy, 'cause you don't know what I can do to you.... (*He answers the phone.*) Yeah.... Yeah, I have him here... I know that, but he doesn't want a lawyer... I know but what can I do; he's a stubborn.... What did his father have to say?... Yeah, okay, well I'll try to make him understand, but I'm not sure he's gonna want to.... Yeah sure, but what do you want me to do? I can't just beat it out of him, can I?... Yeah that's right.... Okay, we'll talk about this again at lunch.... Okay. See ya.... No, not Country Buffet. Somewhere else... I dunno. You choose.

PATRICK

Good news?

VICTOR

Look, I'm only going to tell you this once, my boy...

PATRICK

I'm not your boy...

VICTOR

And that's really too bad, 'cause if you were my boy, you can be damn sure you wouldn't be talkin' to me like that…

PATRICK

You want me to call you sir… grovel in front of you like a whipped dog. Well, don't look at me to prove you're the boss…. You can go play your little games all by yourself and you can…

VICTOR

Shut it! Shut your big friggin' mouth 'cause if you don't shut it I know a few guys who'd be happy to shut it for you pretty damn quick. And by the time you get outta here you'll be sayin' pretty please and thank you and yes sir to guys like me… you got that? At your age it's not the time to start messing around with the law. The law is hard, a lot harder than you think. Have you ever seen the inside of a prison? Maybe I should give you a little guided tour? Do you know what goes on in there? After what you just said to me, you wouldn't have a single tooth left in that gob of yours by now. So you sit down there and you start thinking real careful about what you're doing. You're playing for high stakes here my boy, very high stakes. You're playing with your life and it's a game that could cost you dearly. Your girlfriend's name is Veronica McLaughlin. That's right, isn't it?

PATRICK

She's got nothing to do with any of this. I don't see why…. You gotta dirty everything you touch, don'tcha. I'm the one you gotta deal with. I'm here. Ain't that good enough for you?

VICTOR

It was just a question… just a simple question. Now would you sit down? You're getting on my nerves.

PATRICK

(*sitting*) It's true she was at Cape Enrage with the rest of us, but…

VICTOR

But?

PATRICK

But she didn't do it.

VICTOR

Well if it wasn't her and it wasn't you, that leaves six other people. And one of those is dead, so we're left with five. But four of them saw you leave with Martin, who we found six hours later at the bottom of the cliff, and Sophie told us you were with Martin when he disappeared.

PATRICK

I wasn't with him. That's just what she told you. Why do you believe her, but you won't believe me?

VICTOR

Well if you start talking, maybe we can help you… but the way it is now…

PATRICK

I've told you everything I know and you still don't believe me. I could talk 'til I'm blue in the face and what would it change? So I might as well just keep my mouth shut.

VICTOR

What we want are some details.

PATRICK

What you want is for me to keep talking until I get so messed up you can make me say whatever you want me to. I seen that in a movie once. Guys start explaining and end up screwin' themselves. Well, I'm not gonna play your little game.

VICTOR

The only reason you're…. Nobody said you did it, but the evidence points to you because last Friday you were reported saying (*He looks in his notebook.*) "Martin's gonna get what's comin' to him real soon." Do you remember that?

PATRICK

Yeah, but that… it don't mean anything. I mean I say that about lots of guys… I say it all the time.

VICTOR

Yes, but this was the same Friday you got in a fight with Martin because according to you he was trying to steal your girlfriend.

PATRICK

That's right. It was Veronica herself who told me. He was giving her a lift when all of a sudden he stopped the car and tried to…

VICTOR

Tried to…

PATRICK

Kiss her. She pushed him off and got out of the car…

VICTOR

And it was Veronica who told you this?

PATRICK

Ah, I know what you're thinking. You think it was her fault. That she was leading him on, eh.

VICTOR

Have you noticed the way your girlfriend dresses?

PATRICK

Like that means she was asking for Martin to attack her?

VICTOR

Fine. So what happened then?

PATRICK

When Veronica got to school she was in tears. I waited until lunchtime, then went and hung around his locker. When Martin got there, acting like an idiot as usual, I grabbed him by the throat. I told him if he wanted to get some exercise so badly, he could always do a little workout with me...

VICTOR

Then what...

PATRICK

He wouldn't bite.

VICTOR

What's that supposed to mean, he wouldn't bite?

PATRICK

He played the hypocrite. He told me he didn't know what I was talking about.

VICTOR

And then... what then?...

PATRICK

Well, I shook him around a bit. Just to, you know, refresh his memory. Okay, maybe I gave him a few cuffs, I don't remember anymore. But I know I didn't do anything to really hurt him unless he's like totally soft.

VICTOR

That's what's called taking the law into your own hands; you could be charged for that...

PATRICK

Yeah right... some law...

VICTOR

The law is there to make things clear. I don't know this Martin. I can't be for or against him… but since the dead can't talk… that leaves you. So if you don't talk, then we've got a bit of a problem, don't we?

PATRICK

Okay. Okay. What else you got to ask me?

VICTOR

Your little scuffle didn't go unnoticed, you know. Someone heard you say, "I'm going to rearrange your face and when I'm done with you, you're not gonna feel much like kissing any more girls…" What do you have to say about that?

PATRICK

So?

VICTOR

Well it's up to you to answer. One of your buddies makes a pass at your girlfriend…. Martin was part of your gang no? So you decide to settle the score with him at lunch that day…. That's no better than the way animals carry on, you know…

PATRICK

It wasn't the first time…

VICTOR

Do you know what was going on between Veronica and Martin?

PATRICK

What do you mean what was going on?

VICTOR

I don't know. That's what I'm asking you.

PATRICK

Veronica's the only person who doesn't screw me around or play head games… Martin was…

VICTOR

What?

PATRICK

Nothing.

VICTOR

What I don't quite understand is why you decided just two days later to go on a picnic with him and the rest of your gang.

PATRICK

To make Veronica happy. Veronica and Sophie…

VICTOR

Sophie was Martin's girlfriend, right?

PATRICK

(*nodding his head*) Veronica didn't want things to change between the four of us…

VICTOR

But things had already changed as far as you were concerned?

PATRICK

I just wanted to be alone. I wanted to be alone with Veronica. I wanted to get away from the rest of them.

VICTOR

How was Martin when you saw him that afternoon?

PATRICK

He didn't talk to me. It's hard to tell…

VICTOR

But the two of you were seen going…

PATRICK

You think I was the one who pushed him, don't you? You believe it was me…

VICTOR

I don't believe anything. The jury won't believe anything. The judge won't believe anything. Evidence is all they're interested in and the evidence doesn't look good for you… and you're not telling me anything that changes it. (*The telephone rings.*) Yeah…. Oh she's there. Good…. Yes, send her up…. No, I'm finished with him, for now anyway. (*He hangs up and turns to PATRICK.*) You can go back to your cell now.

Sound of the electric guitar.

Scene Two

Monday 10:45 AM. VICTOR's office.

VERONICA enters. VICTOR is busy with papers, but within earshot.

PATRICK

So do you think I'm guilty too?

VERONICA

You were alone with Martin when it happened, weren't you?

PATRICK

What difference does it make? You've already convicted me.

VERONICA

His mother called me. She was crying. She started by asking me if I knew where you were. I told her...

PATRICK

That I'm in prison. Well, that musta made her happy.

VERONICA

No. Why do you say that?

PATRICK

What do you mean, no? Isn't that what everyone wants? Dump the blame on me?

VERONICA

No. When I told her you're in prison she started to cry. Then she hung up.... (*pause*) Patrick, how are you feeling?

PATRICK

(*pause*) I'm scared. Really scared. (*He takes her hand.*) I've never been so scared in my whole life.

VERONICA

If you believe you're not guilty then that's what you've got to tell them. That's what's important.

PATRICK

No. What's important is that you believe me. That's all that matters.

VERONICA

But I gotta know what really happened.

PATRICK

What do you think happened?

VERONICA

You're the only one who knows.

PATRICK

No. I don't know. I don't know any more than you do.

VERONICA

How come you don't know?

PATRICK

I wasn't there when it happened.

VERONICA

Well, maybe, but you were the last person to be seen with Martin yesterday afternoon. That doesn't look good.

PATRICK

Listen, I was there, but…

VERONICA

Are you telling me you lost sight of him?

PATRICK

He told me he didn't hold it against me or anything, what happened on Friday. He said he would've done the same thing if he'd been in my shoes… I put my arm around his shoulder and I said to him, "Look, Martin, it's not as bad as all that." He told me to give him some space, that he wanted to be alone. I don't know what was going through his head.

VERONICA

What does Martin's death mean to you?

PATRICK

I'm too confused to think. I never thought it'd end like this. I know I should have stayed with Martin. That's what everyone's been telling me since last night.

VERONICA

Why are you confused?

VICTOR

Because we gotta find out the truth in this business.

PATRICK

Yeah, but it always has to be your truth, doesn't it.

VICTOR

All I know is that if it wasn't for the police and the law you'd have to think twice about going out at night alone.

PATRICK

That's just how you like to keep people under your thumb, isn't it. Use fear to keep everyone in their place.

VICTOR

We can talk about this some other time, Okay? Right now I have to talk to Miss McLaugh…

PATRICK

Oh all of a sudden she's not just my girlfriend anymore. You've been elevated to "Miss"… I guess the way you dress doesn't bother him anymore…

VICTOR

You can't stay here, Patrick, okay…

PATRICK

That's right. She's a girl and you think you can make her say what you want. You'll start yelling at her and get her bawling… just like in the movies…

VICTOR

Do you want me to call the constable? Is a little muscle the only thing you understand?

VERONICA

Give it a rest, Patrick. I'm quite capable of looking after myself. I just have to tell the truth. I know you're not guilty.

PATRICK

Why didn't you say that before?

VERONICA

Because you didn't give me a chance.

PATRICK

You really believe I'm not guilty?

VERONICA

That's all I want to believe. The only truth. We'll get out of this. You'll see. Now, go on.

PATRICK

You really believe I'm not guilty?

VERONICA

Y'know, you can't read my mind. That's why it's important to talk to them. To tell them the truth. Let me talk to them. Don't worry. They can't hurt me. You have to stop trying to shield me. I have to defend myself too you know, defend you. I can do it. Trust me.

> *PATRICK takes VERONICA's hand. VICTOR turns his back and studies the file he has in his hand. PATRICK looks at VICTOR while he embraces VERONICA; the gesture comes across like a challenge to authority. PATRICK releases VERONICA and leaves without turning his back on the others. The guitar solo punctuates the end of the scene.*

Scene Three: Manipulation

VICTOR

Miss Veronica McLaughlin. That's right, isn't it? (*pause*) You're Dr. Charles McLaughlin's daughter, aren't you?

VERONICA

Yes, that's right.

VICTOR

How long have you known Patrick?

VERONICA

Two years.

VICTOR

Did you know the victim as well?

VERONICA

Martin?

VICTOR

Yes, Martin?

VERONICA

Yes. He used to live just three doors down from us.

VICTOR

And sometimes he would give you a lift in his car and...

VERONICA

And he tried to kiss me, and Patrick took a jealous fit and that's why you're accusing him, but I can tell you that Patrick would never have gone so far as...

VICTOR

Do you know what that is? That's Patrick Leger's court file. Shoplifting. Car theft. Entering a club with false identification. Writing graffiti on school walls...

VERONICA

Yeah, I know about all that...

VICTOR

And what about your father? What does he think about it all?

VERONICA

My father likes Patrick. For two years, you see...

VICTOR
Since he started going out with you?

VERONICA
Well I know he's going to get out of this.

VICTOR
I think you're very courageous.

VERONICA
It's not courage. It's love.

VICTOR
Would you go so far as to say it was because of love that he threatened Martin Landry last Friday at lunch?

VERONICA
All I know is that he couldn't have... Patrick is not someone who uses his strength to hurt other people. I believe he thought he was doing the right thing. He just wanted to protect me.

VICTOR
What makes you so sure about that?

VERONICA
Because he's had to take care of himself since he was just a kid. Have you talked to his father?

VICTOR
All in good time. But for now, I'm talking to you.

VERONICA
All the bad stuff he's done was just because he needed attention, love. Everything we do in life is more or less either for love or for a lack of love. Patrick is someone who is very fragile. He plays the tough guy just to get attention. But I know he's not really like that. He's really very fragile. I know that because he's told me how he feels about...

VICTOR
Miss McLaughlin, where were you when the crime... or rather, the incident happened?

VERONICA
I was talking to Sophie. Martin's friend. But you haven't let me finish...

VICTOR
Do you get along well with Sophie?

VERONICA
She's not my best friend or anything, but we talk.

VICTOR
Did she know Martin tried to kiss you?

VERONICA
The whole school knew.

VICTOR
Uh huh. And you didn't talk about that?

VERONICA
No.

VICTOR
What did you talk about?

VERONICA
She told me she found a job in a music store. She wanted to quit school. She wanted to know what I thought about it.

VICTOR
That's all?

VERONICA
She asked me if things were going okay between me and Patrick.

VICTOR
And what did you say?

VERONICA
Everything was going… like before.

VICTOR
And how was that?

VERONICA
Fine. I told her things were going fine.

VICTOR
Didn't you think that maybe she was sounding you out to see whether there was something between you and Martin?

VERONICA
Yes, but I pretended not to understand. Martin is like a brother to me. I don't know what he thought he was doing by trying to kiss me.

VICTOR
Yet you went and told Patrick?

VERONICA
For a laugh. I never wanted to make him jealous.

VICTOR
For a laugh…. This had happened before…

VERONICA
Yes, but it was no big deal. It was just a joke.

VICTOR
A joke. Miss McLaughlin, in my day this sort of thing was never a joke. And I know lots of people who wouldn't think it was a joke. As far as I can see, Patrick reacted in a perfectly normal way. What isn't normal is what happened afterwards.

Electric guitar solo. The lights come down on VICTOR's office.

Scene Four: Betrayal

Tuesday, 10:02 AM. PATRICK's cell.

VERONICA
I talked to Sophie last night…

PATRICK
That troublemaker…. Did she talk to you about what happened?

VERONICA
She thinks you're guilty. She says you were jealous of Martin because he was always trying to make me laugh, giving me compliments, little presents…

PATRICK
So? That's normal. Sure Martin used to bug me. I thought he was a flirt, but not to the point of wanting to do him in.

VERONICA
But that's exactly what you said…

PATRICK
So, now you're on their side too? (*VERONICA reacts.*) I thought you believed me…

VERONICA
How could I say anything else? The cops were two feet away from us. What do you think I was going to say?

PATRICK

Fine. Well I guess I got my answer, don't I? I might as well just go crawl under a rock and wait for them to come and lock me up until I…

VERONICA

Oh for the love of…

PATRICK

Love! That's a good one!

VERONICA

Yes, love. That's not what made me change my mind about this. Even if you are guilty…

PATRICK

Oh so you see the idea has crossed your mind.

VERONICA

I'm just saying…

PATRICK

No, I'm sure you're not "just saying" anything. If they manage to pin Martin's death on me, you're going to start having doubts about me too, aren't you? And you know, I'm not so sure there wasn't something going on between you and Martin. The two of you were hanging around together for a long time…

VERONICA

What's got into you Patrick? Why are you talking to me like this all of a sudden?

PATRICK

It's just more than I can take. Being locked up like this is driving me mad. When I saw you didn't believe me, I started to have my own doubts.

VERONICA

I'm only trying to understand. It's just that Sophie…

PATRICK

Sophie? What's she saying now?

VERONICA

She found a letter in Martin's stuff. A letter you wrote to him two years ago when we started going out.

PATRICK

Oh, yeah, that letter. I don't even remember anymore what I said to him in it.

VERONICA

Well, she sure read it. You don't know what you said?

PATRICK

That was the time he took you to the Valentine's dance I think. The time we had a fight. I know I wasn't very happy.

VERONICA

Not just that. You described in detail how you were going to beat him up if he kept "sniffing around me" like you say. And you ended it by saying that the next time would be his last.

PATRICK

I didn't say that.

VERONICA

Sophie gave the letter to the police. Premeditated murder. Don't you realize that's written proof. With your signature on it, Patrick.

PATRICK

So you've already convicted me too.

VERONICA

I'm just trying to understand, Patrick. Put yourself in my shoes. It's true I noticed Martin seemed to avoid me after that night. And I wondered why. I even called him, but he wouldn't tell me anything. And in the letter you told him not to say anything to me because that would just make things worse.

PATRICK

That was for love. I was crazy about you. I'm still crazy about you.

VERONICA

Crazy enough to kill him?

PATRICK

I didn't kill him.

VERONICA

But that's not good enough. They have written proof. What am I supposed to say? I didn't know you'd written that, otherwise I would never have told you that Martin tried to kiss me.

PATRICK

You would have lied to me?

VERONICA

It's not just a question of lying, Patrick. This is question of life and death. This is a lot more serious than a lie.

PATRICK

You just gave yourself away, y'know. You just said that you think I killed him. Eh? Is that right? Well you might as well go now, seeing as I'll be staying here for awhile.

VERONICA

There's no reason to abandon you. Martin is dead now. We can't do anything for him anymore, but you're still alive.

PATRICK

That's not what I want to hear. I want you to believe me. I want to hear you say that I'm not guilty. That as far as you're concerned, I'm not guilty.

VERONICA

I can't say that. Not now. Not right away.

Guitar solo. VERONICA leaves. Lighting in the prison goes down.

Scene Five

Tuesday, 11:08 AM. VICTOR's office. Lighting comes up on VICTOR, stage left. PATRICK passes from one side of the stage to the other.

VICTOR

So, do you know what this is?

PATRICK

More proof. I know. Your final proof.

VICTOR

Why is it you only seem interested in screwing me around and acting the fool while I'm trying to tell you you gotta defend yourself.

PATRICK

What's the point in contradicting you? It's already…

VICTOR

No. It is not already decided. I've heard that one before, you know. And you're wasting your time putting on this little show, playing the cool guy who's in control 'cause I know deep down you're scared shitless. And I know you're just mouthin' off 'cause you got a problem with authority. Well, I'm not your father. You can't just slam the phone down when I call you.

PATRICK

You spoke to my father?

Yves Turbide & Hughes Paulin
Photo by Herménégilde Chiasson.

VICTOR

Somebody had to, the poor guy. And you didn't look like you were going to do it.

PATRICK

What's between my father and me is…

VICTOR

Is between your father and you… yeah I've heard that one before too. But not anymore. Now it's also between you and the law…. (*pause*) Now, listen. Do you really think I'm against you here? Do you really think all I want to do is put you behind bars? Look at me in the eye and tell me that's what you think.

PATRICK

You're still trying to find out if I'm telling the truth or not. What's it to you if I get locked up? You'll still get your pay cheque, you'll still go home at night and sleep in your own bed, eat in restaurants, go for a drink…

VICTOR

It's true I spoke to your father yesterday afternoon. But I think you're wrong to believe that what's happening to you doesn't bother him.

PATRICK

You're both the same, the two of you.

VICTOR

No, we're not both the same. I'm not as old as your father…

PATRICK

It's not a question of age! It's just knowing who makes the decisions. You make the decisions; my father makes the decisions… the law is on your side. Everything is on your side, on his side.

VICTOR

It's not as bad as…

PATRICK

It's been three years since I left home. All my buddies have families. I had to learn how to defend myself, to survive, and it's normal that whenever there's trouble around I'm going to be in the middle of it. And it's normal that the blame will always fall on me. The law… you talk a lot about the law… well, let me tell you what the law means to me. The law is made for those who walk the straight and narrow. The really straight and the really narrow… well lit, well protected. Yeah, nothing would happen to me there, but that's not for me. My place is in the gutter…

VICTOR

Your father told me he wanted to talk to you.

PATRICK

It was no accident that I asked to be placed in a family three hundred miles away from there. I never wanted to see him again. I wanted to forget him. I wanted to forget everything. Can you understand that? Can you understand what it's like to want to erase thirteen years of your life?

VICTOR

Your father has changed. I don't think he's the same man you knew before. Did you know he's stopped drinking?

PATRICK

Why are you so hung up on dragging me into all that again? I just told you I didn't want to go back to that.

VICTOR

Why?

PATRICK

Look, is this why you called me in here? Because if that's why, you're wasting your time. You wanted to show me your letter. Well I've seen it. It's true I wrote the letter. There's no point in hiding the fact. It's my hand-writing.

VICTOR

I really wish you'd stop acting like you think I want to lock you up no matter what. Because it's not true. It's not true at all.

PATRICK

I was raised to mistrust people.

VICTOR

I talked to your father for a long time...

PATRICK

You don't know what I've been through. If you did, you wouldn't talk to me like that.

VICTOR

He's worried about you. He told me that if anything happened to you, he'd never forgive himself.

PATRICK

Yeah well he probably thinks it was me that did it anyway. That I was the one who pushed Martin. So that means there's not many left on my side, is there... besides me... besides me, myself, and I...

VICTOR

Listen to me and listen to me good. The evidence is against you. I'm not going to kid you, that's just the way it is. Any jury is going to have its doubts. But if you decide to collaborate with the law, we can... I don't know... let's just say, limit the damage.

PATRICK
What do you mean, limit the damage?

Scene Six

Wednesday 12:11 AM.

VERONICA is alone on stage when the lights in the prison come up. She takes off her raincoat and sets it on the back of a chair. She shakes the water off her umbrella. PATRICK enters. He sits in front of her, uneasy. He can't find anything to say.

PATRICK
So what's the weather like out there?

VERONICA
Raining. Isn't it obvious?

PATRICK
Oh, right.... What did you do at school?

VERONICA
We had history this morning. I got 95 on my Seven Years War test.

PATRICK
Oh, right... the Seven Years War.

VERONICA
That was when Canada got handed over to the English.

PATRICK
Oh right.... You mean they're not talking about me? They must be. I can't believe they wouldn't be. This is the first time they've had a real-live murderer in the class. That's got to be more interesting than the Seven Years War.

VERONICA
They don't talk about anything else. They're always asking me about you.

PATRICK
Yeah, right. They must be happy they've got me around to make their lives a little less boring.

VERONICA
You're wrong to think like that.

PATRICK
Have they asked you if you're still going to go out with me when I'm in prison?

VERONICA
I didn't tell them anything they didn't already know. But Sophie told them all about the letter. Even when I asked her not to say anything.

PATRICK
Well what do ya expect! The bitch feels offended. Everyone knows her precious little Martin betrayed her in front of the whole school, so now she's looking for someone to take it out on. The bitch is looking for someone to bite. I hate her.

VERONICA
Oh Patrick…

PATRICK
What's with this shit, "Oh Patrick." Don't you see you're wasting your time. Why don't you just go back to the rest of them, 'cause I don't think I'm going too far for awhile here, do you? I have things to do…

VERONICA
You're pissed off at me, eh? Is that it? You're pissed off at me because I love you and it bothers you that I love you. You don't like feeling you need people, Patrick, but you can't go through life without them. You like feeling strong, independent, needing no one. But it's not true that you don't need people because you need me, Patrick. It's the same story with your father…

PATRICK
Leave my father out of this. What is it all of a sudden? It's like he's still…

VERONICA
What…?

PATRICK
Still controlling me.

VERONICA
You don't really believe that's what happened, do you?

PATRICK
I spoke to Victor today.

VERONICA
Yes… and?

PATRICK
He showed me the letter. That about says it all. And he spoke to my father. Seems Victor has a boy too. So like they had lots to talk about raising kids. Now Victor figures my father's just another great guy.

VERONICA

Don't you think it's time you changed things?

PATRICK

What do you mean?

VERONICA

It's possible your father has changed.

PATRICK

Did he call you too?

VERONICA

Well, actually... yes. Yes, he called me.

PATRICK

Oh great. That's just great. And it's obvious you think he's man-of-the-year material too. I bet'cha he even turned on the waterworks for ya. Why not? Nothing like a few tears to grab everyone by the throat.

VERONICA

It's so easy, isn't it, to make a big stink like you do. It's bit harder to grow up, to take responsibility.

PATRICK

Easy for you maybe. Easy to talk like that. Your father...

VERONICA

It's more than that Patrick. You forget that I've done my bit too. I haven't always had my family holding my hand, y'know. You can do what you want with your life; it's up to you. It's your life.

PATRICK

And while I'm waiting for my life, I know just where I'll be spending my time.

VERONICA

When are you going to stop thinking the whole world is out to get you? If I started reciting all the reasons you can invent to mistrust people.... This is serious, Patrick.

PATRICK

I can't forgive guys who pick on people weaker than themselves. That's why I warned Martin that if he touched you again...

VERONICA

And when I try to talk about it you change the subject. Don't you see what you just did there? But since we're on the subject of Martin, I think you should have tried talking to him. I'm sure he would have listened to you. Martin wasn't a

fool. But no, you had to play the tough guy instead. What does that change?
As far as I can see it changes nothing. It doesn't hurt to try loving people, you
know.

PATRICK

You think that's how to stop them from hurting us, eh. Well, you're dreaming in
colour.

VERONICA

Maybe. But at least you should believe me when I say I love you. You should
stop looking for reasons to hide, to be afraid. 'Cause when you do that, you just
convince them they're right. I don't know if you're guilty, Patrick. I don't know
if maybe all of a sudden Martin might've said something to piss you off. I've
seen you do it before. I know that when you get pissed off you completely lose
control. Remember the time you set fire to your math book in the library? You
didn't get caught that time. And what about when you broke the windows
in Mr. Landry's car because he kicked you out of his class? There are lots of
examples like that, but you just never got caught. That's why I have my doubts.
But…

PATRICK

But I didn't kill him. You know, I've always wondered why you got mixed up
with a loser like me?

VERONICA

Because I'm a saint.

PATRICK

(*amused*) Maybe you're right…

VERONICA

If I knew why, believe me I'd tell you. I don't know why myself. And if I could
control it… I'm not sure…

PATRICK

You'd drop me like a hot potato.

VERONICA

It's not easy being in love with you, Patrick. You have to understand that much
at least.

PATRICK

I don't know what I'm supposed to understand anymore.

VERONICA

It's true they're asking me what's going on. And I don't know what to say
anymore because I don't know myself what's happening. You know we were
all just a bunch of friends. Everyone liked everyone. No one wanted to get hurt
and then all of a sudden one of us is gone. One of us is in a grey box with silver

handles on the sides. Imagine it was you. Or imagine it was me. This is the first time in my life death has passed so close, right beside me. I felt his hand on my neck. I understand you're confused Patrick and I understand that things aren't going the way you want them to, but you aren't the only person on the planet. That's really what I wanted to say to you. What I've wanted to say to you for a long time. When I talk to you sometimes I get the feeling you've forgotten you have a heart in that body of yours. But I know that you do have a heart. Even though you're doing everything you can to hide your pain from everyone. You can't understand anymore that there are others in as much pain as you are. I used to love Martin, and when you talk about him the way you just did, you make it all the more painful for me. You make it so painful I want to scream.

PATRICK
Maybe he's the one you should have fallen in love with. I'm just a troublemaker. I never really felt like part of your clique.

VERONICA
My father always taught me to be kind to animals, never to do anything to hurt them, and that an animal who is suffering is the saddest thing in the world because the animal doesn't know what's happening to him. He can't talk about it. He can only cry out his pain. Well when I first saw you all alone in the schoolyard, all alone leaning against the brick wall, I felt you were like an animal with a terrible wound you were trying to hide under your leather jacket. I suddenly wanted to get closer to you. I wanted to heal up your wound so it would stop bleeding. I wanted to take you in my arms to warm you up again. I wanted to stop your hurting. But you didn't want me to see your wound. When animals are hurt they always run away. You're the same, Patrick; you're always running away. You've been running away since that first day. It's like you're afraid of me.

PATRICK
You felt sorry for me, didn't you? You thought you were some kind of angel who could carry me off to heaven. But you're going to find out that I'm too heavy for your wings and you're gonna have to let me drop. Heaven doesn't exist for people like me…. Heaven was made for angels. Maybe that's where Martin is… I hope that's where he is. That's something anyway.

VERONICA
The morning he tried to kiss me, two days before he died, he seemed terrified. He asked me to hold him in my arms, 'cause he was so cold he said. I figured it was just another one of his pranks. He didn't think I was funny. That's when he tried to kiss me. I told him I didn't want him to do that. When he saw it wasn't going to work, that I was going to stay with you regardless, he started to play all sorts of games. He tried to make me lose my temper. That's why I said maybe that's what happened on the cliff. Maybe Martin won in the end. Maybe he ruined your life because as far as he was concerned you had ruined his.

PATRICK
Well he screwed himself because I didn't kill him.

VERONICA

Martin was very fragile.

PATRICK

Don't you see that still makes me the rotten apple.

VERONICA

Fine, but you're still alive Patrick. All we can do for the dead is cry for them and that doesn't change anything. But when you're alive…. It's no good just banging your head against the wall; you only hurt yourself more and more. There are lots of things you can change.

PATRICK

If I change, it means they're right. It's just admitting I was wrong. And that's what they've been telling me my whole life: that I'm wrong.

Electric guitar solo. Lighting change.

Scene Seven

Wednesday 1:27 PM. PATRICK is on the telephone.

PATRICK

I want to speak to Daniel Leger, please…. Yes, that's right, a collect call…. It's his son, Patrick Leger…. Hello? Hello…. Oh it's you, Mom…. Yes, it's…. Yes it's really me…. Where do you think I am?… Stop crying Mom. You know I can't stand it when you do that…. Stop bawling! Otherwise I'll hang up…. Stop it…. Look, tell Dad to give me a call, okay? He knows the number… Mom, stop bawling like that. I'm not dead. It's not the end of the world…. Mom, I can't take it anymore; I just can't take listening to you like this. I know you always figured I'd turn out bad so in your head things are already settled. I have to hang up now. Tell Dad I want to talk to him.

He goes to slam the receiver down, but stops himself and puts it down gently. He continues to speak to the telephone as if he was telling his mother all the things he's never been able to.

Stop bawling. I have all the reasons in the world to be crying, but I'm not. What will happen will happen. It's nobody's fault. It's just the way life is. I didn't want to go with Martin and his gang. I didn't want to have an alcoholic father. I didn't want to be as pig-headed as I am. But I am just the same. What good would it do to bawl my head off? It's not going to change anything, is it? So I'm not going to cry anymore. That would just give them too much satisfaction to think they've broken me, to think they finally got to me and that I should thank them for the lesson they've taught me. Well the rest of you can keep your pity. The whole gang. You'll keep on tellin' people it was me that ruined your life. I like that one. That way you don't have to make any decisions. Well it's not going to happen like that for me. Stop crying, or do like I do. Cry inside. Cry on the inside and hit hard on the outside.

Electric guitar solo. Light on PATRICK dims.

Scene Eight

Wednesday 4:10 PM. VICTOR's office.

VICTOR
So why did you ask Martin to come along with you to Cape Enrage. Weren't you afraid he would upset Patrick?

VERONICA
I wanted them to talk; I wanted them to make peace with each other.

VICTOR
And that's why you invited Sophie and Martin to join you and Patrick up on the cliff, leaving the rest of the gang back on the beach.

VERONICA
That's right.

VICTOR
And you and Sophie stopped along the way to let Patrick and Martin go on ahead.

VERONICA
That's right.

VICTOR
When I questioned Sophie, she told me she left you alone for a few minutes while she went back to the beach to get a coke out of the cooler.

VERONICA
Yeah, that's right.

VICTOR
Why didn't you tell me about that when I questioned you yesterday? You told me Sophie stayed with you the whole time until Patrick came back yelling about having lost sight of Martin.

VERONICA
I don't know. It must have slipped my mind. Maybe I just forgot to tell you.

VICTOR
Maybe you wanted to forget to tell me.

Two versions to choose from:

Version 1:

VERONICA

There's so much going through my head right now…. What happened with Sophie, well that's… that's kinda fuzzy in my mind. But now that you bring it up, yes, I remember. It's true Sophie got up at one point, but…

VICTOR

On the cliff, at about the place we figure Martin must have fallen from, we found this. (*He shows her a small gold chain.*) Do you recognize it?

VERONICA

That's the chain Patrick gave me. I thought I'd lost it. (*She reaches for it.*)

VICTOR

Sorry. I have to hold on to this for now. You'll get it back later. (*Pause, as he takes a book out of his desk.*) Sophie kept Martin's journal, the one he used to drag around with him all the time. She read it and noticed that Martin wrote some odd comments about you. Do you want me to read them for you… January 15, (*He reads.*) "V.—means Veronica, I suppose—doesn't love me. That's clear and I don't love S.—S. must be Sophie.—I hate P.—Patrick—but he's too much of an idiot to take seriously. My love for V. is killing me and I know that one day she will do it for real. I know that she is going to kill me."

VERONICA

That's just an expression. He meant that his pain was going to kill him… I don't know… not that I was really going to kill him. That's crazy to think I'd be able to hurt Martin.

Version 2:

VERONICA

There's so much going through my head right now…. What happened with Sophie, well that's… that's kinda fuzzy in my mind.

VICTOR

On the cliff, at about the place we figure Martin must have fallen from, we found this. (*He shows her a small gold chain.*) Do you recognize it?

VERONICA

That's the chain Patrick gave me. I thought I'd lost it. (*She reaches for it.*)

VICTOR

Sorry. I have to hold on to this for now. You'll get it back later.

VERONICA

Now that you bring it up, yes, I remember. It's true Sophie got up at one point, but…

VICTOR

(*He takes a book out of his desk.*) Do you know what this is. It's Martin's journal, the one he used to drag around with him all the time. Sophie read it and noticed that Martin wrote some odd comments about you. Do you want me to read them to you… January 15 (*He reads.*) "V.—V. means Veronica I suppose— doesn't love me. That's clear and I don't love S.—S. must be Sophie.—I hate P—Patrick—but he's too much of an idiot to take seriously.

VICTOR

May 21. "Last night I saw V. again. She is more beautiful than ever. She and P. do their best to show everybody how happy they are, but I know I'm the one she loves. Right now she's doing everything she can to make me jealous. I'm pretending not to notice. She can't stand Sophie, that's for sure. I'm afraid she's going to turn against Sophie or against me or that she'll ask P. to take care of it for her." This goes on for several pages.

VERONICA

He wanted me to be his girlfriend, his alone. I loved Martin, but… but well it's hard to explain.

VICTOR

One, we found your chain; two, Martin's journal that Sophie turned over to us says…

VERONICA

Don't you see why she's doing this? If she came running to you with the journal it's because she read that Martin didn't love her, that he had never loved her and now she thinks she's been humiliated. She's willing to do anything to get revenge. She's just out to get me because Martin loved me but I didn't love him, at least not the same way he loved me.

VICTOR

Yes, but only as long as he kept himself under control, as long as he confined himself to writing in his journal, you didn't have any real problem. The problems began when he started to chase after you everywhere you went, in front of everybody. That started to get on your nerves, especially when it created a risk that Patrick might discover the double game you were playing.

Electric guitar solo. Lights come down.

Scene Nine: The Final Battle

Wednesday 4:50 PM. VICTOR's office.

VICTOR
> So what I mean is I've got some good news and some bad news. The good news is that you can leave now. The bad news... well...

PATRICK
> I can what?

VICTOR
> Leave. The bad news... is that we've had to.... look, get ready for a shock, okay? We've had to arrest Veronica as the primary suspect.

PATRICK
> What!?

VICTOR
> Veronica. Yes. We have two pieces of material evidence. Evidence that proves she...

PATRICK
> That proves nothing. Are you all totally fucked in the head? You really are missing a few screws, aren't you...

VICTOR
> Watch your mouth, Patrick. You're not out of here yet, you know.

PATRICK
> I've got a file as thick as my arm. When the least little thing goes down, it's normal you finger me. I'm used to it. It's normal... but Veronica, she's not like that.

VICTOR
> Exactly. Hanging around you so much she musta slipped a few pegs.

PATRICK
> Oh I'm so happy to learn that it's still all my fault. I'll never get clear of this, will I?

VICTOR
> Well if you run with dogs, you learn to bark, Patrick. I'm not saying that she did it on purpose. It could've been an accident. But she's just like you. She says it wasn't her. As far as she's concerned there's no way she could be mixed up in this.

PATRICK
> That's obvious. What are you trying to do anyway? Where is she?

VICTOR

We put her in a cell here until she can be transferred to the detention centre.

PATRICK

You've thought of everything, haven't you.

VICTOR

You think I don't have any heart, don't you? You think I live just for the thrill of nailing delinquents at any price. Well it's not quite as simple as that...

PATRICK

Oh cut the crap, Victor, you're gonna make me cry.

VICTOR

Everyday I see broken lives and people bawling because their life has gotten away on them because of some stupid thing they did. A lot of the time they didn't mean to do it; a lot of the time they didn't even want to do it. The worst for them is that they got caught. They can't forgive themselves for that.

PATRICK

I wouldn't want to be in your shoes, Victor. I wouldn't want your job. You talk about justice, about the law. You talk about nothing else. You'd think you were married to the law. Well since I got here, between these four walls, I've done a lot of thinking about stuff. I know I didn't do anything and I know Veronica didn't either. But appearances are against us. For you it's all a question of appearances, isn't it.

VICTOR

What else is there to go on? I can't read your mind; I don't read tea leaves or divine secrets from a deck of cards...

PATRICK

I'd just like to know how you can go home at night, eat supper, watch TV, chat with your kids, sleep with your wife without thinking about all this. Without thinking about the fact that you've just destroyed someone's life.

VICTOR

I agree with you this is not a glorious job I have here, but somebody has to do it. Somebody has to mop up from time to time so the rest of you can live in a clean house. And when you look around you tell yourself you haven't got it so bad. At least here we let people talk.

PATRICK

Right, but you don't listen. Or rather you listen to what suits you best. So what is Veronica guilty of?

VICTOR

Veronica has been accused, okay, accused. That doesn't mean she's going to be found guilty. And if she gets herself a good lawyer, she'll likely be cleared.

PATRICK

When can I get out of here?

VICTOR

Right now, I suppose.

PATRICK

Just like that. One minute I'm guilty, the next minute I'm pure as the driven snow.

VICTOR

Accused, not guilty. Accused. You were accused.

PATRICK

When can I see Veronica?

VICTOR

Tomorrow morning, if you like. By the time you get out of here, visiting hours will be over. You'll have to wait until tomorrow.

PATRICK

That's all you have to say to me?

VICTOR

I think it's a shame everything that's happened to you. Everything you've had to go through… but these things happen…

PATRICK

I'll be fine. This is nothing new. I'll be fine. (*He turns his back on VICTOR.*)

VICTOR

Come with me. We'll get your things.

> *Electric guitar solo. VICTOR exits. Lights remain on PATRICK who picks up his stuff.*

Scene Ten: Failure

Thursday 2:30 PM.

Lights come up on VERONICA's cell. PATRICK is there.

PATRICK

I wanted to come this morning, but I decided to go to Martin's funeral. It was kinda different because Martin's mom decided to have him cremated. It's weird; I still don't think I believe it. I just can't believe that little box can hold all the life and dreams of someone I knew so well.

VERONICA

Were there a lot of people there?

PATRICK

It was packed. The whole school was there. The principal said a few words. The whole church was bawling. Martin's mother was... I didn't think she was going to get through it. His father was there with his new wife. He was bawling too. He covered his face with his hands so no one could see his eyes, but you could tell he was crying.

VERONICA

Did anyone ask about me?

PATRICK

I got there late and I left before the end. I didn't want to see anyone. I sat in the back row.

VERONICA

It's weird, huh. I figured I'd be the one who'd have to go.

PATRICK

I don't know why I went. Funerals aren't my thing. But... I don't know. I just couldn't handle the idea of seeing you in prison.

VERONICA

It's a weird feeling being accused of something you haven't done.

PATRICK

Tell me about it.

VERONICA

Do you think it was me? Do you think I'm the one who did it, who pushed Martin?

PATRICK

Eventually they'll figure out nobody is guilty. As far as I can figure, Martin must have slipped. You remember how it was starting to get dark. It was just as we were about to leave that you had the idea of going for a walk. And up on the cliff the grass is really long; maybe he couldn't see how close he was to the edge.

VERONICA

Since last night, I've thought a lot about what happened out there. I've replayed the whole afternoon in my head like a video. I know it by heart. And you know what I think. I think it was Sophie who pushed Martin off the cliff.

PATRICK

Sophie?

VERONICA

Haven't you noticed how she's the one who's supplied all the stuff the police've used against us. First you, then me. Victor believes her. I don't know how she does it, but whatever she says is taken like gospel. What was she doing showing Martin's journal to Victor? And then her story about the chain I think is a big…

PATRICK

Chain? What chain?

VERONICA

Victor didn't tell you? They found my chain near the spot they think Martin fell from.

PATRICK

The chain I gave you?

VERONICA

Yes that one.

PATRICK

What was it doing there?

VERONICA

Victor says Martin must have snagged it when he tried to kiss me. Because according to him I must have gone to look for Martin when Sophie went to get a Coke from the cooler. But I noticed my chain missing on Saturday.

PATRICK

Okay. Go on…

VERONICA

You're not starting to believe this shit are you? Sophie is crazy. All I know is that I stayed put waiting for you, but I can't prove it. There's nothing says Sophie really went to get that Coke or that she didn't take a detour through the bush.

PATRICK

But what about the chain?

> *At this moment, VICTOR comes in. He has a sheet of paper in his hands. Seeing him, PATRICK turns his back.*

> *Two versions to choose from:*

Version 1:

VICTOR

Sorry to bother you, but Martin's mother brought this for Veronica.

Yves Turbide, Karène Chiasson & Hughes Paulin
Photo by Herménégilde Chiasson.

PATRICK

Well that's a new one, Victor. You don't usually excuse yourself like that. Usually…

VICTOR

(*loudly*) That's enough of your smart-ass remarks, ok! Don't push me too far my boy; you could regret it.

PATRICK

Sorry. 'Specially since Veronica has a few things to tell you about Sophie which might just give you something to think about…

VICTOR

Sophie? What are you talking about?

VERONICA

Oh my God. Listen to this Patrick. (*She reads.*) "I have your chain, Veronica, I have your chain. It came unhooked when I was holding you in my arms and you pushed me away. At that moment, if you only knew how ugly I felt, how clumsy. I have your chain and I would use it to hang myself if it was stronger. I wanted so badly to tell you how I love you, and you pushed me away. All I wanted was to tell you I love you; nothing else matters anymore. I don't love Sophie and I know now that she'll never make you jealous. She just makes me unhappy. You shouldn't have told Patrick because now everyone knows that I love you and that makes it even more painful. Painful to the point that I don't see how I can go on living this useless life. One day you will find this piece of paper and you will understand everything. You will understand all the love I had for you."

VICTOR

When you're ready, you can come by my office. (*He exits.*)

PATRICK

(*pause*) Can you believe there are really people in the world who are so crazy they'd…?

VERONICA

I never realized he could love me as much as that.

PATRICK

That's not love; that's just madness. It's not the same thing.

VERONICA

It's exactly the same thing, the same as madness. Why did you fight with him? Because you were crazy. Crazy for love or crazy jealous, but crazy.

PATRICK

Yes but I'd never kill myself for it.

VERONICA

Because you've never been that unhappy or that much in love...

PATRICK

Veronica, don't start blaming yourself...

VERONICA

I have to live with this. I have to live with his death on my conscience.

PATRICK

Martin would have killed himself anyway. If it hadn't been for you, it would have been for somebody else. It was just something in him.

VERONICA

But you're still alive.

PATRICK

We're both still alive. That's what counts.

Version 2:

VICTOR

Sorry to bother you...

PATRICK

Well that's a new one, Victor. You don't usually excuse yourself like that. Usually...

VICTOR

(*loudly*) That's enough of your smart-ass remarks, okay! Don't push me too far my boy; you could regret it.

PATRICK

Sorry. It's just that Veronica has a few things to tell you about Sophie which might just give you something to think about...

VICTOR

Sophie? What are you talking about? (*embarrassed pause*) Look, there have been some new developments in your case. Not far from the cliff is a hunting cabin. In the course of our investigation we found a witness who told us there was nobody with Martin when he slipped.

PATRICK

(*to VERONICA*) Isn't that what I told you, that he slipped.

VERONICA

We've been telling you that all along. Why do you suddenly believe him?

VICTOR
  His story holds up.

PATRICK
  Yeah, right.

VICTOR
  (*to VERONICA*) Here. Martin's mother brought this for you.

VERONICA
  (*She reads.*) "I have your chain, Veronica. It came unhooked when I took you in
  my arms and you pushed me away. I wanted to tell you I love you; nothing else
  matters anymore. I don't love Sophie and I know now that she'll never make
  you jealous. She just makes me unhappy. You shouldn't have told Patrick, but
  actually I want to shout it to the world that I love you. I wrote this thinking
  about you...
  I said goodbye one morning,
  Leaving nothing behind me;
  I'd hid my pain with joking,
  But feared one day you'd leave me.
  I see you every night;
  You're there in all my dreams;
  Your name my lips delight;
  My life more complete it seems.
  Love is all there is to blame,
  If I love you more and more;
  It plays my heart an awful game,
  But love is what I can't ignore.
  You can try to make me play
  These games that hurt and sting;
  You can try to run away
  As far as dreams can wing.
  But in your heart of hearts you know
  The final word will soon be mine,
  That no matter where you go
  You'll never find true peace of mind.
  Love is all there is to blame,
  If I love you more and more;
  Guardian angels are the same
  As you with keys to heaven's door.
  Love is all there is to blame
  For all I know is pain;
  Love is all there is to blame
  For all my heart is full of pain.

PATRICK
  (*pause*) Can you believe there are really people in the world who are so crazy
  they'd...?

VERONICA

I never realized he could love me as much as that.

PATRICK

That's not love; that's just madness. It's not the same thing.

VERONICA

It's exactly the same thing, the same as madness. Why did you fight with him? Because you were crazy. Crazy for love or crazy jealous, but crazy.

PATRICK

Veronica, don't start blaming yourself…

VERONICA

I have to live with this. I have to live with his death on my conscience.

PATRICK

Maybe it was him you really should have fallen in love with.

VERONICA

That's easy to say: you're still alive.

PATRICK

We're both still alive. That's what counts.

VERONICA

And Martin's dead. Things can never be the same.

PATRICK

(*hugging her*) Let's try to find each other again…

VERONICA

(*breaking away*) It's too easy just to forget.

PATRICK

Well, I can't bring Martin back to life, can I?

VERONICA

I can't believe you could be so cruel.

PATRICK

Sometimes in life it'd be a lot simpler just to be dead, to disappear. But I've always believed that the future would take care of things. Until now, you are the most beautiful thing that's ever happened to me. As for the rest, I'm waiting. I tell myself things are gonna change. What else is there to do? I'm gonna do everything I can to make sure things change.

VERONICA

Some people are more fragile than others. Some people are really fragile.

PATRICK

I didn't know he was all that fragile.

VERONICA

I knew it.

PATRICK

He was another beaten dog.

VERONICA

What do you mean?

PATRICK

You like people when they're hurting. You think you can help them. When things are going well, you don't find them so interesting anymore.

VERONICA

I've always loved people because I needed to love them. When you're in love you don't think about it. You love people because they are who they are. You don't want to change them. I don't know why, but I get the feeling you want me to change.

PATRICK

I didn't say that to hurt you.

> *Electric guitar solo. PATRICK gets up and exits. VERONICA rereads Martin's letter. The lights go down.*

Scene Eleven

> *Friday 11:40 AM. Lights come up on VICTOR's office. He is on the telephone. PATRICK enters without VICTOR noticing him.*

> *Two versions to choose from:*

Version 1:

VICTOR

No, we closed the file yesterday.... Yes that's right.... I made a photocopy of the suicide note and sent it to you by internal mail. I gave the original to the girl.... Well, what can you do. These things happen.... Well, yes, but they're young. They'll forget about it fast enough.... Sure if you want.... Country Buffet?...

I don't like the coffee there. Why not Tim Horton's?... It's not that bad.... Okay, in about twenty minutes. Bye.

Version 2:

VICTOR

No, we closed the file yesterday.... Yes that's right.... The case wrapped up faster than I expected. I was sure it was one of the two, him more than the girl.... Well, what can you do? These things happen.... Well, yes, but they're young. They'll forget about it fast enough.... Sure if you want.... Country Buffet?... I don't like the coffee there. Why not Tim Horton's?... It's not that bad.... Okay, in about twenty minutes. Bye.

VICTOR hangs up and turns around to find PATRICK.

VICTOR

Oh, look at that. I was just talking about you, and the others. We've closed the file. Aren't you pleased?

PATRICK

Has Veronica gone?

VICTOR

Yes, her father came to get her yesterday afternoon.

PATRICK

Did she say where she was going?

VICTOR

I didn't ask her and she didn't tell me. Her father was here. He didn't seem too keen on hanging around either.

PATRICK

I've been calling every fifteen minutes since last night. There's no answer.

VICTOR

She'll be back. Be patient. It won't hurt you to wait. So what are your plans?

PATRICK

I'm moving.

VICTOR

Oh yeah? Where?

PATRICK

I called my father; he's coming to pick me up.

VICTOR

You're going back to your family.

PATRICK

I need to talk to my father. There are things we have to say to each other. We've got to straighten things out.

VICTOR

That's the best thing you could do.

PATRICK

So Veronica didn't tell you anything at all?

VICTOR

Veronica has left for Toronto to stay with her aunt. She didn't leave an address. This'll give you a chance to forget about her. Do something else…

PATRICK

No. That's where you're wrong, Victor. That's where you're very wrong. Veronica and me, we'll get together again. I don't know how. I don't know when. But there's nothing and nobody can keep us apart. Do you hear me? I chose her. I love her. You and all the rest will never understand that. Because it's not logical. But I know that's what's important. That's the only thing I'm certain of. Everything else is pretty mixed up right now. But that I know is the truth. I know it is.

VICTOR

You see, maybe it's not so bad after all. Maybe if all this hadn't happened, maybe you wouldn't be going back to your father.

PATRICK

And I wouldn't have met you? Eh, Victor? Everybody runs away from you Victor. You make everybody afraid.

VICTOR

That's my job. But as far as I'm concerned, I'll never make you scared enough.

The end.

Alienor

Herménégilde Chiasson
translated by Glen Nichols

INTRODUCTION TO *CAPE ENRAGE*

In my opinion, Herménégilde Chiasson's lyrical drama, *Alienor*, is a particularly beautiful and powerful piece. On many levels it is a study of contrasts and the resulting network of tensions instills the play with a formidable sense of energy despite the essentially static nature of the "action." Highly poetic and frequently dreamlike, the play revolves around Etienne who removed himself and his daughter, Alienor, from progressive encroachments of the world to live deep in the woods until a violent encounter with four hunters forces him back into the world on charges of having sexually abused his daughter. In order to protect Alienor's honour, he holds out against the arguments of his lawyer that he might escape prosecution through a plea of mental incompetence. In the end, though, it is Alienor who has the courage to insist on revealing the truth, that it was the hunters who raped her, not her father. The relationship between Etienne and Alienor is revealed through three incredibly beautiful scenes in which Alienor appears to Etienne in dreams and "speaks" to him through song and in dialogue spoken over music.

The interplay of Etienne and Alienor creates a powerful allegory for the creation of a new Acadie, looking forward, but conscious of its foundations. Etienne, representing the past, avoids destruction first by escaping from the world to live in the woods, then later by facing the wrath of the world in a silent martyr-like resistance to injustice. Alienor, engendered by her own past sacrifices, becomes a new symbolic paradigm, a kind of post-modern Evangeline: although raped by the intruders she is able to survive and defeat her opponents by refusing to flee or to be martyred. She believes in building a new world over the ashes of the old world destroyed by their enemies, not to "betray the history of our suffering," but as a way of reconciling past and future: "We must bury the past. We must write it down in a book and bury the book. And the dead will read that book, and they too will finally be able to sleep."

In stark realistic contrast, Etienne's court-appointed psychiatrist, Laurence, engages her former lover, Robert, as Etienne's defence lawyer. These two try to work out their professional allegiances under the cloud of their broken personal relationship. Etienne and Alienor struggle as individuals in face of life-threatening challenges calling upon the stories and dreams that unite them, while Robert and Laurence struggle with very personalized conflicts in a world of facts, numbers and "evidence." The reconciliation of the first pair points to large social and historical significance, while that of the second, based on the eventual revelation of Laurence's deeply repressed memories, suggests the need for profound human understanding. Laurence and Robert do not rekindle their love affair, but understand in the end what a different kind of future might have awaited them had they been able to come to terms with their pasts earlier in their relationship. In both cases, it is the resolution of collective and individual histories which makes room for the reinvention of new life.

The third level of this play is the media interventions of Francoise, a reporter who relates the events of the trial to her "TV" audience. Like the chorus in a Greek tragedy, Francoise's reactions to events and her curiosity about the sordid case reflect the feelings of the audience. But more significantly the audience witnesses the sometimes rather ineffectual media filtering of the events since we see both the trial itself and her reports on it. The ironic gap which grows between our perceptions of events and those of the media underscore the community's collective role in the events depicted onstage. By addressing the audience directly, especially in the character of a news reporter, Francoise's comment on the "community in general" comes to signify not only the fictional community of the play, but also the community of spectators in the theatre, the Acadian collectivity that Chiasson is so consciously writing from and for.

The play presented considerable translation challenges because the intense lyricism had to be balanced against the need to find distinctive character voices while maintaining the narrative energy. As a result, the workshop process was particularly helpful in locating the scene/language dynamics. One example of an image that required working through a considerable number of alternatives, was Etienne's description of the pain he felt at his own helplessness to prevent the violent assault on his daughter: "*Quelque chose comme une boursouflure gravée au couteau sur l'écorce du ciel, sur le corps de la nuit, sur l'enveloppe de mon coeur.*" [lit: Something like a blister etched with a knife on the bark of the sky, on the body of the night, on the envelope of my heart]. The final version, arrived at by listening to the actor's development of the entire scene, alters some of the specific denotative aspects of the image in order to relate the underlying metaphoric structure, potentialize the range of actor delivery through rhythm and vowel combinations, and harmonize with images in related speeches elsewhere in the play. The line now reads, "It's like a blister branded with a knife on the skin of heaven, on the body of night, on the tissue that cradles my heart."

On a simple technical level, sentence length posed surprising difficulties. On one hand Etienne's speeches tend to be composed of very short, almost aphoristic lines which relate closely to his imagistic thought processes. However, in English performance these tended to sound repetitive and choppy, so several compromises were necessary to vary the stage rhythms while maintaining a sense of Etienne's original linguistic patterns. On the other hand, the reporter's speeches were made up of long complex-compound sentences. These were not only almost incomprehensible (not to mention hard to deliver) in English, but seemed out of place given the typical "sound-bite" style of TV journalism. So, again, compromises were necessary to create speakable, justifiable lines while maintaining the "breathlessness" which Chiasson was aiming for in this character.

Indeed, all the characters here struggle to find a voice and that is probably one of the profound unifying features of the play: whether it is Etienne silenced in face of a strange clinical world he doesn't know or want to know, or Alienor trying to break through her father's hard sense of honour and protection to speak her mind, or Robert failing to find the words to express his feelings for Laurence, or Laurence herself suffering the pain of having repressed her own past because she feels there isn't anyone who will listen to her story. Through the contrasts of Etienne and modern society, of past and present, of truth and myth, of justice and revenge, Chiasson explores how communities and individuals come together only through their ability to reveal themselves, their pasts, and their vulnerabilities. But in that coming together they are able to find a future where "we will share nothing less than life itself, our only possession, our unique vengeance."

—GN

** Portions of this preface first appeared in Glen Nichols, "Bard of Acadie: the Theatre of Herménégilde Chiasson" *Port Acadie* 2 (2001): 25-42.

Alienor by Herménégilde Chiasson

Aliénor was produced in 1997 by Théâtre l'Escaouette. It was performed during the winter at the Aberdeen Cultural Centre in Moncton and during the summer at Monument Lefebvre in Memramcook, New Brunswick, with the following cast:

Bertholet Charron	Étienne Landry
Denise Shaw	Aliénor (Winter 1997)
Janine Boudreau	Aliénor (Summer 1997)
Marcia Babineau	Laurence Samson
Yves Turbide	Robert LeBlanc
Katherine Kilfoil	Françoise Francoeur
Alain Doom	Announcer

Directed by Alain Doom. Lighting by Marc Paulin. Music by Jean-François Mallet. Design by Herménégilde Chiasson. Sound effects by Jean-Marie Morin.

The play was published in 1998 by Éditions d'Acadie

This translation of *Alienor* was workshopped and given a public reading in Moncton in March 2002 with the following cast: Nathalie Arseneault, Evie Carnat, Glen Munro, Louise Nichols, Owen Stairs and Shannon Wetmore. Directed by Glen Nichols.

CHARACTERS

Etienne: A man in his sixties awaiting trial. He is a man with great inner strength, but resigned to his fate and with little to say.

Alienor: Etienne's daughter. Moving from adolescence to adulthood, she is defiant, but demonstrates profound compassion for her father whose pain she understands.

Laurence Samson: A psychiatrist in her thirties. She prizes her apparent success in escaping the working-class milieu of her past.

Robert LeBlanc: A lawyer in his thirties. Ambitious with few scruples, he is nevertheless willing to indulge Laurence, who acts as a kind of moral conscience and with whom he is still in love.

Francoise Francoeur: A journalist. She tells the story as it unfolds.

Radio Announcer: Loves sensationalism. The audience hears his voice, but never sees him.

STAGE DESCRIPTION

The stage is open, with no divisions and only a few simple pieces of scenery: tables, chairs, and a bench mark Etienne's cell and Robert's office. The other locations (courtroom, outside the courthouse) are indicated by lighting areas. Stage right a large black and white scrim represents Alienor's forest, blending visually with Etienne's cell. Stage left, there is a projection screen for the reports of the journalist whom we see in front of the courthouse. All changes in time and place are created by lighting effects.

Alienor

by Herménégilde Chiasson

Scene One – The Deserted Village

ETIENNE's cell. ETIENNE Landry is in jail awaiting trial. The man, like a wounded animal, remains passive, reluctant to trust others.

ETIENNE
It all started a long time ago. A long time.

LAURENCE
You must have a vague idea at least.

ETIENNE
All I know is that I was living on some land, in the bush.

LAURENCE
And how big was it, this land?

ETIENNE
It was a big land.

LAURENCE
Yes, but how big? (*pause*) How big was the land?

ETIENNE
It was big. It was a really big land. Big.

LAURENCE
You talk about this land, but every time I ask you about it, the land seems to disappear. As if you're losing your memory.

ETIENNE
If I knew, do you think I would hide it from you?

LAURENCE
I need more details.

ETIENNE
Details.

LAURENCE
You do know what a detail is, don't you?

ETIENNE

Eventually, having to say the same things over and over, you end up…

LAURENCE

You end up… what…?

ETIENNE

You end up no longer knowing if what you're saying is true. You believe it happened. But afterwards…. When you have to tell it to others. It's not the same. When you tell it, it begins to change. The story you want to hear is not the same as mine, not the same as the one I have in my head. (*pause*)

LAURENCE

I don't know anything about your story. If you would like to tell me…. Otherwise, we can stop here…. (*pause*)

ETIENNE

I don't remember the measure of land, okay? I don't remember. I really don't remember…. It's like the snow in winter. Everything is white, and you forget what is under that whiteness. You forget… then one day, it just disappears…. It's the same with us; we too end up disappearing, forgetting everything.

LAURENCE

So you don't remember anything. You lived on that land, you raised your family on that land, you fed off that land, and yet you never bothered to measure it, to know how far it went?

ETIENNE

No… the land went as far as the river. But on the other side of the river, the trees go on and on, and the trees look like trees, the river like the river, the ice the ice…

LAURENCE

Maybe you don't want to remember…

ETIENNE

When you don't know the bush, you can't understand what goes on there…. It's easy to talk sitting by a fire all year round, keeping warm…. It's not like spending a whole life in the bush, seeing the stars go down every morning and come up every night.

LAURENCE

Mr. Landry, it is important that you cooperate with me, otherwise we might as well stop right here and…

ETIENNE

And…?

LAURENCE
    We'll see.

ETIENNE
    What will we see?

LAURENCE
    You've been charged, Mr. Landry. Accused.

ETIENNE
    (*ironically*) Accused.

LAURENCE
    (*firmly*) Yes, accused.

ETIENNE
    Accused in a different world. In your world.

LAURENCE
    You do understand why you are here, at least, don't you?

ETIENNE
    In your world?

LAURENCE
    Yes, in our world.

ETIENNE
    In your world.

LAURENCE
    The court has engaged me to determine whether or not you are fit to stand trial.

ETIENNE
    A trial.

LAURENCE
    One of the techniques I use involves asking the accused to tell me his life story.

ETIENNE
    I have already told you. The rest…

LAURENCE
    The rest? You're keeping it to yourself?

ETIENNE
    The rest is wasted time.

LAURENCE
So far you have told me you were born in a foreign country. You got a job as a sailor on a big boat. You married a Mi'kmaq woman, though you don't recall her name. Then you cleared some land in the forest. Ah yes, you have three children… that's it…

ETIENNE
Alienor.

LAURENCE
Yes, I know. That's your daughter's name.

ETIENNE
I would like to see her.

LAURENCE
You know that's not possible. The court forbids any contact with the victim.

ETIENNE
(*ironically*) The victim!

LAURENCE
That's what she's called.

ETIENNE
The victim.

LAURENCE
In the court documents.

ETIENNE
Where is she now, the victim?

LAURENCE
She's fine. I can assure you she is being well taken care of.

ETIENNE
Alienor, she's all that I…

LAURENCE
All that you…

ETIENNE
All that I have to live for.

LAURENCE
Nobody is going to hurt her.

ETIENNE
Me and her, we share the same blood, the same life, the same broken promise, the same abandoned land, icy, alone...

LAURENCE
The same life? Could you tell me about that life?

ETIENNE
Yes, but it's all mixed up. I don't know which part came before or after. All I know is that I was there. I saw all kinds of things happen, but how can I see it all clearly... not lose the thread?

LAURENCE
Someone who can not tell the story of his life, Mr. Landry, does not appear before a judge. Usually people make sure they avoid that sort of situation.

ETIENNE
When you have a real life, yes, I can see that. You can talk about it, tell it to people. A life, like a story. But when you wait, day after day... when all we have left is the waiting... that doesn't leave much time for talking...

LAURENCE
What are you waiting for, Mr. Landry?

ETIENNE
Night.

LAURENCE
Night?

ETIENNE
At night, I see her...

LAURENCE
Who?

ETIENNE
Alienor. She comes to me. Even more beautiful than in real life. She knows I'm waiting for her. In my dreams. Sometimes she passes by, she stops, she laughs, she beckons me; her voice sweet...

LAURENCE
And then?

ETIENNE
And then, I wake up in your prison, and my rage takes over again. I sit here all day, my eyes rage red, looking at the same iron bars, listening to the curses of the others who are as enraged as I am. Then everyone in there cries out. Everyone cries out.

LAURENCE

Did you live in the forest for a long time?

ETIENNE

Yes, a long time. A very long time.

LAURENCE

Do you want to talk about it? (*pause*) No one can force you. It's your life. You can do what you want with it. (*She gathers up her papers as if to leave.*)

ETIENNE

I was walking in the bush. It was late in the fall. The wind blew cold. Snow was starting to cover the ground. You could hear the guns of the hunters looking for game. The birds had gone; the river was turning to ice. I had gathered the firewood. Winter was coming fast. The land was going to sleep, and I was going to sleep with her.

LAURENCE

Was it a big land?

ETIENNE

(*exasperated*) Yes, it was a big land.

LAURENCE

How big?

ETIENNE

I don't know! You can tell the judge I don't know. That I don't remember anymore. Once, I would have known, but now the village is deserted. The bush has grown back over it. Trees sprang up in the road. Just like that, trees everywhere. Trees to the ends of the earth. As far as you can see; as far as I can imagine: trees.

LAURENCE

Do you know why the village was deserted?

ETIENNE

One morning, someone told us to leave. They wanted to build something. That's what they told us. At the beginning we didn't believe them. We had cleared that land. We thought it belonged to us. We told them that's what we thought. That it was ours. But they had fire-power on their side. At night they started to cruise around the village in their trucks, shooting at the houses. They lit fires in front of the houses, and then they lit the houses on fire. One by one. At night. Everything happened at night. We tried to defend ourselves, but what good are hunting rifles?

LAURENCE

You could have complained. Gone to the law.

ETIENNE

The law. The village was too far away. The law didn't reach that far.

LAURENCE

You let them go ahead?

ETIENNE

In the end the village was deserted. Me, I stayed behind. As long as I could. I stayed. But I was not all alone. I had my family. One night, with my wife and daughters, I took to the bush. At the beginning we thought it wouldn't be for too long. We didn't think it was going to last. We told ourselves that in time they would leave. That we would be able to go home. But they stayed.

LAURENCE

And that's why you stayed in the bush?

ETIENNE

They divided the land among themselves. At night, when we crept to the edge of the clearing, we could see the frames of their houses rising in the moonlight, while the rest of us slept under the stars like animals. After a time, they stopped chasing us. Bit by bit, there were those who wanted to return. They went to work for these new masters, then sometimes the new masters let them build houses. They let them. Small houses. Houses that didn't belong to them. But at least they had a roof over their heads. But me, I was certain that one day, sooner or later, these new masters would lose patience. That they would burn those houses. And that's why I decided to stay in the bush. To not build a house like the others.

LAURENCE

And your wife...

ETIENNE

Dead. She died of a broken heart, of fear or of thirst. She died like someone who swallows her cry. A cry that consumes her in the end.

LAURENCE

Your daughters?

ETIENNE

The oldest perished in the river. It was winter. Her body jammed in the ice. The other one disappeared into the bush. It was a hot July day. She followed an animal. (*pause*) I see them again and again in my dreams. At night. Always the same dream. I'm walking on the ice, and someone starts knocking under my feet. I bend over and see my daughter at my feet. She is knocking on the ice as if she were knocking on a door, but I can no longer open it for her. The ice is as clear as a pane of glass. I reach down to take her in my arms, but I can't. There is ice between us. Then I see her lose her strength. I see her body fall to the bottom of the river, disappear into the depths of the river. Like a rock sinking into darkness. The other one is different. A different dream. Not the same dream. Since she followed an animal, I began to believe they must have married. I dream they come back to see me, him and her, and their children. Children with the head of a fox… but all that is just dreaming. Or nightmares really… nightmares.

LAURENCE

But in reality, you know that… that they are dreams.

ETIENNE

Yes, but I have dreamed it so often I wonder if, deep down, it couldn't be, somehow, the truth. In my dreams it's as if I'm trying to find the end of stories that didn't have time to finish. A beautiful ending… a really beautiful ending.

LAURENCE

And what, for you, would be a really beautiful ending?

ETIENNE

(*pause*) What have they done with her?

LAURENCE

Who?

ETIENNE

Alienor.

LAURENCE

Your daughter is fine where she is. You could have left the forest. Done like the others.

ETIENNE

For that, the world would have had to be remade. A new world…. But me, I had lost the best of worlds. I don't know if you can understand. Then… I decided to hide myself out there. Bury my sorrow there. In the bush.

LAURENCE

But you didn't have to go completely savage!

ETIENNE

It's everywhere. It's in my head, in my body, in my soul. It's there all the time. It doesn't need to be real. It's just there; I see it. The land covered in bush. It's always there. Full of animals. Cruel animals. They have guns. They hunt us. They keep on hunting us…

LAURENCE

Do you have proof of that?

ETIENNE

I can show you the bullet holes in my cabin walls. I saw the holes. I could show them to you.

LAURENCE
Yes, but that was a long time ago.

ETIENNE
There are things that are never forgotten. Even if you wish you could forget them. They're there. They're always there. Filling my head. Solid as ice. Written in my face. In my eyes. On my skin. Then, eventually, they end up taking over everything.

LAURENCE
You have never had a job… or at least I see that you have never contributed to any social assistance plan…. (*pause*) On the other hand, apparently you were seen hanging around the houses. They say as well that several things went missing afterwards…. (*pause*) If you deny nothing, then I can only conclude that it's true.

ETIENNE
Look, you're talking about your world. I don't know that world, and I don't want to know it.

LAURENCE
The court has asked me to evaluate…

ETIENNE
I've already told you the story of my life.

LAURENCE
I have the impression that your story changes every time I meet you.

ETIENNE
Life is like that. Life changes.

LAURENCE
Life maybe, but not the past. The past doesn't change.

ETIENNE
Yes, the past, too, changes.

LAURENCE
How's that?

ETIENNE
Because life changes. Even in the past, life changes.

Scene Two – Taken For a Criminal

Office of ROBERT LeBlanc.

LAURENCE
You know, this time I can't help thinking he's like an animal being led to slaughter.

ROBERT
Well, it's still the best system there is.

LAURENCE
A slaughterhouse?

ROBERT
Look, you can't just open the doors and let all those guys back into circulation. It's fine to have big ideas, but at some point you have to draw the line.

LAURENCE
I'm not criticizing. It's just that in this case, it's different.

ROBERT
For whom?

LAURENCE
Perhaps if he could count on the help of a good lawyer. Someone like you, for example.

ROBERT
I'm warning you. My fees are rather steep, and your fellow doesn't seem to be too…. Anyway, if everything he says is true, it will not be an easy case.

LAURENCE
No, it's not going to be easy.

ROBERT
So what is it then… I mean why you? Why is he so interesting to you?

LAURENCE
He intrigues me. He's not transparent.

ROBERT
Criminals are never transparent.

LAURENCE
I find it hard to think of him in those terms.

ROBERT

Yes, I've heard you before. Criminals are sick, and if they are sick it should be doctors taking care of them.

LAURENCE

Did I say that?

ROBERT

In that case, all the judges, all the lawyers, even you, everyone would end up on EI tomorrow morning.

LAURENCE

I don't know if you realize it, but this case could bring you a lot of publicity.

ROBERT

I'm not so sure it's the kind of publicity I'm looking for. It's a delicate situation.

LAURENCE

I see you winning this case hands down. I think you are the ideal person because you can give the accused a sense of confidence, make him understand he has to defend himself and that you're there to help him. I've seen you in action and I know you can do it. After all, I wouldn't have called you if I wasn't sure.

In the courtroom. The trial is underway.

ROBERT

Mr Landry, you say you have spent most of your life in the forest.

ETIENNE

That's right.

ROBERT

For many people such a thing is difficult to believe since even the animals barely survive the winters we have, all the more so for human beings who are not used to such harsh conditions.

ETIENNE

I managed. I managed to survive.

ROBERT

Let's go back to your daughter. Mr. Landry, your daughter, even though she is of school age, has never received any education. In fact, the little she has learned, she seems to have learned from you. Is that correct?

ETIENNE

She learned about life.

ROBERT

Could you elaborate?

ETIENNE

Don't you think that's enough? What else is there to learn?

ROBERT

Your Honour, may I have a word with my client? (*He approaches ETIENNE.*) Listen, Mr. Landry, I'm asking you all these questions in order to give you a chance to cooperate with me. If the prosecutor asks them, he will be a lot tougher than I am. By answering them now, we avoid his badgering you later on. I guarantee he won't let anything get past him.

ETIENNE

Yes, but you're asking me to say things I have never said to anyone. In front of all these people who are looking at me as if I belonged in a cage. I see them and I know they've come to see the man who was found in the bush.

ROBERT

Look, Mr Landry, don't worry about that. Talk to me. Only to me. Forget they're out there.

ETIENNE

I'm ashamed. I'm ashamed of my misery, ashamed of my poverty.

ROBERT's office.

LAURENCE

By the time the trial gets underway, I promise you'll have all the evidence you need. If it makes you feel any better, I can tell you, if nothing else, his world is a world I know. I was born there, I grew up there. He will talk.

ROBERT

You mean to say you were born in the forest? I don't believe you.

LAURENCE

The difference with me is that there was a road to get out on. A dirt road. In the summer, every time a car passed, everything disappeared in a cloud of dust. But it was a road. I followed that road and I got out. I stayed out for a long time. A long time... to the point that when I went back I didn't recognize anyone anymore.

ROBERT

Is that why he intrigues you so much?

LAURENCE

You might say that. There are aspects of him which make me think of my own father. When he's there, I can feel the forest coming closer. The way he looks at me... a mixture of soft and hard. Something troubling, animal-like. Something which bothers me, which I can't quite put my finger on, or at least can't make sense of.

Courtroom.

ROBERT
Doctor Samson, for about a week now, you have been having long conversations with my client, and you have decided to recommend that he is fit to stand trial. Is this correct?

LAURENCE
Yes, it is.

ROBERT
Were you not struck by certain gaps in my client's statements?

LAURENCE
No, not really.

ROBERT
Not really?

LAURENCE
Your client seemed quite lucid to me.

ROBERT
Lucid? Are you certain about that?

LAURENCE
Yes, his statements were consistent through repeated questioning.

ROBERT
Indeed. Let's talk about some of these statements. My client claims that he has lived his whole life in the forest. Most of it at least. Presently, he has no fixed address because he lives in the forest. Is that correct?

LAURENCE
That's what he told me.

ROBERT
Doesn't it seem strange to you, in this day and age, to meet someone living like a wild animal, sleeping under the stars, hunting for food, dressing in stolen clothes, and so on and so forth?

LAURENCE
It must be said as well that your client, who is also my patient, insisted on going through with this trial.

ROBERT
Did he tell you why?

LAURENCE
Because he would rather be seen as a criminal than as someone mentally incompetent. Those are not his exact words, but it's what he meant.

ROBERT
And even that didn't seem strange to you?

LAURENCE
I believe that for him dignity is more important than the punishment he risks bringing on himself.

ROBERT
Dignity ahead of punishment. Strange idea of justice, don't you think? (*He turns, as if addressed.*) Yes, Your Honour, I will withdraw that comment. (*to LAURENCE*) Didn't you find it strange that he should insist on such a position?

LAURENCE
It's not my job to guess at his motives.

ROBERT
Your Honour, the diagnosis of Doctor Samson raises several doubts, even for people like you and me who are simple laymen in the field of mental health. Mr. Landry says, for example, that shortly after the birth of his third daughter, some men came to the village. At night. According to my client, they were armed and fired point-blank at the walls of the houses. So this was when he decided to flee into the forest with his family. However, there is no mention of such an incident anywhere, in any text, any newspaper article, or even in the memory of the people I consulted. At the very least this is strange.

ROBERT's office.

LAURENCE
I see Landry everyday, and every time it's like a vision, a memory that surges up from I don't really know where.... Sometimes I think it's gone and then, poof! There it is again. I'm not kidding; it's got so I dream about him at night.... That's what happens I guess when we let things drag on too long. But anyway, I think it's over. It is over. Course, that's easy to say, but harder to believe, and even harder to change.

ROBERT
The idea is to talk to the right person, but I don't know if I'm the right person to listen.

LAURENCE
In my situation, I don't have anyone to talk to. I don't have any family, no husband; I wonder sometimes if I even have any friends close enough to listen to me. You're the only one left. I'm not frightening you I hope?

ROBERT
Look, if that's what it's come to, it's not because…

LAURENCE
Let's not get into that again, okay? That's not why I called you. Well, actually, yes…

ROBERT
Because I'm the only lawyer you know so intimately!

LAURENCE
What are you saying?

ROBERT
I'm just wondering why you chose me.

LAURENCE
It's not quite right, I know that.

ROBERT
(*disapproving*) You know very well that what you're doing here is illegal.

LAURENCE
Confiding in you?

ROBERT
If the court discovers that as an impartial medical officer you took it into your own hands to find a lawyer for one of your patients, that would mean…

LAURENCE
Are you going to turn me in?

ROBERT
No. No. Listen… it's for your own good.

LAURENCE
So what have you decided?

ROBERT
I'm going to think about it.

LAURENCE
What's there to think about?

ROBERT

First, my fees. Then I don't know anything about this guy apart from what you've told me, and I've a few doubts on that score. Finally, it's just not my kind of case.

LAURENCE

Doubts? What doubts?

ROBERT

Do you know many lawyers who would take on a case without knowing if they're going to win or lose?

LAURENCE

What's with this idea of having to win all the time?

ROBERT

I didn't know he was so important to you.

LAURENCE

This trial is going to attract all sorts of attention.

ROBERT

That's what you say.

LAURENCE

I'll send you his file. As far as the fees, let's just say that the publicity will be worth a lot of money. People will see your face every night on the TV. It's the kind of trial that can change a career.

ROBERT

And make you look like a circus animal.

LAURENCE

So what's new? We're all animals in a circus.

ROBERT

Publicity. All the same, it's not a murder trial.

LAURENCE

Murder, that's boring. This is the sort of thing the public wants; the kind of story that lifts them up out of their ordinary world. It's a bizarre situation, with extraordinary characters. That's what people like. Imagine. Everybody's going out today to rent a couple of videos, and curling up on their couch to watch them. Then imagine that between the movies, you appear on the same screen to show them a real-life story about a man found in the bush living like an animal. For the public, it's like *The Jungle Book* all over again. And you. Every night, you'll be there, in their living rooms; it'll be you who'll talk to them about this man, who'll make them understand how ordinary their lives are. You'll tell them about someone bigger than them, bigger than all of us.

Scene Three – A Rather Curious Story

In front of the court house. The journalist is recording her report for the camera.

FRANCOISE
The man arrived accompanied by two police officers, and a rather curious situation seems to have developed. In this sort of trial the evidence is usually presented pretty quickly, but this time the case appears set to drag on because the defence, who wants to prove the accused is unfit to stand trial for reasons of mental incompetence, finds itself opposed to the medical opinion of Dr. Laurence Samson who argues to the contrary. This morning the court heard the testimony of the accused as he recounted in detail his story which the prosecution claims makes absolutely no sense.

The defendant maintains that he spent his life in the forest after being driven off his land. Although he can't remember exactly when these events took place, he claims armed men terrorized him and his family to the point where he, his wife, and three daughters had to abandon the village where they were living. Nevertheless, when asked this morning to provide details or even an approximate location, he wasn't able to do so. As a result, according to the prosecution, there doesn't seem to be any reason to believe such an incident actually ever took place.

Another curious fact is that Landry claims his wife died in the forest. All this information is contained in the report of Dr. Samson, the physician who recommended Etienne Landry fit to stand trial. Dr. Samson was also called to the stand for a good part of the morning, and the defence hammered her with some really tough questioning.

At times the statements of the accused caused several people in the courtroom to laugh or smile; for example, Landry claims his oldest daughter still lives at the bottom of the river while his second daughter followed an animal into the forest, married this animal and has had children with him.

As a matter of fact, according to the physician who was assigned to the case, Dr. Laurence Samson, it was the accused himself, Etienne Landry, who insisted on going through with the trial because, he insists, his story is true. He decided to take the opportunity offered him here to declare it publicly, and, obviously, present evidence to the court.

The lawyer for the defence, Robert LeBlanc, seems more or less at odds with the wishes of his client, since throughout the morning he kept insisting that the trial should never have taken place. We will learn more tomorrow when the proceedings resume, and the witnesses for the prosecution, the four hunters who discovered Landry, take their turn in the witness box.

Scene Four – Your Voice Betrays You

Robert's office.

ROBERT
It's impossible. It just doesn't stand up. I can't build a defence like this. You told me that you would have all the evidence for me, but here we are and I realize I have nothing. The trial starts tomorrow and I have nothing. Tomorrow I'm going to go there and make a fool of myself. The trial is all over the papers. (*He shows a copy of the paper.*) Don't you get it? It's like a big show. I'm going to make a spectacle of myself. No, but I don't understand, Laurence. That's not a file. It's nothing but a pack of questions that add up to nothing. It's a bunch of reflections on life in general. The judge will not be amused deciphering the state of Etienne Landry's soul. He will render his judgement based on what he hears. It's not as if I had a jury I could jerk a few tears out of. No, it's just between the prosecutor, the judge, and me. And me, I'll be going around in circles like a chicken with its head cut off. It's gonna be great... just great!

LAURENCE
Listen, Robert, don't you think you're being a little melodramatic? I have confidence in Landry. When he gets there, when he sees the court, the people, how serious it all is, especially when he sees the witnesses, he'll start talking.

ROBERT
You really think so?

LAURENCE
He's got to say something. Oh yeah, he'll talk. I believe he'll talk. I know he's going to talk. I'm sure he's hiding his story, but he can't hide to the point of dying for it.

ROBERT
Yes, but Laurence, that's intuition talking, half an impression. And justice is far from being impressionistic, believe me. I have seen people get off scott-free over stupid little points of procedure, even when there was absolutely no doubt in anyone's mind they were guilty. No, I don't see how we can get out of this one other than by pleading mental incompetence. (*pointing to the file*) And with what's in there, it's possible. I only have to open it up to any page, and any court will concede to the evidence.

LAURENCE
I don't want to do that.

ROBERT
(*Nonchalantly, he opens the file. He reads a bit chosen at random.*) Question: What kind of relations have you established with the animals of the forest? Answer: I am an animal among other animals. Any judge hearing an answer like that will clear him straight away. Otherwise...

LAURENCE

Look, we're dealing with someone here who doesn't speak our language, Robert. Someone who speaks in images. A kind of Native. His wife was Native, wasn't she?

ROBERT

Whether you like it or not, I'm going to plead mental incompetence.

LAURENCE

Well, that's fine with me; I'll simply testify otherwise.

ROBERT

Go ahead, and we'll see which of the two of us wins.

LAURENCE

Let's be sensible about this.

ROBERT

I don't have any choice. Tell me if I have a choice.

LAURENCE

In a case like this, you know as well as I do that I will have the final word.

ROBERT

The final word… that could cost you dearly. It could cost you your reputation as a physician.

LAURENCE

You didn't use to speak to me like that. I get the feeling you're looking for revenge…

ROBERT

No, Laurence, don't drag our relationship into this. It has nothing to do with it. This is strictly professional.

LAURENCE

It's your tone of voice that gives you away, you know.

ROBERT

That's just the lawyer in me talking. It's someone different. It's not someone that I take to a restaurant or to bed… It's not even someone I like particularly well. It's someone I leave and pick up again at the court house, but there…. Listen, it was you who decided one fine day, for reasons I'm still trying to understand, to leave both the lawyer and the lover…. Mind you, I don't hold it against you, even if I never have understood. It's over and done with. Everything ends eventually. That's the worst thing about it…

Scene Five – My Everlasting Gift of Song

ETIENNE's cell. ETIENNE is alone in his cell. ALIENOR appears to him in a dream, in the forest.

ETIENNE

Everyone is asking what I was doing there, in the bush. As if I had dreamed it all. As if I could have dreamed such misery, such hardship, such fear. As if I had the courage or the wisdom or the patience to invent such misfortune.

ALIENOR

(sung) It's as if the world no longer exists,
As if our life is forever gone.
In your heart burns a fire no one knows,
In your eyes the darkest night is seen.

ETIENNE

There was no point telling them you were my daughter. They just told me to get up. They told me to get up and I got up. You too, you got up. And that's when they pulled us apart forever. They took my place in our bed. Alienor, my dear girl, they have killed us many times, but never like this time, never for all time, never for forever. It's like a blister branded with a knife on the skin of heaven, on the body of night, on the tissue that cradles my heart.

ALIENOR

(sung) In the sky the sun has hidden itself;
All their bitter rage they spilled in me.
And that rage erupted in your life,
And death made its home in your heart.

ETIENNE

Their insolence is scorched into our walls. Their hate will fan our rage, our burning rage. I will live the rest my life with your fear on my skin. Cursing those who conspired to break us. I curse them for life. Even when I am left with no more words and I will have to invent new ones. My fury will burn for a lifetime in the fire of their hell. My eyes are red with anger, with tears, with shame. My girl, remember that afternoon for the rest of your life, that afternoon heavy as death.

ALIENOR

(sung) The sun is extinguished in the rain,
And the world knows no more where you live.
So sometimes when you cry it's a howl
Against those who laughed at your resistance.

ETIENNE

There was no point telling them you were my daughter…. They answered by emptying their rifles into our walls. And that's when I saw the bush swell up as far as eye could see, swallow me completely, until it erased all my memory. That day I understood. I understood I would never get out. That the bush would be my shelter, my prison, my tomb. That the bush was as boundless as death. Since then I have forgotten the measure of our bush. It would be like giving them the secret of death. Like wanting to measure time. Measure earth. Measure sky, stars. Measure life. But me I know that on that day, time stopped. For life. For all time. Stopped.

ALIENOR
(*sung*) But life for you is not only a game:
It's a knife driven into your skin,
A dark cloud bringing shivers to your back,
A wound that never speaks its name.

ETIENNE
When they picked up their guns again, when they saw how much damage they'd done… they started to look for a way of explaining their hate. They looked around for something else to dirty. They contrived that I was the guilty one. The truly guilty. There was no one else around. You became my victim. They had to protect you from me. The four of them. It took the four of them to protect you. They walked on their hind legs. Their story stood up. My story seemed lame.

ALIENOR
(*sung*) In your dreams you dream again of me;
I am always there somewhere near you;
I am close to your heart in your voice;
When I walk your footsteps are my path.

ETIENNE
I should have cried out louder than their guns, my dear girl. Louder than my fear. My cry would have been loud enough to stop them cold. Turn them into stone. But I chose to keep quiet and suffer in silence. That is the crime I want to be tried for. The crime of silence. To be delivered of this shame, a branding red-hot iron in my head. I will tell them nothing of you, my girl. I will carry in me our terrible story. Our suffering. For life. That will be our secret, our music, our song. The song I give to you forever which will sing of my rage always, on earth as in heaven.

Scene Six – Such compelling Silence

ROBERT's office.

LAURENCE
I have the image of that man's face stuck in my head, his eyes follow me, his silences which go on and on…

ROBERT

That can't be! You must have transferred something to him from your childhood.

LAURENCE

He's like my father, I know. But why him? Why at this point in my life? Just when I thought I had come to terms with all that?

ROBERT

Because your father took off with your secret.

LAURENCE

What do you mean, my secret?

ROBERT

Everybody has a secret, otherwise we'd just give up. Even the worst criminals have a secret, something which keeps them hanging on to life.

LAURENCE

You mean like an ideal or something?

ROBERT

In any case, Etienne Landry is certainly someone filled with secrets; the difference is that nobody seems able to break through his secrets, not even you, with all your science. As for me? I really don't see how I can do it.

LAURENCE

It's because of him that I've spent my life running away from anyone who got close to me, slamming doors, shutting people out.

ROBERT

And me, I was one of those victims too, I suppose?

LAURENCE

That was part of it. Part of a system of self protection.

ROBERT

As a psychiatrist you're the best one to know your own faults.

LAURENCE

More like a deep wound.

ROBERT

Okay. So I don't use very sophisticated language when it comes to these things. After all, to each his own, eh… otherwise…

LAURENCE

Let's not go there, okay?

ROBERT

It's not something that can be so easily forgotten, you know.

LAURENCE

Let's go back to Landry.

ROBERT

Even there, I still don't understand why you're trying so hard to help him.

LAURENCE

Why do you think I do this job?

ROBERT

To the point you're ready to risk your reputation as a psychiatrist?

LAURENCE

Landry's risking a lot more. And besides, when you get right down to it, what am I really risking? Like you, what are you risking? Losing face? Having to say, "I'm sorry, I was wrong." What is it, this fear of being afraid? It seems to me that life is an awful lot more than that. It seems to me that at one time in our lives we wanted a lot more than that. How is it we ended up accepting so little? How did we get to this point?

ROBERT

Because people change.

LAURENCE

Yes, but eventually that ends up sounding like an excuse.

ROBERT

Who is this guy anyway? He just seems to have come out of nowhere, out of nothing. With a story that doesn't stand up. With a life that doesn't make sense.

LAURENCE

With a silence so compelling we want to listen, for once. Listen to the silence around him. A long time ago I left that silence, made sure I was always surrounded by noise. That way, I didn't have to listen to the silence. Listen at all. Like when I was living in the forest and would listen to the wind, listen to the wind speaking to me. And when I saw him, I knew he came from that world, that he came from the universe I had run away from, and that maybe it was time for me to make peace with that world, make peace with him.

Scene Seven – Erase the Shame From My Eyes

ETIENNE's cell.

LAURENCE
Do you know why it happened? (*pause*) Don't you want to tell me why?
(*ETIENNE shakes his head from side to side.*) Let's look at the facts again.
On the afternoon of October 10th, four men who were looking for shelter
in an abandoned cabin surprised you in bed sleeping next to a young woman.
According to their testimony, it was you yourself who told them later that this
young woman was your daughter.

ETIENNE
If that's what they said…

LAURENCE
You do realize you have been charged with a very serious crime, don't you?

ETIENNE
Is it a crime for a father to love his daughter?

LAURENCE
There are limits.

ETIENNE
They condemned us to live like animals. That's how we were living, like animals.

LAURENCE
Even when your wife was alive?

ETIENNE
Since she was a child. I used to take her in my arms to warm her up, to console
her, to protect her from the evil that loomed round us all the time. All fathers
do that.

LAURENCE
When she was a child, yes. But later?

ETIENNE
In the bush, life is fragile. You can never let your guard down.

LAURENCE
In the bush.

ETIENNE
The strong eat the weak.

LAURENCE
Don't you think she'd have been better off if she didn't have to live like that?

ETIENNE

The life I gave her was my own life also.

LAURENCE

You talk as if you were God the father, as if you created her yourself from a handful of earth. What about your wife in all this? You never speak of her.

ETIENNE

My wife died bringing into the world my daughter's body. I was the one who gave her all the rest, everything that fed her spirit, her heart.

LAURENCE

Being a father is a big responsibility.

ETIENNE

I always made sure she had everything she needed.

LAURENCE

Including affection.

ETIENNE

What exactly do you think your questions or my answers are going to change?

LAURENCE

If the court proves that you had sexual relations with your daughter, you will be punished. Why is it like that? It's a long story. The world will not change from one day to the next. Society has put in place mechanisms to protect itself. The court is...

ETIENNE

Will the court be able to erase the shame from the eyes of those who are guilty?

LAURENCE

Those who are guilty? I don't understand what you're getting at?

ETIENNE

He who saw, then lost his sight?

LAURENCE

Those who are guilty? That's a new one.

ETIENNE

Let's just forget I said anything.

LAURENCE

Up until now, you've been the guilty one... er... the accused...

ETIENNE

Are you going to ask for a trial?

LAURENCE
They have to charge you since…

ETIENNE
You have your witnesses. What are you risking?

LAURENCE
That's true. Four. Four witnesses.

ETIENNE
Good people.

LAURENCE
Good people. I don't know, but…

ETIENNE
They look like soldiers.

LAURENCE
Ordinary guys really.

ETIENNE
Who find themselves in the bush.

LAURENCE
Once a year.

ETIENNE
To kill animals.

LAURENCE
Just to have a good time.

ETIENNE
Trustworthy men.

LAURENCE
Typical men.

Scene Eight – Echoes From the Courthouse

In front of the courthouse.

ANNOUNCER
It's 5:22, or twenty-two minutes past five o'clock if you don't like digital time; eight minutes to six in Newfoundland. It's time to join the well-known Francoise Francoeur who has agreed to take a few minutes out of her busy

schedule to tell us about today's events at the courthouse where Francoise spent this morning at the trial of Etienne Landry. Francoise, are you there?...

FRANCOISE
(*in a familiar tone*) I can't hear a damn thing. What's the problem?

ANNOUNCER
I think we'll have to come back to this report from Francoise Francoeur... ah! They tell me the problem has been fixed. Can you hear me, Francoise?

FRANCOISE
Yes, yes. I'm here.

ANNOUNCER
So Francoise, can you tell us what happened there this morning?

FRANCOISE
The public galleries of the courthouse were full this morning for the continuation of the trial of Etienne Landry. The defendant seemed agitated and exhibited sudden mood shifts several times creating a commotion in the courtroom. The judge even had to suspend proceedings for fifteen minutes when the prosecution called the first witness to the stand. Landry started to sob so loudly that it was hard to follow the questioning.

ANNOUNCER
Does anyone know what set off this emotional outburst in the accused?

FRANCOISE
No. In fact, our only link with this type of behaviour on the part of the accused still rests with the psychiatrist, Dr. Samson, who once again was taken to task pretty severely by the defence for having brought to trial a man who is not able to defend himself and who, furthermore, doesn't even have the stamina to handle the judicial procedures involved in such a trial.

ANNOUNCER
Yes, but if he's already in such a state, will Landry be able to stick it out to the end? We seem to be dealing with some rather disconcerting behaviour here. Perhaps you could tell us a bit about the testimony of the men who discovered Landry?

FRANCOISE
This morning we heard the testimony of the four men, the four hunters, who described in detail the reasons for their intervention. In fact it seems to have been a question of protecting the young victim, the daughter of Etienne Landry whose name cannot be divulged here under the law for the protection of minors. Moreover, several people in the courtroom found themselves unable to hold back their emotions on hearing details of her situation, the unsanitary conditions, and the terrified expression of the young girl when the four armed men appeared. Here again, we saw Landry lower his head several times, sobbing

and repeating loudly that the testimonies were full of untruths. According to the witnesses, it would seem that Landry was keeping the girl in total seclusion, forbidding any contact with strangers or with family and friends.

Scene Nine – Looking My Accusers Straight in the Eye

ETIENNE's cell.

ROBERT
Mr. Landry, I have some bad news for you. Despite everything I have done to plead mental incompetence for you, it appears that Dr. Samson has decided to the contrary. We don't have much control over it. So that's how things stand. In the meantime I have some questions to ask you.

ETIENNE
I was the one who asked her.

ROBERT
Asked what?

ETIENNE
I asked her to decide what she decided.

ROBERT
Okay, but usually it's the doctor's decision, not the patient's. What you've asked her to do could jeopardize her career, you know, because the court pays her to make decisions based on the expertise she is supposed to have, not according to the wishes of the accused.

ETIENNE
You shouldn't speak like that because it was me who asked for the trial.

ROBERT
Fine, but how, exactly, do you want me to defend your case?

ETIENNE
Maybe there is no case to defend.

ROBERT
Well, then all you have to do is plead guilty. When the trial begins, the judge will read the charge. He will ask you if you plead guilty or not-guilty. You can simply answer "guilty" and the judge will pass his sentence.

ETIENNE
No. I insist on having a trial. If I'm going to be condemned, I feel I must be accountable for my actions.

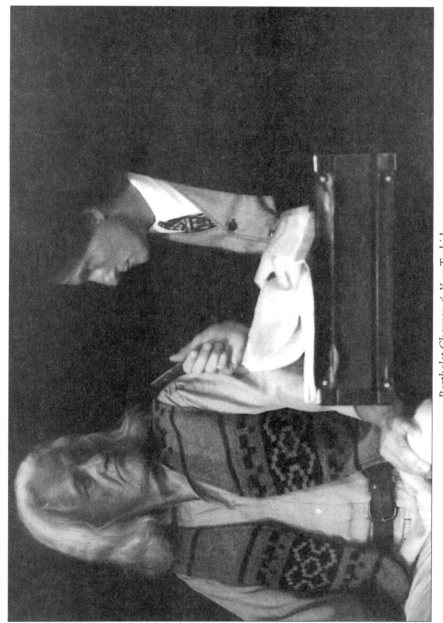

Bertholet Charron & Yves Turbide
Photo by Herménégilde Chiasson.

ROBERT

No, no, no. It doesn't work like that. I am your lawyer. I am supposed to defend you.

ETIENNE

(*pause*) I want to look my accusers straight in the eye.

ROBERT

Would you prefer to defend yourself? That is another option, you know. You could tell your own version of the events and…

ETIENNE

I prefer that someone else speak on my behalf.

ROBERT

Even if you hardly know me.

ETIENNE

They say I can trust you.

ROBERT

Is that what Dr. Samson told you?

ETIENNE

As far as I was concerned, I didn't want a lawyer at all. All I wanted was to see the faces of those who have dragged me here. See them in their own world, as they saw me in my world. See them puff themselves up one last time, satisfied with the good they think they have done.

ROBERT

I know you didn't want a lawyer, but you've got one, even if it can't be said you chose me exactly. In any case, I hope that we can make a good team and that we end up with good results, for me, and especially for you.

ETIENNE

We will talk. And when two people really talk together, they usually find a way of understanding each other.

ROBERT

I appreciate the confidence you have in me. That doesn't happen everyday. And since we're talking about trust, there is a question I always ask my clients when I take on a case. It is very important, as much for me as for you, because we are going to have to work together to prove your innocence. What you are going to tell me won't go beyond these four walls, but it is vital for me to know the truth. Mr. Landry, did you or did you not have sexual relations with your daughter?

ETIENNE

(*indignant*) What would make you believe a thing like that?

Scene Ten – You Will Say Nothing

ETIENNE's cell. ETIENNE is alone in his cell. ALIENOR appears to him in a dream.

ALIENOR
(*She speaks over a musical background.*) You were walking peacefully in the darkness of your dreams when men's cruelty raised a storm so great your eyes closed themselves against the pain crashing down upon us. The world compels us to answer their cruel questions. All in order that they may lie down in their beds, sure and certain that the dark night will take them in her arms, that the night will tell them they are safe where they are, having done what they had to do, having said what they had to say, having understood what they had to understand.

(*sung*) The silence of the night disappears with the dawn,
The music of the birds a cry without hope.
You watch your prison walls alone,
Knowing well what they will never know.
How you fought from summer to the spring;
Our life was lost and hid from sight.
The battle that we conquered to survive,
All these words that you cannot express.

(*She continues to speak over the music.*) You will say nothing, father. You will say nothing. You will take what they have left us in the belief you're making yourself a cloak of dreams from it. With your memories as weighty as stones in the pockets of that cloak. Each stone a memory. The others will forget your name, but you, you will remember theirs forever. To prevent your memory from being lost in theirs, you would write it everywhere, if you knew how to write. However, it is the others who will write your story. But they will forget to include your dreams, your courage, the way you had of lifting your eyes to the sky, of caressing the grass with your footsteps, of leaving great silences between your words to give life a chance to catch her breath.

(*sung*) With nothing to say to them, only asking yourself
Why these questions without answers, why this remorse?
You would like to stop yourself and cry,
But your tears are mingled with your memories.
You cry out in nights full of despair,
For they will erase our history.
You know better than me that it's too late;
The sun is swallowing your voice.

(*She continues to speak over the music.*) You bend your neck, father, you tilt your head towards the earth which is filled with the song of all living things. You hang your head reminding yourself of their insults, the violence of their words, the harshness of their questions. There is no crueler beast in the forest.

We know that now. You will never again get to speak to them. They will never again hear what you are saying. And in the evening, when they take you back to your cage, you will measure just how solid is their trap, how hard and cold. You made the mistake of not knowing the rules of the game. And for that crime, you will be guilty for a long time to come.

(*sung*) A day is coming when they've done and they've said so much
That they will buy from us our secret and our life.
Finally forced to leave this place,
What'll we do, what will we say to them?
As we stand before our world in flames,
We keep silent waiting for the worst
Without knowing if help will come our way;
This way fear could chase away our love.

Scene Eleven – Fear is Like a Disease

ETIENNE's cell.

LAURENCE
Just the same, a fairly large number of stains were found on your daughter's clothes and in her bed which suggests that sexual relations almost certainly took place. You were seen by four men, four hunters, whose testimonies, taken separately, are perfectly consistent. The judge is going to base his decision on apparent facts, and in this case, the facts are far from inconclusive. (*pause*) Have you thought about your daughter?

ETIENNE
My daughter knows my reasons.

LAURENCE
And does she accept them?

ETIENNE
What?

LAURENCE
The reasons? Does she accept your reasons?

ETIENNE
Last night I dreamed of her. She reproached me for my silence. I saw her going away, moving away from me. Moving towards your world. I felt betrayed. And I understood that already she has forgotten the rage I showed her.

LAURENCE
Let's get back to the events of the day you were discovered. If I understand this right, you were lying next to your daughter when you heard gun shots around the cabin where you were sleeping. You got up to see what was happening.

Courtroom.

ROBERT
Your Honour, yesterday my client revealed some rather disturbing information to Dr. Samson. Due to the nature of this information, I am asking the court for permission to recall Dr. Samson to the stand. My client is aware of the information which Dr. Samson is prepared to disclose. Yes, I know that, Your Honour, but this is exceptional testimony which has the potential to completely change the outcome of this trial.

ETIENNE's cell.

LAURENCE
And then you saw four armed men who started to shoot at the walls of your cabin. I have a lot of difficulty believing that.

ETIENNE
They were drunk. Drooling like rabid dogs. My daughter was scared to death. I took her in my arms and lay on top of her.

Courtroom.

ROBERT
And so he stretched over her so that she wouldn't be hit by one of their bullets?

LAURENCE
That's correct.

ROBERT
And then?

Etienne's cell.

ETIENNE
And then they opened the door and they saw us there. They thought they.... They thought they saw what they invented later.

LAURENCE
Invented? (*pause*) That's the first time you've used that word.

ETIENNE
My daughter's face was white with fear. I could feel her body trembling. She was holding me so tightly I could hardly breathe. I started to get scared myself. Fear is like a disease, you know. It is something that spreads from person to person. It spreads with each breath. It was like I caught her fear all of a sudden. I said to myself they're going to kill us. I was afraid of them killing us. And they did. She was right to be so afraid. Because they did kill us.

LAURENCE

Not for real. Not completely anyway.

ETIENNE

There can be many deaths in one life, and the last is not always the worst.

Courtroom.

ROBERT

So, the latest testimony of Etienne Landry would undermine the testimony of the four witnesses for the prosecution who claim they found Landry lying on his daughter which made it appear there most likely had been sexual relations taking place?

LAURENCE

According to Etienne Landry, the witnesses have greatly exaggerated the situation. According to him, the four men had consumed so much alcohol they were certainly in no condition to gauge the significance of their actions.

ROBERT

And did he talk to you about the semen stains found in the bed and on his daughter's clothes?

LAURENCE

As far as I know, those semen stains have not been analyzed.

ETIENNE's cell.

ETIENNE

They decided to pull us apart. They might as well have cut our arms from our bodies. Then they... they...

Courtroom.

LAURENCE

Then they raped her in front of him.

In front of the courthouse.

FRANCOISE

Well, quite a dramatic turn of events yesterday at the trial of Etienne Landry. Although Dr. Samson had already given her testimony, a new version of the events was relayed to her by the accused just before the start of the day's proceedings. According to Landry, it was the four hunters, until now the principle witnesses for the prosecution, who actually committed the crime in question. We know that Landry is accused of incest with his daughter, but according to him, it should be the four hunters, the ones who surprised him in his daughter's bed, who in fact, again according to Landry, committed the crime of which he is unjustly accused.

ANNOUNCER

Is there any proof of this? It is rather curious that Landry didn't mention all this before. It makes me wonder if he didn't do it on purpose.

FRANCOISE

In fact, an oversight in the investigation has come to light which risks costing the prosecution dearly. It appears there has been no analysis of the semen stains found in the victim's bed. You'd think such an oversight would be unlikely in this day and age, and I presume the prosecution will have to find some pretty solid answers to these questions when the trial resumes.

ANNOUNCER

Yes, certainly. It's all quite incredible, isn't it. How did the prosecution react when confronted with this omission?

FRANCOISE

Without a doubt they were so certain of the testimony of the four men, whom they simply considered above suspicion, that the prosecution just didn't bother to go any further in the establishment of proof. You have to understand the context, that according to the four hunters, it was a matter of protecting and freeing a child who otherwise risked spending her life in the forest. But all this is still nothing but speculation. It is now up to the court to weigh the pros and cons of this case.

ETIENNE's cell.

ETIENNE

Do you believe me now?

LAURENCE

It's not the kind of story one hears everyday.

ETIENNE

Now, I have nothing left. I have given you my story, my truth.

LAURENCE

Now you know the peace of mind that comes from having told someone.

ETIENNE

But you, what are you going to do with my story?

LAURENCE

Do you want me to speak to your lawyer about it? (*pause*) Do you give me permission to speak to him about it?

ROBERT's office.

LAURENCE

He told me he didn't want to tell his story in public.

ROBERT
But why?

LAURENCE
Because he asked me if I believed him. But I can't say if I believe him or not. As soon as that comes out at the trial, what will I look like in all this?

ROBERT
At this point, I have no way, or nearly no way, of defending him. It'll be a massacre. What have we got to lose?

LAURENCE
I wonder if there has been an analysis of the semen stains they found on the clothes and in the bed.

ROBERT
I'll find out, but there must have been. It's elementary.

LAURENCE
Because if the results show that he...

ROBERT
He'll have to take the stand.

LAURENCE
I've never seen anything like this. Someone with so little interest in defending himself.

ROBERT
You could take the stand on his behalf.

LAURENCE
Me?

ROBERT
You could repeat what he told you. Nothing else.

LAURENCE
The judge will certainly wonder what I'm doing there.

In front of the courthouse.

FRANCOISE
Responding to shocking new developments in the case, the judge has called a two-week recess to see if there is cause to begin proceedings against the four witnesses who would then become the four new defendants. Between now and then the defence will have their work cut out for them if they want to prove that the four witnesses are in fact the four assailants.

ANNOUNCER
So the suspense continues to build, if we can say that. How would you describe this first part of the trial?

ETIENNE's cell.

ETIENNE
Just imagine if the same thing happened to you. The same thing that happened to my daughter.

LAURENCE
Why are you asking me that?

ETIENNE
Just to know. Because you live in a different world. A foreign world.

LAURENCE
You think it's really so different?

In front of the courthouse.

FRANCOISE
Etienne Landry seemed visibly tired when he was escorted out of the courtroom today, and it wasn't possible to get close enough to ask him any questions. However, according to the prosecution, the new testimony is worth considering even if Landry's statements so far have left everyone thinking he is a pretty unusual character who has become quite disturbed by everything that has happened to him over the last few weeks. As you will recall, Landry claims to have taken refuge in the forest where he then spent much of his life, following the burning of his home and the expropriation of his land.

Scene Twelve – I Thought I Saw a Ghost

ROBERT's office.

ROBERT
Rape cases are so much easier than cases of incest.

LAURENCE
Easier for whom?

ROBERT
For me.

LAURENCE
How's that? A case is a case, isn't it?

ROBERT
> Rape is simpler to prove.

LAURENCE
> They're still victims, as much in one as in the other.

ROBERT
> The important thing is that justice be done.

LAURENCE
> Justice. Sometimes I ask myself where people got such an idea.

ROBERT
> It's not that bad an idea.

LAURENCE
> Still, you have to believe in it. Have faith.

ROBERT
> Or fear. Because everyone knows that justice has a long reach.

LAURENCE
> Nevertheless, it would be so much simpler if we all just believed in freedom. If we had the courage to be free.

ROBERT
> Or responsible. In the meantime there is justice to protect the weak by making the powerful afraid.

LAURENCE
> And you think it works?

ROBERT
> It's the best we have.

LAURENCE
> Sometimes, I wonder what's going to happen to Etienne Landry when he leaves our world.

ROBERT
> Our protection, you mean.

LAURENCE
> They say an animal who has been raised among people will be killed when it returns to the wild. His smell betrays him.

ROBERT
> Why would the forest refuse to take him back?

LAURENCE

No, he's the one who will refuse to take back the forest, but because he doesn't know how to get by in our world, he'll be devoured at every turn. Devoured by us. Even without our intending to. That's what makes me so sad.

ROBERT

Not much you can do about it.

LAURENCE

But you see I, I've always believed that we could reinvent our lives.

ROBERT

And me, I've always believed that we have to do the best we can with what we have.

LAURENCE

We really are on two different planets, aren't we; the two of us, two different stars.

ROBERT

Well, all celestial bodies attract one another. That's how the universe keeps going round and round.

LAURENCE

Why do you think it didn't work out for you and me?

ROBERT

I don't know. We were incompatible, I know that. It was chemical. I've never understood. The stars... it's too far away for us to really say!

LAURENCE

In my opinion it was a lot more than that. The day I took off out of the bush was the day the bush started to chase me. And that...

ROBERT

You mean to say we can never escape the environment we grew up in? Come on!

LAURENCE

The forest is not just an environment, a setting; it's a world, a whole universe. It's a magical place, and I understand Landry when he talks about the animals that change places with people. Sometimes, I tell myself the beast is never far away, and that we have to feed it, clothe it, tell it all will be well, even when it beds down in caves heated with electricity. I understand Landry. Every word he says to me is a reminder.

ROBERT

Is that why he resembles your father, or at least makes you think of him...

LAURENCE
> It's more than that.

ROBERT
> More than that. How?

LAURENCE
> I understand everything Landry describes because I have lived it. I just
> pretended not to understand in order to get him to talk.

ROBERT
> It's true this is an interesting case. It's as if we've found a dinosaur at the end
> of the twentieth century.

LAURENCE
> There are things like that which we bury or lock up or burn, thinking we've
> gotten rid of them for good. Then suddenly, it's there again like a hologram: in
> a corridor, in a prison cell, or on the seat of a car. All of a sudden the memory
> comes back to us, the smells, the sounds, even the taste which life has left in our
> mouth. It all comes back. Landry is my childhood. What I swore I had buried
> forever.

ROBERT
> Yes, but why him? Why now, so suddenly?

LAURENCE
> Because the more he talks, the better I understand what happened to me. He
> unsettles me; he questions me. Even if it is me who is asking the questions,
> I have the feeling he has all the answers. Everything I've put up with until now,
> the arrangements I made with myself in order to keep going, the peace that
> I had given myself, all that is crumbling away.

ROBERT
> It's that bad?

LAURENCE
> You don't understand, Robert. The forest is more than just a bunch of trees
> growing together; it's all the mystery of life which dawns, struggles and makes
> a place for itself. Here, this will always be a small, very fragile place, carved out
> of asphalt and concrete. But what I know, and what Landry knows, is that the
> forest can come back at any time. The forest has no need of us to survive. No,
> it's the other way around. And me, I betrayed the forest, or rather I left it
> behind because something happened which I buried in the forest. And now it
> has come back. It is Landry who has found it, and who has come back to make
> me face it again.

ROBERT
Don't you think you're exaggerating? Landry is a lost soul, a wild man who has strayed into the city. For sure he will continue to be important as long as we continue to believe in his stories, but between you and me...

LAURENCE
It would be so simple if he were just another crazy old man. We could cure him, and everything would go back to the way it was before. But me, I know that he carries with him our memory. His own, mine, and also that of all those who believe the past is a succession of pleasant stories and that everything will be taken care of in the future. Between the two, there's nothing but living and waiting. It would be so simple, so beautiful to believe that everything will be taken care of and there will be justice for everyone.

ROBERT
The first time you saw Landry, did you know he had been accused of incest?

LAURENCE
Yes. What's that got to do with this conversation?

Scene Thirteen – May Life Avenge Us

ETIENNE's cell.

ETIENNE
My dear, I have told them our secret. I told your story, our unhappy story.

ALIENOR
The time has come, father, to bury our pain.

ETIENNE
Yes, but where? In what land? And even buried, will it wander again?

ALIENOR
We are going to bury our old life and reinvent a new one right here. Here we will give a new name to the world. So that the world will continue to be ours. We will belong in this new world, fill it with beauty, remake it in our image, in the image of our courage. Build a new world over the one they put to the torch.

ETIENNE
What have we done to make them think we have been so courageous? What have we to show the world other than the wound that refuses to heal?

ALIENOR
We must bury the past. We must write it down in a book and bury the book. And the dead will read that book, and they too will finally be able to sleep.

ETIENNE
To write such a book, you have to know how to write.

ALIENOR
I will learn.

ETIENNE
To write forgetfulness.

ALIENOR
I will write so we never forget.

ETIENNE
No, you too are going to forget. You have already started to forget.

ALIENOR
I will never betray the history of our suffering, even when they insist that happiness comes from forgetting. Never believe that their world will triumph over our spirit. Nothing, no, nothing can diminish the dignity of our spirit.

ETIENNE
Are you going to forget how they hurt you?

ALIENOR
We will be avenged, father, by life.

ETIENNE
They get richer even by our poverty!

ALIENOR
We'll just have to make sure that life avenges us.

ETIENNE
Where do you find the strength to say something like that after they have dirtied everything?

ALIENOR
For a very long time you have guarded your rage like a refuge. Eventually you made a trophy of it. Showing the world the scars of your dignity. They have re-opened your wound, it's true. I saw them. The wound that I do not have. Not yet. This wound that I don't want to bear, that I will never be able to bear.

ETIENNE
What else do I have to give them but the hate they left in me?

ALIENOR
You must speak to them. Learn their language. Answer with their own words.

Bertholet Charron & Janine Boudreau
Photo by Herménégilde Chiasson.

ETIENNE

And you think that's how life will care enough to avenge us?

ALIENOR

They can do nothing against us. We will find the words. And we will learn how to say them so that such a wrong can never happen again.

ETIENNE

That's it. The pain. The pain that comes from seeing the same wrongs committed again and again.

ALIENOR

I will be with you. You will be with me. I will look ahead. You will look behind. And the two of us, we will measure the breadth of the land, the reach of our wealth. Nobody will come again to rob us, nor to lie about us. Nobody will sell us like slaves. We will return to the forest on our own terms, and we will come out again embraced in light. And my children will walk in that light. And they will play in that light. And their lives will be their own. For a long time. Forever. Their own. We will share nothing less than life itself, our only possession, our unique vengeance. I will forget the forest, yes. The rain, the cold, the snow, yes. But never believe that I will forget the beating of your heart, the words of your song, nor the warmth of your arms.

(*sung*) We will look everywhere,
To the ends of the earth;
We have been so afraid,
A fear so profound.

(*She speaks over the music.*) In the darkest hours you will hear my voice;
I will hold your hand tightly; I will walk in your footsteps.
I will say the things that you have so wanted to say;
I will laugh at the things which brought us so much death.

(*sung*) We will look everywhere;
Life will be expanded
To frontiers of our hearts,
To the reach of our arms.

(*She speaks over the music.*) If not for me, do it for yourself and those to come.
The time has come to stop our flight;
The time has come to retake the blue of the sky;
The time has come to live our rebel life.

(*sung*) We will look everywhere;
See the other forests,
Discover all the joy
Of the deepest secrets.

Scene Fourteen – A Thousand Years in My Head

Courtroom.

ROBERT

Yes, I know, Your Honour, but my work has focused on finding a way of reversing the charges and I believe the lab results show irrefutable proof. To conclude, my client wishes to take the stand for reasons which he will explain to you. Thank you, Your Honour. (*He turns to ETIENNE.*) Okay, go ahead. It's okay. Go ahead.

ETIENNE

It was a long time ago, many lifetimes ago. I believed I was living all alone in a great land, that I was living all alone in a land with poverty as my neighbour, with ignorance as my neighbour. That I was living all alone with forgetfulness. I lived a long time on that land. And that land was peopled with trees. And I stayed among the trees, believing that I was part of the land, the only land I would ever have. A long time. It was like that for a long time. Until, in time, I reached the limits of fear, of poverty, of ignorance. For a long time I believed that the past was the only world where I was safe. Then these men woke me from my dream to drag me into their hell. Until then I believed that the bush was the only place where I could live in peace. I learned about fear in the bush. It was there that I hid myself after centuries of running away, of keeping quiet. I glided through the night like a fox, slipping away from the wolves when they attacked in packs. Then one afternoon, a pack of wolves came armed, like they always came armed, to tell me that I was an animal, and that they had the arms to prove it.

In front of the courthouse. LAURENCE and ALIENOR off to one side.

LAURENCE

The fact that he saw you in the courtroom this morning must surely have helped give him the courage he needed to say what he had to say.

ALIENOR

I don't know what he was like before the death of my two sisters and my mother, but I have the impression that he has never pulled himself out of that trap. He has always seen himself like a wounded animal, an animal bleeding to death in a trap, in the winter, in the forest. He has learned to do without words.

FRANCOISE

(*making her report from her usual place*) The trial of Etienne Landry resumed this morning in front of a full courtroom. The defence had no difficulty getting the charges reversed, given the results of the laboratory analysis of the stains found at the crime scene. Originally these had been presumed to be Landry's semen, but following the testimony he gave two weeks ago, everything has changed. As you remember, he confided in his psychiatrist who then relayed the information to the court, throwing the trial into disarray. And that's how the four witnesses who originally signed the complaint against Landry now find themselves opposite him in the prisoner's box. A complete reversal of the situation.

ROBERT's office.

LAURENCE
Just imagine that suddenly one day you disappear. You escape completely. Escape from everything that hurts you.

ROBERT
Yes but you have to want to, that's the hard part. You have to really want to.

LAURENCE
You have to know terrible pain to want to hide yourself so far away.

ROBERT
The difference is that for us, we come back.

LAURENCE
Maybe that's what pain is: not being able to go back.

In front of the courthouse.

FRANCOISE
Dr. Samson, you have had numerous contacts, numerous meetings with Etienne Landry; would you say that he has suffered a great deal from these proceedings?

LAURENCE
But what is suffering, after all? I tend to believe that it is different for each of us. The threshold of pain, for example, is never the same for everybody.

FRANCOISE
Yes, but you would agree with me that since we are dealing here with an individual who has spent his whole life in the forest, who suddenly finds himself one day in an arena, if not a circus, he must have felt rather hounded, lost, at the very least anxious, wouldn't you say?

LAURENCE
In my professional opinion, there is nothing normal and nothing abnormal. The story of Etienne Landry has troubled a lot of people because we, all of us, are used to a certain way of life. But if we were to go into the jungle, for example, I am sure that we would find people there who live exactly like him, and maybe at that point we'd become the curiosities.

Courtroom.

ROBERT
Do you recognize the four men in front of you there?

ALIENOR
Yes.

ROBERT
Could you tell the court if these are the same men who raped you. (*The lawyer turns as if called, but the audience doesn't hear the voice of the prosecution who is objecting.*) Could you tell the court if these are the same men who attacked you?

ALIENOR
Yes, I recognize them.

ROBERT
Could you tell the court the circumstances of this attack?

ALIENOR
It was hot that day. All day long we heard gunshots in the forest. That was how we knew fall had arrived. It was like the gunshots had woken us from summer. Those days, we tended to stay indoors. We were afraid of being mistaken for wild animals. They could have shot at us. That's what had already happened. My sister...

ROBERT
Go on.

ALIENOR
That's how my second sister was killed. She got lost in the forest and.... In the spring, I found her body floating down the river with the ice.

ROBERT
Did you tell your father about it?

ALIENOR
Much later, but he preferred to believe that she got lost in the forest and that one day she would come back to see him with her children.

ROBERT
Let's go back to the afternoon of the crime.

ALIENOR
I went and lay down on my bed.

ROBERT
You didn't sleep in your father's bed?

ALIENOR
No. We each had our own bed. My father didn't want to see me here, in court. In order to protect me from the people he believes want to hurt us. That's the same reason they found him lying on top of me. Because he was afraid one of their bullets would hit me. He would sooner die than see someone hurt me.

In front of the courthouse.

FRANCOISE

We have finally been able to hear from Etienne Landry's daughter. Over the course of most of the morning, she described many, sometimes contradictory, details about the circumstances surrounding the attack she suffered. The very touching testimony was interrupted several times when the young victim's emotions overwhelmed her. She was clearly distressed recounting the details of the brutal manner in which she was attacked. One could sense the intense embarrassment and anxiety felt by the four accused men in the prisoner's box, as well as by the members of their families who were seated discretely throughout the courtroom.

ETIENNE's cell.

LAURENCE

How are you holding up seeing your daughter in court? (*pause*) I believe it will be difficult for her.... After this drama, she'll have to regain confidence in herself, in life.

ETIENNE

If there ever is a life after all this. If ever. It will have to be a new life.

LAURENCE

It will be difficult for her to trust people again.

ETIENNE

I know something about that. I have been mistrustful all my life. The only person... is my daughter. My little girl with a body as light as the wind, eyes as bright as the moon, a voice as sweet as the rain...

LAURENCE

She is a woman now. With a body full of vengeance. She will take revenge on all men. Even on those who want nothing more than to love her.

ETIENNE

What makes you believe a thing like that?

LAURENCE

Because. Because I too, I... I suffered the same way.

ETIENNE

You should have said so before.

LAURENCE

I've been saying it to everyone ever since it happened, but there's been no one to hear me.

ETIENNE
Your father didn't help you, like me...

LAURENCE
No, because... because...

ETIENNE
No.

LAURENCE
Yes.

Courtroom.

ETIENNE
A week after that, I saw my daughter again. I found her changed. She was no longer the child whose hand I held in the woods, and I understood the fear and the rage and the misery written on her body. I had chosen to hold my peace because I thought there weren't words to express that rage, and even more, that there was no one to listen to my words anyway. But my daughter made me understand that I had to speak up. I don't know what's going to happen to these four men who find themselves humiliated, like they humiliated me in front of my daughter. I could spit in their faces like they spit on my daughter's body. But what good would that do me? In the forest, all the animals obey their own law. The law of their species. What, then, is the law of our species? I ask you. What is our own human law? It is from that law that I ask today for justice. That's all I had to say.

In front of the courthouse.

FRANCOISE
The trial ended with the testimony of Etienne Landry who asked to take the stand, and who made a sort of public confession in which he spoke of, among other things, his connection to the crime his daughter suffered. It was pretty emotional testimony, which he concluded with some rather puzzling comments about justice. He declared, among other things, "In the forest, all the animals obey the law of their own species. What, then, is the law of our species?" At that point he addressed the judge directly by asking him, "What is our own human law? It is by that law that I ask today to be judged." And so the judge rendered his decision today by condemning the four accused to six months in custody and six months community service, a rather light sentence for a rather, shall we say, odious crime. But the judge based his decision on the fact that it was a first offence for the four men; as well he considered the esteem they are held in, or were held in, one never knows, by the community in general.

The end.

Alienor – My Gift of Song

Musique © Jean-François Mallet, 1997.

Alienor – Revenge

Musique © Jean-François Mallet, 1997.

Alienor – Silence of the Night

Oct. 30/07

Oct. 30/07